SKELTON: THE CRITICAL HERITAGE

THE CRITICAL HERITAGE SERIES

GENERAL EDITOR: B. C. SOUTHAM, M.A., B.LITT. (OXON.)
Formerly Department of English, Westfield College, University of London

---

For a list of books in the series see the back end paper

SKELTON

THE CRITICAL HERITAGE

Edited by
ANTHONY S. G. EDWARDS
Associate Professor of English
University of Victoria

ROUTLEDGE & KEGAN PAUL
LONDON, BOSTON AND HENLEY

First published in 1981
by Routledge & Kegan Paul Ltd
39 Store Street,
London WC1E 7DD,
Broadway House,
Newtown Road,
Henley-on-Thames,
Oxon RG9 1EN and
9 Park Street,
Boston, Mass. 02108, USA
Printed in Great Britain by
Redwood Burn Limited, Trowbridge & Esher
Compilation, introduction, notes, bibliography and index © Anthony S. G. Edwards,
1981

British Library Cataloguing in Publication Data

Skelton, the critical heritage. – (The critical
heritage series)

1. Skelton, John, ca. 1460–1529 – Criticism and
interpretation
I. Edwards, Anthony S. G.   II. Series
821'.2   PR2348   80–41988
ISBN 0–7100–0724–8

General Editor's Preface

The reception given to a writer by his contemporaries and near-contemporaries is evidence of considerable value to the student of literature. On one side we learn a great deal about the state of criticism at large and in particular about the development of critical attitudes towards a single writer; at the same time, through private comments in letters, journals or marginalia, we gain an insight upon the tastes and literary thought of individual readers of the period. Evidence of this kind helps us to understand the writer's historical situation, the nature of his immediate reading-public, and his response to these pressures.

The separate volumes in the *Critical Heritage Series* present a record of this early criticism. Clearly, for many of the highly productive and lengthily reviewed nineteenth- and twentieth-century writers, there exists an enormous body of material; and in these cases the volume editors have made a selection of the most important views, significant for their intrinsic critical worth or for their representative quality—perhaps even registering incomprehension!

For earlier writers, notably pre-eighteenth century, the materials are much scarcer and the historical period has been extended, sometimes far beyond the writer's lifetime, in order to show the inception and growth of critical views which were initially slow to appear.

In each volume the documents are headed by an Introduction, discussing the material assembled and relating the early stages of the author's reception to what we have come to identify as the critical tradition. The volumes will make available much material which would otherwise be difficult of access and it is hoped that the modern reader will be thereby helped towards an informed understanding of the ways in which literature has been read and judged.

B.C.S.

Contents

Acknowledgments

I should like to thank the following copyright-holders and publishers for permission to quote from various works: the estate of Humbert Wolfe and the Hogarth Press for permission to include an extract from 'Notes on English Verse Satire' (1929); the estate of E. M. Forster and Edward Arnold Ltd for permission to include Forster's essay John Skelton from 'Two Cheers for Democracy' (1950); the 'Times Literary Supplement' for permission to include Edmund Blunden's essay (1929); the estate of Richard Hughes and Chatto & Windus Ltd for permission to include the Introduction to Hughes's 'Poems by John Skelton' (1924); the Oxford University Press for permission to include the passage on Skelton from C. S. Lewis's 'English Literature in the Sixteenth Century (excluding Drama)' (1954) by C. S. Lewis Reprinted by permission of Oxford University Press; Robert Graves for permission to reprint his essay An Incomplete Complete Skelton from the 'Adelphi' (1931); the estate of W. H. Auden (Professor Edward Mendelson) for permission to reprint Auden's essay from 'The Great Tudors' (1935); G. S. Fraser for permission to reprint his essay from the 'Adelphi' (1936).

I am also grateful to the various scholars listed in my Bibliography whose work has made my own task much easier. I owe a particular debt to Professor Robert S. Kinsman of the University of California at Los Angeles who has generously shared his knowledge of Skelton with me.

Introduction

There are obvious difficulties in any attempt to present
John Skelton's critical heritage. As Patricia Thomson has
reminded us in the case of another sixteenth-century poet,
Sir Thomas Wyatt, there were virtually no 'masters of
criticism' before the Restoration.(1) It is not until the
publication of the second volume of Warton's 'History of
English Literature' in 1778 - nearly 250 years after Skelton's death - that we find the first extended evaluation
of the poet. Before that, the materials for an understanding of the changing critical appreciation of Skelton
are highly fragmentary. One has, in the main, to rely on
passing allusions, brief comments, and such inferences as
can be adduced from the evidence of Skelton's influence on
the literature of his own and subsequent generations.
   It is the fragmentary nature of much of Skelton's critical heritage that poses the greatest problem. Indeed,
much of the sixteenth- and seventeenth-century material I
have been able to assemble can only be termed criticism by
the most elastic use of the term. Dispassionate, or even
considered, judgments of his work are (at best) very rare.
The chief problem is that Skelton's reputation, both
during his own lifetime and subsequently, has been inex-
tricably bound up with controversy, personal, political
and aesthetic. Comparatively little of the early comment
on his work is free from this identification of Skelton
with partisan causes of various kinds.
   But in some ways it is this very tendency to attract
controversy that makes Skelton's reputation such a reward-
ing subject for study. By focusing on this particular
figure it is possible to follow, in a revealing way,
fluctuations in literary taste from the sixteenth century
through to our own age. When one attempts to trace the
vicissitudes of his critical status, Skelton emerges as a
valuable representative figure, reflecting changing

aesthetic and cultural responses to certain forms of
literary expression, notably satiric and popular verse.
    Much of the subsequent controversy about Skelton is
mirrored in the contemporary responses to his work.
Initially, for his contemporaries he seems to have been a
symbol of all that was surpassing in English scholarly
achievement and poetic excellence. Caxton, in the earliest recorded comment on Skelton, in the Preface to his
translation of the 'Aeneid' (1490), links Skelton's
scholarship and his poetic skills and uses them as a way
of vindicating the reliability of his translation (No. 1):

> For hym I knowe for suffycyent to expowne and englysshe
> euery dyffyculte that is therein ... And also he hath
> redde the ix. muses and vnderstande theyr musicalle
> scyences and to whom of theym eche scyence is appropred.
> I suppose he hath dronken of Elycons well.

Even though this passage smacks rather of a publisher's
blurb, it none the less affords a revealing insight into
Skelton's contemporary reputation. At the age of (probably) little more than thirty his name could be invoked
with the apparent expectation that it would provide a
guarantee of the merits of Caxton's edition.
    Other evidence exists to confirm this contemporary view
of the 'scholarly' Skelton. Caxton's Preface touches on
some of it. We are told that Skelton has already translated 'the epystlys of Tulle' (now lost) and 'the boke of
dyodorus syculus', a weighty universal history. (2) And
he had been 'late created poete laureate' at Oxford, a
distinction primarily of academic significance. Similar
awards were to follow from the universities of Louvain and
Cambridge, probably in 1492 and 1493 respectively. And
about 1496 he was appointed royal tutor to the future
Henry VIII, (3) a position which was to provide new opportunities for didactic and scholarly writing. (4)
    Praise for this aspect of Skelton's achievement is
reiterated in the comments of Erasmus who met him on his
visit to England in 1499, while Skelton was still a member
of the royal household. Erasmus acclaims him as 'that
incomparable light and ornament of British letters' in his
prefatory comments to a poem in honour of Prince Henry
(No. 2a).
    But from this point Skelton's reputation as a scholar
seems to cease to concern his critics. It is not until the
nineteenth century, in the comments of James Russell
Lowell (No. 46), that we hear any more praise of Skelton
as scholar.
    For it seems evident that by 1499 Skelton has already

begun to acquire a significant reputation as a poet. Few
of his poems can be dated with certainty before this year
- only his 'Elegy on the Death of the Earl of Northumberland' (1489) and his allegorical 'Bouge of Court' (1498) -
but his poetry was evidently known, at least in some
degree, by Erasmus when he visited England in 1499. There
survives in a manuscript in the British Library, MS Egerton 1651, a poem headed 'Carmen Extemporale' (No. 2b) by
Erasmus in praise of Skelton's verse. Dated Autumn 1499,
it lauds Skelton in the most fulsome terms. He is said to
surpass Orpheus and is compared to Virgil. His talents
are said to come from Calliope, the chief of the muses.
The praise is extravagant and wholly disproportionate to
what appears to have been Skelton's poetic achievement at
this time. To some extent at least Erasmus' encomium must
be seen as the effusion of a courteous visitor to the
court of Henry VII, disinclined to afford any possibility
of offence to his powerful hosts.

To some extent - but Erasmus' acclaim cannot be wholly
discounted. For there does seem to be evidence that within the next ten years Skelton had established himself as
one of the leading contemporary English poets. Before
turning to that evidence it may be helpful to speculate a
little on how Skelton came to achieve such popularity.

Only one of his works had been printed by 1500, and no
more appear to have been printed until about 1513. And it
must be borne in mind that printings of early books were
generally extremely small. How then would Skelton have
been read by Caxton, Erasmus and those other contemporaries whom we will consider next? There is no simple answer
to this question. But it is worth recalling that, in the
late fifteenth and early sixteenth centuries, the printed
book (first brought to England by Caxton) was not yet
firmly established as the most potent force for the dissemination of literature. It would, indeed, have been
most probable that Caxton had read Skelton's 'Tulle'
and 'dyodorus syculus' in manuscript. The latter work,
in fact, survives now only in that form (in a copy in
Trinity College, Cambridge). There are other circumstances
tending to support the view that manuscript circulation
was probably more influential in the dissemination of
Skelton's earlier works than were printed books. Chief
among these is the actual milieu in which he created
many of his earlier works. For at this period of his
life Skelton was mainly associated with the King's court
and with courtly circles. Within such circles much of
his verse was doubtless produced for specific local occasions, most obviously ones requiring entertainment. For
example, the comic lyric 'Mannerly Margery Mylk and Ale'

survives only in a manuscript (British Library MS Add.
5465) together with its music. And 'Against Garnesche'
was a 'flyting' written at 'the kynges most noble
commaundement'; we gather this from the only surviving
contemporary copy which is again a manuscript (British
Library MS Harley 367). The work itself is a comic,
satiric attack on one of King Henry VIII's courtiers.
Skelton's place within this courtly milieu may well have
defined the manner and extent of the dissemination of a
number of his earlier works, serving to restrict them, in
the main, to a relatively small audience most of whom en-
countered his works in manuscript. Such an intimate
relationship between poet and audience was in no sense
untypical in the early sixteenth century. It is worth
recalling that, a generation later, none of Wyatt's poems
and only three of Surrey's appeared in printed form
during their lifetimes.

Such circumstances make the growth of Skelton's poetic
reputation particularly striking. For example, 'The
Great Chronicle of London' (c. 1510) links him with
'poettis of such ffame' as Chaucer and his own contemporaries Thomas More and William Cornish (No. 4). The
allusion to Skelton is a brief one. But that in itself
seems suggestive of the status of Skelton's poetic reputation and credentials needed no further documentation.(5)

Others were equally ready to link Skelton with great
poets of the past. Henry Bradshaw, in two saints' lives
written around 1513, 'The Life of St. Radegunde' and 'The
Life of St. Werburge', links Skelton with both Chaucer and
Lydgate in terms which are designed to suggest an equality
amongst them (No. 5). These laudatory references are
interesting for several reasons. Although few of Skelton's works can be confidently dated within the period
1500-13, it would seem on the evidence of Bradshaw's praise
praise that he was probably writing quite extensively
during this time. This is the more noteworthy since between approximately 1503 and 1512 Skelton seems to have
left the court for relative exile as rector of Diss in
Norfolk. And yet his works seem to have been circulating
sufficiently extensively for a monk in the north of England (Bradshaw lived in Chester) to have been familiar
with them.

In Skelton's middle years, when he returned to court
c. 1512 after his years of exile at Diss, there seems to
be a change in the nature of his audience and in the
manner in which his works circulated. It is from this
time that Skelton's works began to achieve a more general
circulation in print as he was called upon to fulfil his
newly designated role as 'orator regius' (the King's

orator). His 'Ballade of the Scottish Kynge' (c. 1513)
was the second of his works to be printed - after a fif-
teen year hiatus since 'The Bouge of Court'. This was
followed by 'Elynor Rumming' (1521), 'The Garland of
Laurel' (1523), 'Dyuers Ballettys Solacious' and 'A
Comely Coystroun' (both published c. 1527, but including
material written much earlier), and 'A Replycacion against
certain scholars' (c. 1528). The decision to print these
particular works suggests a desire to give wide dissemination to particular aspects of Skelton's achievement, in
particular to those most closely identified with the
'orator regius': that is, those works which stress courtly
attitudes or 'establishment' positions. 'The Ballade of
the Scottishe Kynge' and 'A Replycacion' are both 'public'
works proclaiming orthodox political positions. 'The Garland...' and 'Dyuers Ballettys...' demonstrate a concern
with courtly attitudes and values. It is only in 'Elynor
Rumming' and 'A Comely Coystroun' that Skelton's distinctive comic/satiric vein achieved print during his lifetime. This was doubtless because their humour and satire
were directed at targets of little or no political significance. Skelton's great political satire on Wolsey,
'Colin Cloute' has come down to use in what are probably
its earliest forms in two fragmentary manuscripts (British
Library MSS Harley 2252 and Lansdowne 762). It seems that
such works were felt to be too volatile in subject matter
and treatment for a publishers to risk circulating them in
print, at least while author and subject were still alive.
    There is earlier evidence of contemporary sensitivity
to the subject-matter of Skelton's verse. It is ironic
that the only one of his contemporaries with whom Skelton
is linked by Bradshaw is the poet and translator Alexander
Barclay - 'religious Barkeley' or 'preignaunt Barkley' as
he is called. For it was Barclay who, a few years previously, had struck the first controversial note concerning
Skelton's reputation. In his poem 'The Ship of Fools'
(1509) he introduces a tersely dismissive comment on
Skelton's 'Philip Sparrow'. 'Wyse men loue vertue, wylde
people wantones', he claims, placing Skelton's poem firmly
on the side of 'wantones' together with the 'Iest ...
[and] tale of Robyn hode' (No. 3). This is the first
criticism of Skelton's 'wantonness' or 'lewdness'. What
Barclay means by such terms is not altogether clear. But
it is interesting that he should equate Skelton's works
with such popular literature as the 'tale of Robyn hode'.
Such equations were to recur in the sixteenth and seventeenth centuries. Skelton the scholar all too quickly
became a Skelton synonymous with popular and folk literature, with all the attendant implications of licence and

disorder. It is particularly ironic, in the present instance, that such criticism should be levelled at 'Philip
Sparrow', the one poem of Skelton's which future generations were to admire with barely a dissenting voice.

The basis for Barclay's disapproval of Skelton is not
known, but it seems not to have been limited to his dislike of 'Philip Sparrow'. He wrote a work entitled
'Contra Skeltonum' ('Against Skelton') which has not survived. (6) And there is a passage in one of his 'Eclogues'
which may perhaps be an attack on Skelton; it reads in
part: (7)

> Another thing yet is greatly more damnable,
> Of rascolde poetes yet is a shamfull rable,
> Which voyde of wisedome presumeth to indite,
> Though they haue scantly the cunning of a snite:
> And to what vices that princes moste intende,
> Those dare these fooles solemnize and commende.
> Then is he decked as Poete laureate,
> When stinking Thais made him her graduate.

A passage in Barclay's 'Life of St. George' (1515) contains a disapproving reference to 'he which is lawreat'
which may also refer to Skelton. (8)

Presumably Barclay's gibes are responses to comments of
Skelton's own, now unfortunately lost. One can only speculate on their content. Certainly Skelton seems to have
been eager to involve himself in controversy with his
fellow writers. An indication of this is provided by the
verses of William Lily, the grammarian (No. 6). Again, we
lack the verses of Skelton's which engendered them, but
the virulence of Lily's attack bears testimony to the
force of the former's satire. It is unwise to attach too
much importance to such an attack in the critical tradition, especially given the lack of any clear context in
which to evaluate it. But together with Barclay's comments, Lily provides the first hint of controversy surrounding Skelton's reputation. These are the first inti-
mations of what is to follow in reaction against Skelton's
satiric mode later in the century.

But the final known contemporary judgment of Skelton
casts no shadows across his reputation. Robert Whittington, another grammarian, wrote a poem in praise of Skelton
which was published in 1519. Whittington was a fellow
laureat of Oxford, and possibly also a friend of Skelton's
so his praise must be taken with a pinch of salt. Moreover
his poem, whilst lengthy, is too generalized in its
response to Skelton's work to be of much assistance in
establishing the critical heritage. He is praised

elaborately for his rhetorical skill, which is said to
surpass that of such stock figures of rhetorical excellence as Demosthenes and Ulysses, and is finally addressed
as 'culte poeta' and 'Anglorum vatum gloria' (No. 7).

This note of acclaim seems to exhaust the contemporary
judgments of Skelton. Already, however, in the relatively
small body of critical comment available from his own
lifetime, it is possible to discern something of the
diversity of responses that Skelton was subsequently to
prove capable of exciting. The polarities of critical
discussion, of praise and disapproval, were already firmly
established before his death.

One can only speculate on the lack of any critical commentary on Skelton during the final decade of his life.
It may well be connected with his involvement in political
controversy during the 1520s, particularly with his
attacks on Cardinal Wolsey, the King's chief advisor.
Although he and Wolsey were subsequently reconciled, it
may be that those in a position to comment on Skelton's
talents found it safer, both for themselves and for him,
to remain silent.

This is speculation, as is so much of our attempt to
understand the relationship between poet and audience in
Tudor England. But even on the meagre evidence that does
exist it seems safe to assert that Skelton's situation as
poet contrasts strikingly with that of his late medieval
predecessors and of other early sixteenth-century poets.
Some of his late medieval predecessors were able personally to supervise the copying and dissemination of their
poems. The 'Confessio Amantis' of Chaucer's fourteenth-
century contemporary John Gower underwent several revi-
sions in this way. Certain fifteenth-century poets were
able to go even further and act as their own 'publishers'.
Such writers as Thomas Hoccleve and John Capgrave copied
their works themselves and supervised their circulation.
There is, in contrast, no evidence of such a developed,
or even a particularly organized, manuscript tradition of
Skelton's works. Most of those works for which manuscripts survive exist in unique copies, none of which can
be directly connected with Skelton himself. This also
contrasts with the textual situation of sixteenth-century
courtly poets such as Wyatt and Surrey, whose works had a
solely manuscript circulation during their lifetimes.
Unlike them, Skelton's works did not have an audience
restricted to a narrow coterie in which works could be
manageably passed from hand to hand in manuscript without
requiring any more permanent or extensive dissemination.

This is partially due to the fact that the growth in
Skelton's reputation coincided with the development of

printing in England. As I have indicated, there was a
steady increase in the demand for his works during the
latter part of his life, a demand which could not be
adequately met by manuscript copying. This demand was
itself doubtless a result of the diversity of Skelton's
literary productivity, ranging as it did from courtly
verse to low comedy, from orthodox political affirmations
to politically volatile satire. Skelton was the first
English writer whose works excited interest across a wide
social spectrum during his own lifetimes. Interest continued to grow after his death in 1529. This is evidenced
by the numerous posthumous sixteenth-century editions of
his works.

But even so, there is no significant critical comment
on his work between the 1520s and the 1550s. It seems
that the evident interest in Skelton was expressed in
other forms than direct critical statement. In particular, the biographical or pseudo-biographical tradition of
Skelton probably began to emerge even before his death
with the publication of the 'Hundred Merry Tales' in 1525;
number 41 concerns Skelton. This tradition was both
crystallized and given new impetus by the publication of
the 'Merry Tales', attributed to Skelton, in 1567. (9)
It led to the development in verse and prose of the figure
of the libertine eccentric who had married in defiance of
the Church and defended his own paternity in the face of
his parishioners' disapproval - most of which may not be
far from the truth. The influence of this biographical
tradition and its remarkable vitality can be seen in the
various jest-book accounts of Skelton, such as those in
'Tales, and quicke answers, very mery, and pleasant to
rede' (n.d.) (10), as well as in the form of anecdotes in
such works as John Parkhurst's 'Ludicra sive Epigrammata'
(1573) (11) and John Chamber's 'A Treatise against Judicial Astrologie' (1601). (12) In its most extreme
elaboration and degeneration 'Dr Skelton' appears in the
jest-biography 'The Life of Long Meg of Westminster'
(1620) as the lover of the eponymous heroine to whom he
speaks in his 'mad merry vain'. (13) In other forms the
biographical tradition saw the linking of Skelton with
another jest-figure, Scoggin. I will return to this
point.

Another important indication of the esteem in which
Skelton was held can be found in the number of imitations
his work seems to have inspired. Even before his death
his influence can be detected in Roy and Barlow's 'Rede
Me and Be Nat Wrothe' (1528). (14) And in the 1530s and
1540s the playwright John Heywood was clearly influenced
by Skelton. (15) Indeed, the distinctive Skeltonic verse

seems quickly to have gained popularity, especially for
polemic purposes. Several controversial tracts survive in
this verse form from the 1540s and 1550s and other works
continue to be written in Skeltonics until near the end of
the century. As late as 1589 a poem on the Armada
appeared entitled 'A Skeltonicall Salutation' and was
actually written in Skeltonics. These are not the only
indications of Skelton's influence in the late sixteenth
and early seventeenth centuries. But before discussing
such indications it is helpful to look at the actual
critical commentary on Skelton's works following his
death.

The first writer to offer any such discussion was the
scholar, book collector, religious controversialist and
playwright, bishop John Bale. Bale, in fact, left several
accounts of Skelton in his various biographical and
bibliographical compilations. In his first biographical
register of English writers, 'Illustrium Maioris Britanniae Scriptorum' (1548), he includes only a brief comment
on Skelton among the final additions to his book: 'Skeltonus poeta laureatus sub diuerso genere metri edidit'
(Skelton, poet laureat, composed in various kinds of
verse'). (16) But in his manuscript work, the 'Index
Britanniae Scriptorum', he offers a much more extensive
account. (17) This latter account appears with only
minor variations in his 'Scriptorum illustrium maioris
Brytanniae' (1557). This account (No. 8) provides the
first biographical sketch of Skelton and the first posthumous description of the canon of his works. Bale also
offers some critical comments, most of them basically
sympathetic to Skelton. He is compared favourably with
Lucian, Democritus and, most interestingly, with Horace,
with whom he is identified by virtue of his capacity to
utter criticism from behind a mask of laughter. Indeed,
Bale lays particular stress on Skelton's satiric and
controversial roles. As a controversialist himself,
Bale was perhaps more readily able to offer a sympathetic
discussion of Skelton than many of his critics.

For Bale, Skelton was primarily a satirist, attacking
reprehensible abuses. This view recurs, albeit in a more
vivid and fantastical form, in William Bullein's comments
in his 'Dialogue against the Fever Pestilence' (1564).
The only satires he singles out for comment are those
against 'the cankered Cardinall Wolsey'. But his opinion
of Skelton is, by implication, very high. For Skelton
is linked in Bullein's grouping once more with Chaucer and
Lydgate, joined now by the third of the triumvirate of
famous medieval poets, John Gower (No. 9).

This praise, however, pales in comparison with the

elaborate compliments offered by Thomas Churchyard in his
poem prefacing the publication of Skelton's 'Pithy,
Pleasaunt and Profitable Works' in 1568. This poem (No.
10) places Skelton against a wide-ranging literary tradition. After invoking classical and European traditions
through references to Marot, Petrarch, Dante, Homer, Ovid
and Virgil, Churchyard goes on to maintain that

> But neuer I nor you I troe,
>   In sentence plaine and short
> Did yet beholde with eye,
>   In any forraine tonge:
> A higher verse a staetly style
>   That may be read or song
> Than is this daye in deede
>   Our englishe verse and ryme

English literary history is then recounted: 'Piers Plowman', Chaucer, Surrey, Vaux, Phaer and Edwards are all
mentioned before Churchyard turns to Skelton, 'The blos-
some of my frute'. But his actual comments are dis-
appointingly feeble. Skelton is 'Most pleasant euery
way,/As poets ought to be'. The most distinctive feature
of his observations is the fact that once again the
satiric vein is singled out: 'His terms to taunts did
lean'. To some extent Churchyard's poem is merely a blurb,
a puff for the edition it precedes. But, it does confirm
a sense of Skelton's achievement consistent with the views
of Bale and Bullein.
    Indeed, others were perfectly ready to sustain Church-
yard's view of Skelton as one of the pre-eminent poets of
past or present. In his poem 'The Rewarde of Wickedness'
(1574) Richard Robinson describes a visit to Helicon where,
after seeing Homer, Virgil, Ovid and Chaucer, he comes
upon 'Skelton and Lydgat' with Wager, Heywood and Barnaby
Googe. A similar encounter takes place in the anonymous
poem 'A poore knight his Pallace of private pleasures'
(1579). There the narrator visits the 'camp' of Cupid
where he encounters many great poets including (once again)
Homer, Virgil and Ovid together with Hesiod and Euripides.
He also sees Chaucer, 'the cheafest of all English men',
and also 'There Goure [Gower] did stand, with cap in hand,
and Skelton did the same'. Both poems link Skelton, as
did Churchyard, with the greatest writers of classical and
English literary tradition.
    This was the high point of sixteenth-century acclaim.
Henceforward, the favourable view both of Skelton's satire
and of his poetic status was increasingly questioned,
either directly or by implication. The comments of John

Grange, for example, in his 'Golden Aphroditis' (1577)
praise Skelton in a curiously backhanded manner, talking
of his 'wryting of toyes and foolish theames' and his
'gibyng sorte' (No. 11). But Grange was, none the less,
sufficiently affected by Skelton to echo and even borrow
from his works. (18) In the same year, Holinshed in 'The
Laste volume of the Chronicles' speaks rather patroniz-
ingly of 'John Skelton, a pleasant Poet'. (19) And less
than ten years later, in 1586, William Webbe also damns
him with faint praise as a 'pleasant conceyted fellowe'
(No. 12). Both Grange and Webbe do, however, continue to
pay perfunctory tribute to Skelton as a satirist. But in
the light of what is to follow it is significant that
Grange speaks of Skelton's 'ragged ryme' as appropriate
for his satiric mode.

For, in 1589, the first wholesale assault was made on
Skelton's reputation, an attack which primarily took
issue with just such questions of Skelton's satiric
propensity and metrical idiosyncrasy. Puttenham's 'Arte
of English Poesie' (No. 13) contains an explicit denigration of these aspects of his poetic achievement. As a
satirist he is 'sharpe' but with 'more rayling and scoffery than became a Poet Lawreat'. Indeed, he is linked
with those who among the Greeks 'were called *Pantomimi*,
with vs buffons'. It may be that in this judgment Puttenham was influenced by the jest-book figure of Skelton,
the lively, sometimes coarse buffoon of the 'Merry Tales'.
A more obvious factor is Puttenham's preference for more
'courtly' poets such as Surrey, Wyatt, Vaux, Phaer and
Edwards. Whereas less than two decades previously Skelton
had been compared favourably with several of these
figures, now he is contrasted with them to his disadvantage.

Of greater critical interest was Puttenham's denigration of Skeltonic metre as the work of a 'rude rayling
rimer & all his doings ridiculous'. Such criticism is an
attack on the most distinctive feature of Skelton's verse
technique, his use of 'Skeltonics' - short, irregularly
stressed lines, characterized by extended rhymes. For
Puttenham this was the style of the 'common people' which
he rejected in favour of the 'concord' of the 'courtly
maker'. The terms of Puttenham's criticism were to affect
subsequent views of Skeltonic verse from the 1590s and
into the early decades of the seventeenth century. Its
effect can be detected, for example, in Gabriel Harvey's
various references to Skelton in the 1590s. He tends to
present him as a grotesque figure who, like his own enemy
Greene, would 'counterfeitan an hundred dogged Fables ...
and most currishly snarle ... where [he] should most

kindly fawne and licke' (No. 14b). Elsewhere, Harvey de-
picts Skelton as a 'madbrayned knave' (No. 14a) of bizarre
predilections, as a melancholy fool and a poet of limited
technical skill. (20) Others in this period place similar
stress on his alleged metrical infelicities. Hall, in
1598, speaks of his 'breathlesse rhymes' (21) - but does
nevertheless seem to have been influenced by Skelton in
his own satiric writings. (22) And Francis Meres, in
'Palladis Tamia', also published in 1598, reiterates
almost verbatim Puttenham's strictures on Skelton's verse.
(23)
     Others were even more explicit in stating their dis-
approval of Skeltonics. For example, William Browne in
the first ecloque of 'The Shepherd's Pipe' (1614) complains that 'Skeltons reed' does 'iarre' (No. 20). Also
Nicholas Breton in 1612 'Cornu-copiae or Pasquils Night
Cap' talks of Skelton's 'ruffling rimes' which are 'emptie
quite of marrow', before going on to join the small band
of critics who can find something unpleasant to say about
'Philip Sparrow' (No. 18).
     This disapproval of 'Philip Sparrow' is the more re-
markable since admiration of this poem seems to have en-
dured even during this relatively low ebb in Skelton's
critical fortunes. One indication of this regard is the
number of poets who appear to have been influenced by it.
Both Gascoigne (in 'Weeds', 1575) and Philip Sidney (in
'Astrophel and Stella', 1591) produced imitations of the
poem. Its influence can also be found in parts of Sidney's 'Arcadia'. Shakespeare alludes to it in 'King
John'. And manifestations of this influence by imitation
were to continue into the seventeenth century. John Bart-
let in his 'Book of Airs' (1606) produced a version of
'Philip Sparrow' as did such later poets as William Cart-
wright, Richard Brome and Robert Herrick. (24)
     Other works of Skelton's failed either to excite much
comment or exert any influence in the late sixteenth and
early seventeenth centuries. The chief example of such
failure is the poem 'Colin Clout', which was, on the evidence of separate editions produced, the single most popular work of Skelton's during the sixteenth century. (25)
But it seems to have been rarely singled out for comment
or imitation. The most famous indication of its influence
is Spenser's introduction of the figure Colin Clout into
various poems, notably The Shepherd's Calendar (1579).(26)
Otherwise there is little apart from a friendly, but
qualified, reference by Drayton (No. 16c) to indicate any
on-going interest in the poem.
     There are, however, some more generalized indications
of Skelton's reputation and influence to be detected in

the drama of the period. Both Christopher Marlowe, in
'Dr Faustus' (1604), and Ben Jonson, in 'The Devil is an
Ass' (c. 1611), introduce passages into their plays which
reveal a discernible Skeltonic influence. (27)   Jonson
includes Skelton as a character in his masque 'The Fortunate Isles' (1625), where he is linked with the jest-book
figure of 'Scogan' (otherwise 'Scoggin'). Before this
the figure of Skelton had made another dramatic appearance
in Anthony Munday's 'The Downfall of Robert Earl of
Huntingdon' (1601). Here as on previous occasions Skelton
is identified with the Robin Hood of folk literature.
Skelton appears initially 'in propria persona' and again
later in the play as Friar Tuck. In the latter guise he
speaks passages in Skeltonics - until Little John pleads
with him: 'Stoppe master *Skelton*: whither will you
runne?' (28)   Skelton may also have appeared, again linked
with Scoggin, elsewhere in the drama of the period. (29)
     The general tendency of these appearances is to iden-
tify Skelton with a comic, low world of popular culture.
This identification takes two distinct forms. First,
there is the use of Skeltonics in a way which generally
tends to suggest tediousness and clumsiness, and their
inappropriateness for serious verse. Secondly, there is
the identification between Skelton and Scoggin (also
Scogin, Skogan). The origin of the identification between
the two figures is obscure, but appears to have begun soon
after Skelton's death. (30)   The actual figure of Scoggin
appears to have been based on a confusion involving the
fourteenth-century Henry Scogan, a friend of Chaucer, and
the legendary John Scoggan, sometimes claimed to have been
Henry VII's fool. Nor is it clear how these two iden-
tities first became intertwined one with another and subsequently with that of Skelton. But the equation seems to
have been an attractive one for writers and critics of the
sixteenth and seventeenth centuries, and it is one that
served to further diminish Skelton's claim to considera-
tion as a serious poet.
     But the general disparagement of Skelton seems to have
attracted special attention to one particular work, 'The
Tunnyng of Elynor Rumming'. This bawdy tale of an ale-
wife was viewed as epitomizing the work of the 'low'
Skelton and excited a considerable amount of comment in
consequence. Some comment was denigrating. Nashe, writing in 1600, speaks rather contemptuously of the 'riffe-
raffe of the rumming of Elanor'. (31)   Arthur Dent's 'The
Plaine Man's Pathway to Heaven' (1601) links 'Ellen of
Rumming' with other 'vaine and friuolous bookes of Tales,
Iestes, and lies', equating the poem with contemporary
jest-books and other popular works which are dismissed as

'so much trashe and rubbish' (No. 15). More subtle, but
equally critical, on somewhat different grounds, is the
use of Skelton's poem in Ben Jonson's masque 'The Fortunate Isles' (1625). (32) In this masque Skelton appears
as a character ('skipping Skelton') together with his
comic alter ego Scogan and speaks lines adapted from
'Elynor Rumming'. (33) His function as character and as
speaker of his own verses is clearly a comic and/or burlesque one. He earns the approval of Merefool, a character who, as his name suggests, represents values which are
rejected in the total context of the masque. Skelton and
his poem become, for Jonson, representative of certain
kinds of literary values which he chooses to dismiss,
values which seem to see the poem as synonymous with vulgar and inept versification. (34)

Elsewhere there are some comments which express admiration for the poem, either directly or indirectly, because
it is possible to identify it with popular literature.
'Elynor' is echoed in 'The Cobbler of Canterbury' (1590),
a collection of droll tales. (35) It is also mentioned
with approval in a later adaptation of that work, 'The
Tinker of Turvey' (1630). In the Preface to the latter
the Tinker encounters an ale-wife: (36)

I asked her who brewed that nectar, whose malt-worm so
nibbled at my pericranium, and she said herself, for
old Mother Eleanor Ruming was her granddam and Skelton
her cousin, who wrote fine rhymes in praise of her high
and mighty ale.

Others were even more positive in their praise. Drayton,
for example, describes 'Ellen of Rumming' as one of the
'English bookes ... that ile not part with', linking it
with such other favourite works as (once again) 'Robin
Hood' and 'Bevis of Hampton' (No. 16a). (37)

The single most extensive manifestation of the appeal
of 'Elynor Rumming' during this period is in the burlesque
poem 'Pimlyco, or Runne Red-Cap' (1609), a work which examines both Skelton and his poem. Concerning the latter,
the anonymous author finds much to praise. Although he
recognizes that 'Elynor' may be 'of so base account', by
virtue of its 'low' subject-matter, he can find prece-
dents in Virgil and Ovid to justify the exploration of
humble themes (No. 17):

Since then these *Rare-ones* stack'd their strings,
From the hie-tuned acts of Kings
For notes so low, less is thy *Blame*....

The author is clearly drawn to the 'liuely colours' of
Skelton's poem; he goes on to quote most of the first 250
lines of it.

However, affection for Skelton's poem does not appear
to extend to Skelton himself. He is seen as belonging to
an age 'when few wryt well' and is linked to other (un-
named) contemporary poets who have only 'empty Sculles'.
Clearly the response to 'Elynor Rumming' is, in this instance, an ambivalent one. The author seems intrigued by
the dichotomy (as he sees it) between Skelton's status in
his own time as poet laureate and the nature of the poetic
subject-matter that won him his status. Although he finds
the subject-matter attractive it seems to him inadequate
for such status.

This sense that Skelton is not a poet to be taken seriously emerges elsewhere in the early seventeenth century.
Michael Drayton, for example, had an evident affection for
Skelton's works. His praise of 'Elynor Rumming' and
'Colin Clout' has already been mentioned. He was sufficiently influenced by Skelton to attempt a 'Skeltoniad'
and other poems in Skeltonics. (38) But elsewhere he reveals a defensive attitude towards Skelton's verse. In
his 'Ode to Himselfe and the Harpe' he suggests that 'tis
possible to clyme ... although in SKELTON'S Ryme' (No.
16b). The comment seems to reflect a contemporary doubt
about the viability of the Skeltonic verse form as a
vehicle for serious poetry. Similar doubts are expressed
by Humphrey King in his 'An Halfe-penny-worthe of Wit ...'
(1613) when Skelton is joined with other 'merry men' whose
verses are suitable only for unserious subjects, such as
tales of 'Robin Hoode/And little Iohn' (No. 19).

The prevailing critical perspective on Skelton during
the early seventeenth century offers only a trivialized
view of his art. His main claim to interest then was in
his depiction of low life. (39) The attitude of 'Elynor
Rumming' appears to have been especially influential. It
was the last of Skelton's works to be reprinted during
the seventeenth century, in the famous edition of 1624,
with a picture of Elynor the ale-wife herself and prefatory verses by the ghost of Skelton lamenting the current state of English ale. (40)

This view of Skelton as the irresponsible madcap
achieves its fullest and most unsympathetic presentation
in 'The Golden Fleece' by 'Orpheus Junior'. (41) The
exact nature of this curious work resists summary definition. Published in 1626, it is an odd combination of
historical complaint and travel literature. Near the end
of the third part, Skelton and Scoggin appear to inter-
rupt a sonnet by St David in praise of Charles I. They

are identified as 'the chiefe Advocates for the Dogrel
Rimers by the procurement of *Zoilus, Momus* [figures of divi-
sion and protest] and others of the *Popish Sect*' (p. 83).
(42) There follows a three-way exchange in verse between
St David, Scoggin and Skelton (pp. 84-92). On the next
day, however, the latter confess their faults and are censured by Lady Pallas (p. 93). The burden of her strictures is an attack on the satiric style and mode as
embodied in these two figures. She argues that 'a simple
course Poeme inriched with liuely matter and iuyce, ought
to be preferred before an heroicall swolne verse pust vp
with barme or froth of an inconsiderate wit' (p. 94). In
other contexts the argument might serve to defend criti-
cally such a poem as 'Elynor Rumming'. But here the
thrust of the attack is directed at the notion of satiric
writing, 'For it is easier to finde faults, then to mend
them, to pull downe a house, then to build one vp' (ibid.).
And ultimately 'all *scoffing companions*, and base ballet
Rimers', including Scoggin and Skelton, are banished from
Parnassus (p. 95).

In 'The Golden Fleece' the current elements of criticism of Skelton tend to converge. Here appears the comic
grotesque figure of the 'biographical' tradition, demonstrating his predilection for lewd verse and also func-
tioning as the divisive satirist (recalling the 'Pantomimi'
criticism of Puttenham). Whilst the account is in no sense
critical, it does indirectly reveal a great deal about
contemporary critical thinking.

After this point, comment on Skelton tends largely to
disappear. An indication of this lack of interest is provided by 'A Banquet of Jests' (1639) which talks of Skelton's 'meere rime, once read, but now laid by' (No. 22).
(43) But the future trend had already been anticipated in
the comments of John Pits in his posthumously published
'Relationum Historicarum de Rebus Anglicis' (1619). Much
of his account of Skelton is biographical, probably deriv-
ing from Bale. But his value judgments appear to be his
own (p. 701):

Lingua enim periculosum loquacibus malum. Sermo
salsus saepe vertitur in mordacem, risus in opprobrium,
iocus in amaritudinem, et dum tibi videre false sub-
monere, carpis acerbe.

His language had dangerous evil in its utterances. His
nimble speech was often turned into jest, laughter into
opprobrium, mirth into bitterness, and while he would
pretend to be submissive, he spoke cruelly.

Once again Skelton the satirist is dismissed. And the
disapproval of some of his works seems to have led to a
general disinclination to read any of them. A little
later, in 1622, Henry Peacham is more succinctly dismissive of Skelton's claims as a poet. In 'The Compleat
Gentleman' (No. 21) Skelton is treated in the course of a
survey of English poetry as 'a Poet *Laureate*, for what
desert I could neuer heare'.

Henceforward, criticism of Skelton becomes primarily
biographical. This tendency in the critical tradition is
exemplified by the works of Fuller and Anthony à Wood.
Admittedly both were writing what were primarily biographical reference works, but, even allowing for that
fact, their choosing not to discuss Skelton as a creative
artist is striking. Fuller's 'Worthies', published in 1662
(No. 24), is not altogether unsympathetic to Skelton, but
he is seen solely in biographical terms. His life is
presented in dramatic contours - the satirist with '*wit*
too much' fighting against larger forces than he is capable of resisting. In this drama there is no sense of
Skelton's verse. None of his works is mentioned. Skelton
the man is the sole figure of interest.

In à Wood's 'Athenae Oxonienses' (1691-2) there is not
even that dimension of interest. À Wood lists references
to various John Skeltons and gives an account of the canon
(which is probably not based on any first-hand knowledge).
But the only comment on the verse is sharply disapproving:
'...yet the generality said, that his witty discourses
were biting, his laughter opprobrious and scornful, and
his jokes commonly sharp and reflecting' (p. 21). The
terms of à Wood's criticism strikingly recall Pits's
earlier comments. It seems doubtful whether à Wood had
actually read Skelton.

Elsewhere there is abundant evidence of a more general
neglect. No editions of Skelton's works were published
between 1624 and 1718. Hence it is not surprising that
the only copy of his poems that James Howell could find in
1655 was an extremely battered one 'skulking in *Duck-Lane*,
pitifully totter'd and torn'. Nor is it surprising that
Howell should have found little merit in Skelton's
poems, apart from a few lines of 'quaint sense', for (as
he notes) 'the Genius of the Age is quite another thing'
(No. 23). And Samuel Holland in 'Wit and Fancy in a Maze'
(1656) felt it necessary to gloss the mere mention of
Skelton's name - and to do so in highly inaccurate terms.
After observing that '*Skelton, Gower*, and the Monk of
Bury [Lydgate] were at Daggers-drawing for *Chawcer*'
(p. 102), he adds a marginal note to Skelton's name:
'Henry 4. his Poet Lawreat, who wrote disguises for the
young Princes'.

What infrequent discussions there are damn the works
with faint praise. Edward Phillips in 1675 presents
Skelton as 'accounted a notable Poet ... when doubtless
good Poets were scarce'. He then proceeds to attack
Skelton's style ('miserable loos, rambling') and his
'galloping measure of Verse'. Like Howell, Phillips can
only discover Skelton 'in an old printed Book, but imperfect' and can only give a very selective account of the
canon (No. 25). His comments demonstrate the absence of
serious critical interest in Skelton during the late seventeenth century. Such faint influence as can be perceived
manifests itself in the odd attempts at Skeltonic imitation
as those in 'The Old Gill' (1687) (44) and by John Bunyan
in his 'Booke for Boys and Girls' (1686). (45)

    Various other references to Skelton during the latter
part of the seventeenth century confirm the evidence of
critical neglect. William Winstanley's account in 'Lives
of the Most Famous English Poets' (1687), pp. 42-3, is
merely a conflation of the accounts of Phillips and
Fuller, and has no independent value. There is slightly
more interest in a brief passage in Thomas Rymer's 'Short
View of Tragedy' (1693), since Rymer makes there the
earliest comment on Skelton the dramatist, contrasting his
work unfavourably with the devotional drama of Europe.
But, as with other seventeenth-century critics, it is
doubtful whether Rymer had read much Skelton, since his
only Skelton citation is from the poem 'Why Come Ye Not to
Court?', which he refers to as a drama. (46)

    From this point there follows a lengthy period of
silence broken only by two reprints, that of 'Elynor
Rumming' in 1718 (to which I will return) and the 1736
reprint of the 1568 edition, the first collected edition
of Skelton's works for over 150 years. This collected
edition seems to have prompted the most famous of all
critical denigrations of Skelton. Alexander Pope in his
'Imitations of Horace' (1737) made his dismissal of
'beastly Skelton' (No. 27a). Elsewhere Pope is equally
dismissive: 'there's nothing in them [Skelton's poems]
that's worth reading' (No. 27b). Pope's responses to
Skelton climax the contempt and neglect that constitute
this phase of Skelton's critical heritage. Even Dr Johnson's subsequent dismissive criticism of Skelton's lack of
'great elegance of language' appears quite positive by
comparison (No. 29).

    Yet even before Pope the tide had begun to turn.
Almost the first sign of renewed interest was the reprinting in 1718 of 'Elynor Rumming', (47) the first edition of
any of Skelton's works since 1624. The Preface to this
edition has been justly described by its discoverer as

'of some importance in the history not merely of Skelton's
reputation but even of eighteenth century critical
tastes'. (48) Skelton is praised for his 'just and
natural Description'. Those who would wish to object to
the lowness of the poem's subject-matter or its antiquity
are met by the affirmation that it merits the attention
of 'Persons of an extensive Fancy and just Relish' who may
appreciate 'a Moment's Amusement' (No. 26). Once again,
'Elynor Rumming' becomes a critical touchstone. But here
an unusual degree of critical independence is apparent in
the evaluation of the work, a willingness to articulate
criteria for admiration amid the general atmosphere of
distaste and neglect.
    Other approving voices, of equally independent spirit,
were to follow. The reprinting of the poems in 1736
appears to have brought Skelton to the notice of Mrs
Elizabeth Cooper. In 'The Muses Library' (1737) she hails
him unequivocally as 'The Restorer of Invention in *English*
Poetry!'. Her acclaim is subsequently somewhat qualified
by her feeling that he was 'much debas'd by the Rust of
the Age He liv'd in', particularly in his verse forms -
thus harking back to a preoccupation of much pre-Restora-
Restoration criticism. But elsewhere she shows further
evidence of her highly individual judgment. She is the
first critic to single out for particular praise 'The
Bouge of Court', 'a Poem of great Merit' which is worthy
of comparison with 'the inimitable *Spencer* [sic]'. Mrs
Cooper had clearly read at least some of Skelton's poems
with a measure of care and a freshness of insight which
evidently had some influence on her own age (No. 28).
For, a little later, Theophilus Cibber in his 'Lives of
the Poets' (1753) (49) reprints her comments with only
minor additions - although without any acknowledgment of
his source.
    However, such a spirit of admiration as that displayed
by the 1718 editor and Mrs Cooper is not evident in the
first extensive critical appraisal. In 1778 Thomas
Warton, critic and poet, published the second volume of
his monumental 'History of English Poetry', a work which
marks the beginning of modern Skelton criticism (No. 30).
It cannot be said that Warton is particularly sympathetic
to Skelton. In his introductory biographical sketch he
notes Skelton's 'ludicrous disposition' and further
announces at the outset of his discussion that 'It is in
vain to apologise for the coarseness, obscenity, and
scurrility of Skelton, by saying that his poetry is tinctured with the manners of his age. Skelton would have
been a writer without decorum at any period.' Warton goes
on to compare him unfavourably with Chaucer and to note

some of the disapproving comments of the late sixteenth
century. His essential conclusion is also disapproving in
accord with the critical temper of his own age: '[Skel-
ton's] genius seems better suited to low burlesque, than
to liberal and manly satire.'

Elsewhere, Warton does find particular passages he can
single out for praise, including (once again) the 'Bouge of
Court' where Skelton shows himself 'not always incapable of
exhibiting allegorical imagery with spirit and dignity'.
But the main stress in Warton's discussion falls on the
variable quality of the verse: 'No writer is more unequal
than Skelton.' The lack of sympathy with Skelton's
achievement is evident. Warton is temperamentally an
antiquarian, always ready to be deflected from his discussion into by-ways of curious knowledge - the biography
of the earl of Northumberland, medieval tapestries,
macaronic verse (omitted in No. 30). But his work, for
all its limited sympathy and understanding of Skelton's
verse, is of genuine importance. It forms the first
extended criticism of Skelton's poetry buttressed by any
analysis and illustration. Even Warton's antiquarian
tendencies have their value; he is able to provide the
only account of Skelton's play 'The Nigromansir', now
lost. (50) With Warton there is, for the first time in
the critical heritage, an attempt at a reasoned analytical
approach to Skelton's work which also endeavours to look
at the totality of his oeuvre. Whilst the results of this
approach do not lead to any more favourable response to
Skelton, there is at least an attempt to control and limit
instinctive prejudice by reason and scholarship.

Warton's example did not make itself quickly felt. The
continued willingness to disparage Skelton is reflected
in a review of his 'History', which, commenting on Skelton,
observes: 'Yet even in [his own] age Skelton's manner was
deemed gross, illiberal and obscene; and now all will agree
with Pope in styling it *beastly*.' (51) Little more than a
decade later Philip Neve dismisses Skelton as a 'rude and
scurrilous rhymer'. The only merit in Skelton Neve is
prepared to acknowledge is the 'justness of his satire' in
his attacks on Wolsey (No. 31). The shadow of earlier
critical postures still lay long over current attitudes.
Just as the review of Warton is influenced by Pope, so
Neve recalls the biographical accounts, particularly that
of Fuller, of the previous century.

In the early nineteenth century, the tempo of critical
interest began to quicken a little. In 1810 Chalmers re-
issued the 1736 edition of Skelton as part of his collected edition of the English poets. This edition formed
the subject of an unsigned review by Robert Southey in the

'Quarterly Review' for 1814 (No. 32), which deals in part
with Skelton. After criticizing Chalmers's choice of copy
text and his editorial procedures generally, Southey proceeds to a brief but forcefully argued defence of Skelton
as satirist. He is compared to Rabelais, and Southey concludes that Skelton was 'one of the most extraordinary
writers of any age or country'. Some years later, 1831,
Southey reiterated his critical support for Skelton in
the introduction to the texts of 'Colin Clout' and 'Philip
Sparrow' included in his 'Select Works of the British
Poets'. There he argues that the poems are 'worthy of
presentation, as illustrating in no common degree, the
state and progress of our language, and the history of
a most important age, and for their intrinsic merit
also' (p. 61). In both comments Southey offers a broader
critical response to Skelton than hitherto, encompassing
editorial and philological concerns (particular problems
in relation to Skelton) and also offering a widened
historical sympathy. His comparison between Skelton and
Rabelais (also reiterated in the 'Select Works') was to
prove particularly influential, and was made again and
again during the nineteenth century.

But in the shorter term Southey's review of Chalmers
seems to have had the effect of stirring up renewed
interest in Skelton. This interest is evidenced in part
by the comments of William Gifford, editor of the
'Quarterly Review' and a friend of Southey's, who included
an approving comment on Skelton in his edition of 'The
Works of Ben Jonson' in 1816 (No. 33). Gifford showed
himself familiar with at least some earlier criticism and
with the 'stupid' 1736 edition. Himself a scholar and
satirist, he praises Skelton's scholarship and defends
him against the charge that his satire is vulgar.

A less whole-hearted spirit of admiration can be found
in the comments of another poet, Thomas Campbell, in his
'Specimens of the British Poets' (1819). Campbell takes
particular issue with the views of Southey: 'it is surely
a poor apology for the satirist of any age to say that he
stooped to humour its vilest taste, and could not ridicule
vice and folly without degrading himself to buffoonery'
(No. 34). The continuity of earlier attitudes can also be
found in the first North American edition of Skelton's
works in the same year. Ezekiel Sanford in his 'Life of
Skelton' prefaced to this edition is willing to praise his
'originality', but his Skeltonics are denied the title
of poetry, being seen as making his poetry 'excessively
monotonous and dull' (No. 35).

But in other quarters there were continuing indications
of a renewed interest. The first edition of his play

'Magnificence' to appear since the sixteenth century
appeared in 1821, published by the aristocratic biblio-
philes of the Roxburghe Club. The following year saw the
publication of what was, in effect, an anthology of Skelton in the 'Retrospective Review'. The conclusion of this
article presents a response to his work which is remarkably sympathetic:

> In judging of this old poet, we must always recollect
> the state of poetry in his time and the taste of the
> age, which being taken into the account, we cannot help
> considering Skelton as an ornament of his own time, and
> a benefactor to those which came after him.

Yet in such a response the note of patronage is still very
apparent; when all has been said, Skelton is still, to the
author, chiefly 'a fit subject for the reverence and the
researches of the antiquarian' (No. 36).
    Even so, the appreciation of Skelton as a vital, impor-
tant poet was continuing to grow in the early part of the
nineteenth century, particularly among his fellow poets.
Within a year of the appearance of the 'Retrospective
Review' article Wordsworth characterized him as 'a demon
in point of genius' (No. 37a). This may be taken as a
considered judgment. For Wordsworth left evidence of his
own study of Skelton in a sonnet which echoes part of 'The
Garland of Laurel'. (52) And in the 1830s he lent
encouragement to Dyce in the preparation of his edition,
discussing with him at some length such questions as
Skelton's genealogy and bibliography. (53)
    In the 1820s comes Coleridge's enthusiastic (albeit
inaccurate) praise of 'Richard Sparrow' in his 'Table
Talk' (No. 38a). Such praise is reiterated in his posthumously published notes on Shakespeare's 'King John' where
the work (now correctly titled) is admired as 'an exquisite and original poem' (No. 38b).
    It is tempting to speculate on the role of Robert
Southey in this renewed appreciation of Skelton, particularly by nineteenth-century poets. Southey was, of course,
course, associated with Wordsworth, Coleridge and Gifford,
all of whom praised Skelton after he had written on him.
Campbell's comments were an explicit response to Southey's
praise. It was Southey's 1814 review of Chalmers's edition which prompted Dyce to undertake his monumental edition of Skelton's poems. (54) And, as will become
apparent, traces of his influence can be discerned in
later nineteenth-century criticism. All in all, Southey's
work towards the critical rehabilitation of Skelton seems
to have been an important but largely unremarked feature

in the history of Skelton criticism.

Southey's pioneering work of reclamation foreshadowed the more extensive and more favourable critical examinations of the 1840s. The first of these was by Isaac D'Israeli in his 'Amenities of Literature' (1840). This was the most extensive attempt yet made to vindicate Skelton from the harsh criticisms of posterity (No. 40). The often vilified Skeltonic is hailed as 'airy but pungent'. Skelton himself is seen as 'too original for some of his critics', particularly Puttenham and Pope. And D'Israeli seeks to justify Skelton's 'personal satires and libels' as worthy of modern study on the grounds that they transcend their occasion: 'for posterity there are no satires nor libels. We are concerned only with human nature'. D'Israeli comes closer than any previous critic to perceiving the fact (if not the exact nature) of the satiric persona in Skelton: 'He acts the character of a buffoon; he talks the language of drollery.... But his hand conceals a poniard; his rapid gestures only strike the deeper into his victim.'

D'Israeli's judgments were independent and forcefully argued. He formulates the extensive grounds for the appreciation of Skelton that had hitherto been adumbrated. Other equally independent minded critics shared his enthusiasm. Two years later, Skelton won the support of Elizabeth Barrett Browning. In an article in the 'Athenaeum' she found herself attracted by his 'strength' and his 'wonderful dominion over language' which is 'the very sans-culottism of eloquence'. Those qualities of his satire which had previously earned critical disapproval are singled out by Mrs Browning for admiration. Skelton is, for her, 'the Juvenal of satyrs!' whose eccentric metrics are justified by their subject-matter. In a different vein, the 'Bouge of Court' earns admiration. And (pace Dr Johnson) Skelton is presented as an 'influence for good upon our language' (No. 41). Thus with breathless compression does Mrs Browning present her fresh and vigorously expressed opinions, opinions which challenge much of received thinking about Skelton.

But amid the signs of an excited rediscovery of Skelton's poetry there were those critics who still adhered to earlier critical views. Henry Hallam's 'Introduction to the Literature of Europe...' published in 1837 speaks of his 'original vigour' but dismisses his 'attempts at serious poetry' as 'utterly contemptible' (No. 39). Agnes Strickland interpolated a biographical judgment of Skelton into her life of Katharine of Aragon (1842): he is adjudged a 'ribald and ill-living wretch'. No mention is made of his poetry (No. 42).

Entrenched habits of response died hard. But any
justification for such casually dismissive criticism was
undercut by the appearance in 1843 of Alexander Dyce's
two-volume edition of 'The Poetical Works of John Skelton'.
This edition was a remarkable achievement which has still
not been superseded. It includes complete texts of all
works which there seemed grounds for attributing to
Skelton, with editorial apparatus and extensive annotation
- the latter providing the first serious effort to lift
the veil covering the many obscurities of Skelton's verse.
The work was prefaced by authoritative surveys of
Skelton's life, reputation and early influence. Dyce's
'Skelton' is a tour de force of nineteenth-century
scholarship, the foundation upon which all modern study
of Skelton rests. As the 'Gentleman's Magazine' put it in
reviewing his edition in 1844: 'In the whole catalogue of
English poets there was not one whose work called more
loudly for an editor than Skelton, nor could they have
fallen into abler or more careful hands.' (55)
     Contemporary reviewers were not slow to perceive the
value of Dyce's pioneering work. His edition provided the
occasion for a lengthy article in the 'Quarterly Review'
in 1844 (No. 43) which was, in effect, the first attempt
at an overall systematic and sympathetic critical survey
of Skelton's works. Most of the major works are discussed
including the 'Elegy on the Duke of Northumberland',
'Philip Sparrow', 'Elynor Rumming', 'The Bouge of Court',
'Magnificence', 'Colin Clout' and 'Why Come Ye Not to
Court?'. Serious attempts are made to deal with some of
the major critical problems concerning Skelton. He is
vindicated from the attack of Pope through a comparison
between his own satiric role and that of Swift. And, as
for Mrs Browning, Skelton's vitality proves attractive.
He is 'the only English verse-writer between Chaucer and
the days of Elizabeth who is *alive*'. Qualities which had
previously earned disapproval are now praised as necessary
functions of his poetic raison d'être: 'His whole value is,
as a vulgar vernacular poet, addressing the people in the
language of the people'. Indeed, considerable stress is
placed on the role in his verse of 'the popular expression
of a strong popular feeling' possessing a fundamental
'truth'. In acclaiming Skelton as 'the father of English
doggerel' the 'Quarterly Review' is not offering a pejora-
tive judgment, but is rather responding to his oeuvre with
sympathy and a constructive historial sense. The 'Quarterly Review' article provides a fitting accompaniment to
Dyce's edition, presenting a detailed demonstration of the
essential interest and importance of Skelton's verse.
     This article is the more remarkable since in general

the response to Dyce's enormous labour of scholarship was
not great. In critical terms the results were negligible.
But his edition may have had some effect in extending
awareness of Skelton's work to North America. It may not
be coincidental that shortly after his edition appeared
it is possible to detect the first signs of Skelton's
influence there. Melville, for example, may conceivably
have been affected by 'Philip Sparrow' in the course of
the composition of his novel 'Mardi' (written in 1847-8).
(56) And around 1855, James Russell Lowell produced an
American edition of Skelton based on Dyce. (57) Lowell
has left the earliest testimonials to Skelton's excellence
by a major American critic. He described Skelton at one
point as the one 'genuine English poet [of] the early years
years of the sixteenth century' (No. 46a). On another
occasion, he joins the line of critics who had found
'Philip Sparrow' worthy of admiration (No. 46b). But
these are, admittedly, faint signs. There are few indications of serious American interest in Skelton before the
twentieth century.

   The situation was not significantly different in other
parts of the world. Some foreign critics were conspicu-
ously unsympathetic. A virulent response came from the
French critic and historian, Hippolyte Taine. Taine seems
to follow the 'Quarterly Review' writer in stressing
Skelton's commitment to 'life', but aligns himself fundamentally with those, like Hallan and Strickland, who were
repelled by the nature of that life and its alleged
failure to achieve a meaningful formulation in art:
'beneath the vain parade of official style there is only
a heap of rubbish' (No. 44).

   It is rare, in fact, to find a nineteenth-century
critic who had studied Dyce's edition with profit and
could approach Skelton with the requisite historical and
critical sympathy. An attempt that is particularly striking in its efforts to meet these demands is an unsigned
article in the 'Dublin University Magazine' for 1866 (No.
45). It attempts to see Skelton in the context of his
age, against the contemporary social, religious and political background. Seen in such a context Skelton's
satires become profoundly and significantly serious.
'Elynor Rumming', for example, 'is the saddest of Skelton's works; there is no relenting, no hope in it....
Like Hogarth's "Progress," it pictures infatuated man
under the sway of passion, recklessly sacrificing his all
to morbid propensities'. But not all of Skelton's
achievement is distorted by such didactic solemnity. He
is compared intelligently with Butler, Swift and (ironic-
ally) Pope, as well as at length with Rabelais. And there

is a perception of the link between Skelton's satire
intention and the aesthetic of his verse. It is observed
of 'Colin Clout' that

> Skelton's metre is all his own; the words spring from
> line to line like so many monkeys, pointing, grinning,
> chattering, howling, biting. The similes have that
> pitiless pungency which Butler afterwards evinced.
> The whole is breathless and fierce as a panther's
> attack.

Beneath the rhetoric there is demonstrated a sense of the
energy and force of Skelton's satire, justifying the con-
tention that 'In Skelton the satire of the age reached
its acme, and after his disappears. He raised it to intense poetry, melting and modelling it with the fire of
his original genius'.
  Such a detailed defence and sustained enthusiasm for
Skelton is unusual, especially when linked to an attempt
to place him in an historical perspective which explains
and justifies his satiric activity. Indeed, the very
vigour with which it prosecutes its critical concerns
places it apart from the general trend of commentary on
Skelton in the later nineteenth century. Elsewhere, if
he was no longer denigrated, he was not afforded such
extended attention.
  The prevailing attitudes are represented in the comments of John Churton Collins (No. 47). In 1880 he
included a brief selection of Skelton's works in T. H.
Ward's anthology 'The English Poets'. In his Introduction
to this selection Collins reflects current critical
orthodoxy concerning Skelton. He compares him (yet again)
with Rabelais, praises 'Philip Sparrow' and 'Elynor
Rumming', the latter for its 'sordid and disgusting
delineation of humble life' in the manner of Swift and
Hogarth. Also singled out for comment are 'the complete
originality of his style ... the variety of his powers ...
the peculiar character of his satire ... the ductility of
his expression'. The chief value of such remarks (unsup-
ported as they are by any analysis) is that they distil
what were then felt to be the distinctive features of
Skelton's achievement. Collins presents Skelton as a
figure who is acceptable and explicable largely in terms
of his relationship to a tradition of satiric realism,
particularly identifiable with the eighteenth century.
  Critical discussion seems to have been satisfied to
accept Skelton in such terms during the rest of the century. Critical comments are few. Augustine Birrell,
the critic and essayist, commented in an aside in his

essay on Poets Laureate that Skelton 'was a man of original genius'. (58) In 1897, James Hooper offered a survey
of Skelton's critical reputation in the 'Gentleman's Magazine'. (59) But the main activity had become scholarly,
rather than critical, and was taking place in Europe,
particularly Germany, rather than in the English-speaking
world. Beginning in 1881 with H. von Krumpholz's study of
'Magnificence', there followed a series of literary, lin-
guistic and textual studies that provided the first
serious attempts at a scholarly examination since Dyce's
edition. (60)

This trend towards scholarly study continued into the
early years of the twentieth century. A number of studies
were undertaken by the American professor, J. M. Berdan.
(61) A few German and English scholars also made contri-
butions, the most notable being R. L. Ramsay's edition of
'Magnificence', published by the Early English text
Society in 1908. But there are scant traces of any critical interest.

This apparent lack of interest was ended by an upsurge
of critical concern for Skelton from the 1920s, not expressed by professional critics or scholars but by a
generation of young poets who perceived the relevance of
Skelton to their own craft. Chief among these was Robert
Graves, who spearheaded the revival of interest. Graves
seems to have first read Skelton in 1915 or 1916 (he has
left conflicting accounts). (62) The earliest clear
evidence of his response is his poem 'John Skelton'
included in 'Fairies and Fusiliers', published in late
1917. (63) The poem concludes on this note of affection-
ate admiration:

> But angrily, wittily,
> Tenderly, prettily,
> Laughingly, learnedly,
> Sadly, madly,
> Helter-skelter John
> Rhymes serenely on,
> As English poets should.
> Old John, you do me good!

'Old John' seems to have become Graves's particular
poetic mentor during the 1920s and 1930s. One indication
of this is that between 1921 and 1938 ten of Graves's
books are prefaced by quotations from Skelton. (64) And
Skeltonic influence can be found in a number of his poems,
most notable in his longest single poetic work 'The
Marmosite's Miscellany' where the indebtedness to Skelton
has been made explicit. (65)

This is not the place, however, to attempt to assess
Skelton's influence on Graves's poetic oeuvre. It is sufficient to note that it has been pervasive. But few
literary critics have reiterated their feelings about
Skelton's achievement with such frequency and eloquence.
In this regard he enjoys an important role in Skelton's
twentieth-century critical heritage. For over forty years
he has vigorously championed the claims of Skelton's
genius and encouraged others to do likewise.

The earliest of his critical comments that I have been
able to discover occurs in an article on Neglected and
Recently Rescued Poets in 1920. There he observes that
Skelton 'is, I suppose, the most submerged of the poets
who held the undisputed laurels of their day'. (66)
Subsequently, Graves strove to bring Skelton to the surface. Scattered through his works from the 1920s to the
1960s are various comments and analysis of Skelton's work.
In 1925 Graves published an enthusiastic review of Richard
Hughes's edition. (67) In the same year he included an
analysis of 'Speak Parrot' in 'Poetic Unreason' (pp.
171-3). He returned to Skelton in the following year in
his essay on The Future of Poetry where, with Shakespeare,
he is proclaimed as 'one of the three or four oustanding
English poets'. (68) The next year, 1927, saw the publication of Graves's own little selection with a combative
preface announcing it as 'the first popular pamphlet of
[Skelton's] verse since Elizabethan times, and is intended
to call attention to the astonishing power and range of
the truest of our neglected poets'. (69) And in 1931 he
published the review article of Philip Henderson's edition
(No. 51).

Graves's interest in Skelton seems to have declined
during the 1930s and 1940s. (70) But from the late 1940s
he shows a renewed concern with Skelton's poetic status.
There is an admiring passage in 'The White Goddess'
(1948). (76) 'The Common Asphodel' in the following year
praises Skelton as 'the last of the classically educated
English poets who could forget his Classics when looking
at the countryside and not see Margery Milke-Ducke as
Phyllis and Jolly Jacke as Corydon' (p. 255). In 'The
Crowning Privilege' (1955) Graves asserts that Skelton
'showed a stronger sense of poetic calling than almost any
of his successors' (p. 12). This is a theme to which he
returns in his most extensive critical discussion in his
'Oxford Addresses on Poetry', where he maintains that 'the
earliest and clearest example of the dedicated poet is
John Skelton', who forms the subject of the first of his
addresses.

Graves speaks at the beginning of this Oxford address

of his first discovery of Skelton: 'What heightened my
shock of delight was that nobody else, it seemed, had felt
as I did about him during the past four centuries.' This
echoes the earlier, almost proprietorial concern for
Skelton's reputation which informs his 'Adelphi' review:

> The first and most enthusiastic modern rediscoverer [of
> Skelton] was, let me say at once, myself; and if I had
> not done so much to create a demand for a Complete
> Skelton this book would not be here for me to review.

Here we see Graves bringing to bear his own distinctive
understanding of the complexities of technique involved in
an adequate appreciation of this neglected poet:

> Why has Skelton been forgotten so long? It has not
> been merely because of his reputation for beastliness -
> Urquhart's translation of Rabelais has always been
> deservedly popular among the educated class. It is
> that he has always been too difficult, not only in his
> language, so full of obsolete words, but in his metres,
> which became unintelligible as soon as the iambic
> metre and syllable counting overcame the native
> English style of writing musically in stresses.

It is primarily on the grounds of their failure to compre-
hend the complexities of Skelton's metrics that Graves
attacks the work of the other editors, Richard Hughes
('the sort of book that needed only an intelligent
scribe') and more especially Philip Henderson. Henderson
is severely handled for his treatment of scansion, his
inconsistent modernization and his imperfect scholarship.
Graves's treatment of Henderson's edition is harsh and
even unfair. The questions he raises in his review about
a modern understanding of Skelton's text are not ones for
which a dogmatic dismissal of Henderson are appropriate -
as Henderson himself was quick to point out. (72) But the
importance of Graves's essay is that it does raise such
questions, albeit in an unduly ad hominem manner, questions which are fundamental to an informed appreciation of
Skelton's art.
  Graves's excited rediscovery of Skelton is found not
only in his own often expressed admiration. His influence
also served to direct other young poets towards Skelton.
Chief among these was Richard Hughes, Graves's former
schoolboy protégé. One manifestation of Hughes's own
admiration for Skelton was his select edition of his
poems which was (as we have seen) to earn Graves's disapproval. But Hughes's Introduction (No. 48), like

Graves's own work, is marked by a new technical appreciation of Skelton's verse. Indeed, he argues that 'simply
as a rhythmical technician [Skelton] is one of the most
accomplished the language has even known'. Both Graves
and Hughes implicitly challenge earlier views of Skelton
as interesting primarily on historical grounds, as a
satirist and commentator on his age. Instead, Skelton
is now presented as intrinsically important; his satiric
function is de-emphasized. Hughes argues that 'Skelton
is a poor satirist compared with his powers as a poet'
and contends that his chief achievement lies in 'the
value of his original work'.

Evidence of this new critical perspective can be found
elsewhere. Louis Golding, the American poet and critic,
urged the value of his prosodic achievement: 'This poet is
significant almost entirely in virtue of such of his
poetry as is written in his own inalienable metre,
written ... in the "Skeltonic doggerel".' (73) The
'historical' Skelton of earlier criticism was being
replaced by Skelton the technician. The admiration for
Skelton's doggerel was again taken up by another poet,
Humbert Wolfe, in 1929. Using Churton Collins as his
whipping boy, Wolfe is prepared to make enthusiastic
claims for Skelton as versifier: 'Doggerel! I wish that
we had more English poets capable of writing it' (No. 50).

This re-evaluation of Skelton's achievement continued
to gain impetus. In June 1929, Edmund Blunden published
a long article in the 'Times Literary Supplement' to mark
the 400th anniversary of his death (No. 49). Blunden was
another friend of Graves. Indeed, he links himself expli-
citly to the earlier work of critical 'recovery' undertaken by Graves and Hughes. He is prepared to confront
the problem of earlier hostility to Skelton shown particularly in Pope, Warton and Strickland, as well as the technical and historical difficulties facing a modern reader
of his verse. Blunden also raises the question of Skelton's character, which has, he asserts, 'been scribbled
upon with an indolent vaingloriousness'. His defence
against all these criticisms and problems is to insist on
the essential accessibility of Skelton's verse to a modern
reader: 'for our part we observe that a great deal of his
writings is as natural in style and as clear in significance as could be wished'. And he proceeds to develop
this defence through an examination of several of the
major works including 'The Garland of Laurel', 'Colin
Clout', 'Philip Sparrow' and 'Magnificence'.

Blunden's other main concern is to continue the work of
his fellow poets in vindicating Skelton as metrist. He
praises Skelton's 'metrical independence', his 'volleying

succession of rapid rhythms' and the fact that his verse is 'founded on a decisive feeling for accent'. And his campaign against the 'philosophical and cloistered iambic' leads to comparisons with Butler and Byron in his 'audacity and urgency'.

The importance of Blunden's essay in the rehabilitation of Skelton is readily apparent. It was published as a front-page article in a major literary weekly, offering both a wide-ranging vindication of the man and a detailed discussion of some of his major works. Such sympathetic exposure in a leading journal of wide circulation and influence was a sign of the more friendly critical temper of the times.

There were also further indications that Skelton was beginning to emerge from the admiration of a small but discriminating coterie to gain a more general interest. In 1931 Dent brought out a commercial edition of Skelton's poems - the first complete edition since Dyce's. It was edited by yet another young poet, Philip Henderson, and although his work, as we have seen, was criticized by Graves it is still in print and remains the text in which most readers now encounter Skelton. With modernized orthography and moderate annotation, Henderson places Skelton within the compass of the general reader of poetry.

Specialist scholarly activity had not been idle either. the 1930s saw a steady stream of significant Skelton research led by the work of L. J. Lloyd, William Nelson, I. A. Gordon and H. L. R. Edwards, which collectively constituted the first major attempt at clarification of the life and works since Dyce's edition. (74)

But in terms of the critical tradition one piece of work written during the 1930s stands out. W. H. Auden's essay John Skelton was written for inclusion in the anthology 'The Great Tudors', first published in 1935. It is clear the views he expresses there are the product of an extended interest in Skelton; his earlier prose and verse both suggest that Auden had studied him with some care. (75) But the fruits of this study achieve their fullest, and best, critical expression in the essay reprinted here (No. 52), abounding in fresh and stimulating insights focused into a balanced assessment.

Predictably, as with the other twentieth-century poets who have studied Skelton, Auden is especially concerned with his metrical techniques. He seizes on such features as the 'tempo' which is 'consistently quicker than that of any other English poet'. Skeltonics are praised for their 'natural ease of speech rhythm'. But Auden's perceptions are not restricted to an appreciation of aspects of Skelton's technique. He goes on to challenge received

critical views on the nature of Skelton's achievement:
'Skelton's work is abuse or flyting, not satire', he
argues, linked to a 'capacity for caricature'. The effect
of such factors is to enhance the 'physical appeal' of his
poetry. Skelton becomes, in Auden's terms, 'an entertainer' rather than a 'visionary'. Auden is evidently
concerned to balance sympathy and admiration for Skelton
against a sense of the nature of great poetry. Such
careful discriminations provide an invaluable corrective
to contemporary excesses of enthusiasm as well as to
earlier excesses of denigration. If by the highest standards of poetic excellence Skelton is found wanting, the
nature of his achievement is none the less warmly
acclaimed. Auden's essay represents the most judicious
and balanced assessment of Skelton's poetic status so far.

His essay also marks the beginning of a movement towards a more qualified and discriminating evaluation of
Skelton, a movement which was to continue into the 1950s.
Thus, G. S. Fraser, writing in 1936 for 'Adelphi' (No.
53), develops the view that Skelton was a comic yet
fundamentally serious artist:

> But the scenes he chooses are often not intrinsically
> funny. It is rather that he deliberately makes them
> funny, that he sustains the reader's amusement with
> his own energy of vision. On a much greater scale,
> of course Rabelais did the same sort of thing.

His final judgment, following on generally unfavourable
comparisons with Rowlandson and Butler, is another care-
fully measured evaluation:

> He created no tradition.... He is quite unique in
> his kind. The great stream of English literature
> would have taken much the same course if he had never
> written. But ... Skelton will always remain an
> example for poets caught up in the coils of a tradi-
> tion, a decent way of writing, which they feel to be
> constricting their lives. It is better, always, to
> be a buffoon than a bore.

In some respects the notion of Skelton as 'buffoon poet'
is not a new one. It is foreshadowed in Warton's criticism of Skelton over 150 years previously. And it can,
of course, be found earlier than that, in the sixteenth-
century biographies and pseudo-biographies of the poet.

But here it is erected into an aesthetic appreciation
of the postures and qualities of Skelton's verse, for
which it is possible to have genuine, if circumscribed,
admiration.

The same sympathetic, restrained admiration can be
found in the last two articles in this collection, those
by E. M. Forster and C. S. Lewis. Forster's essay (No. 54)
was originally given as a lecture to the Aldeburgh Festival in Suffolk in 1950, and is particularly entertaining
in its discussion of Skelton's East Anglian poems, notably
'Philip Sparrow', 'the pleasantest [poem] Skelton ever
wrote'. Forster's general thesis is that Skelton 'belongs
to an age of transition' or 'an age of break up'. This
makes him, for Forster, 'difficult' or (as he characterizes Skelton at the outset) 'extremely strange'. Such
comments may suggest an unhelpful generality superficial-
ity to Forster's view of Skelton. But, in fact, writing
as a non-specialist for a popular occasion he offers a
deft account of Skelton's oeuvre from the perspective of
a discriminating, independent critical intelligence. Yet
his ultimate conclusions accord with those of other mid-
twentieth-century critics, such as Auden and Fraser: 'On
the whole he's a comic - a proper comic, with a love for
improper fun, and a talent for abuse.' The judgment is
perhaps distorting. The stress on the comic aspects of
Skelton's art fails to account satisfactorily for large
portions of his poetic corpus. But Forster's observations do help to provide a view of Skelton which reveals
him as both accessible and alive to the intelligent
general reader. As such, his lecture has a real, albeit
restricted, value.

C. S. Lewis, writing in 1954 for the Oxford History of
English Literature (No. 55), is more concerned to confront the larger critical problems of Skelton's achievements. He examines first the question of the nature of
the aesthetic success of the Skeltonic, particularly in
relation to Skelton's most praised poems, 'Philip
Sparrow' and 'Elynor Rumming'. Lewis's conclusion here
anticipates his more basic reservations about Skelton's
art. The Skeltonic, he argues, is validated aesthetically
'because - and when - this helter-skelter artlessness
symbolizes something in the theme. [E.g.] Childishness,
dipsomania, and a bird.... When it attempts something
fully human and adult ... it fails.' Indeed, for Lewis,
Skelton's poetic success is often a fortuitous affair:

> Skelton does not know the peculiar powers and limi-
> tations of his own manner, and does not reserve it,
> as an artist would have done, for treating immature
> or disorganized states of consciousness. When he
> happens to apply it to such states, we may get
> delightful poetry: when to others, verbiage. There
> is no building in his work, no planning, no reason

why any piece should stop just where it does ... and no
kind of assurance that any of his poems is exactly the
poem he intended to write.

Such then it is urged, is the charm of Skelton - 'he is
always in undress ... the gifted amateur'. The judgment
is offered as an explicit disagreement with Graves's earlier praise during his 'rediscovery' of Skelton. In fact,
Lewis's assessment marks the extreme point in the swing of
the critical pendulum so far during the twentieth century.
Skelton ceases to be even a comic or a clown, for Lewis;
instead he becomes an unwitting versifier whose achievements are effected as much through inadvertence as
through design.
    Surprisingly, there have been no significant attempts
to rebut the critical position assumed by Lewis. Rather,
since 1954 such attention as Skelton has received has
tended to be scholarly rather than critical. (76) Much
significant work has been done to elucidate the many historical and textual problems which still surround Skelton's poetry. In particular, Robert Kinsman, in a series
of studies beginning in the early 1950s, has done much to
sharpen our sense of the historical perspectives through
which Skelton must be understood. (77) He has also com-
piled a fine selection of Skelton's verse and a study of
the canon. (78) There have been several book-length studies, including works by Italian, French and American
scholars. (79) But it will probably not be until the
appearance of the projected new editions of Skelton by the
Penguin and Clarendon presses that there will be any fresh
stimulus towards major new critical re-evaluation.
    It would be fruitless to speculate on the form such a
re-evaluation will take. But it if is at all influenced
by the past it will doubtless be marked by either an emphatic affirmation or a rejection of the values identified
in Skelton's poetry. For Skelton has always been a controversial figure, capable of attracting vehement sup-
porters and detractors in equal measure. Most often such
vehemence has been aroused in literary figures of authority and distinction whose opinions cannot be lightly dismissed. The direction of Skelton criticism has been cru-
cially affected by the views of such men as Puttenham,
Pope, Southey and Graves. But even more poets and men of
letters have felt inspired by Skelton to judgments of
genuine independence. Caxton, Barclay, Drayton, Elizabeth
Barrett Browning, Wordsworth and W.H. Auden are only the
most obvious examples. Not all such judgments are favourable; but they testify to a engagement and concern, which
is, even at its most negative, an oblique tribute to
Skelton's verse.

Skelton has always been a difficult writer for critics
to place. Few professionals from Warton to C. S. Lewis
have felt altogether comfortable with him. He disconcerts
by the nature of his innovative genius, particularly in his
blending of new verse techniques with complex modes of
satire, and by the remarkable forms these elements are
given. Such a fusion is particularly challenging in the
demands it places on the readers of Skelton's poetry.
All that can be said with any certainty is that Skelton
will continue to challenge future generations as effect-
ively as he has the past.

Notes

1 'Wyatt: The Critical Heritage', ed. P. Thomson (London,
   (1974), p. 1.
2 This work has been edited for the Early English Text
   Society by F. M. Salter and H. L. R. Edwards (London,
   1956).
3 The best sources for Skelton's biography are the studies by H. L. R. Edwards, 'Skelton' (London, 1949) and
   M. Pollet, 'John Skelton, Poet of Tudor England' (London, 1971).
4 He produced at least one didactic prose treatise for
   the prince. This has been edited by F. M. Salter in
   'Speculum', IX (1934), pp. 25-37.
5 For discussion of this allusion see R. S. Kinsman,
   A Skelton Reference, c. 1510, 'Notes & Queries',
   CCV (1960), pp. 210-11.
6 It is listed among Barclay's works in Bale's 'Scriptorum illustrium Maioris Brytanniae (Basle, 1557),
   p. 723.
7 'The Eclogues of Alexander Barclay', ed. B. White
   (London, 1928), p. 165: 4th Eclogue, lines 679-86.
8 Ed. William Nelson (London, 1955), vv. 113-19.
9 Both the 'Hundred Merry Tales' and the 'Merry Tales'
   are reprinted in Dyce's edition of 'The Poetical
   Works of John Skelton' (London, 1843), I, pp. lvii-
   lxxv.
10 The relevant extract from this work is conveniently
   printed in Dyce, I, pp. lxxv-vi.
11 'Short Title Catalogue' (hereafter STC) 19299, p. 103.
12 STC 4941, pp. 99, 113.
13 The 'Life' is conveniently reprinted in C. C. Mish,
   ed., 'Short Fiction of the Seventeenth Century' (New
   York, 1968), pp. 84-113.
14 See William Nelson, 'John Skelton, Laureate' (New
   York, 1939), p. 232.

15 Cf. J. W. McCain, Heywood's 'The Foure PP': A Debt to
    Skelton, 'Notes & Queries', CLXXIV (1938), p. 205, and
    also the references to Heywood's 'Play of Love' cited
    there.
16 The comment occurs among the latest 'Additio' (Sig.
    Sss iiv).
17 Bodleian Library MS Selden supra 64; this has been
    edited by R. L. Poole and M. Bateson (Oxford, 1902),
    pp. 253-5.
18 See Nelson, pp. 230-1, for details.
19 STC 13568, p. 1612.
20 See Harvey's 'Pierce's Superogation' (1593), p. 75
    (STC 12903), for the reference to Skelton as a
    'Malancholy foole'. Concerning Skelton's limited
    technical skills, Harvey records his father's facility
    in imitating an 'owld Ryme, of sum Skeltons, or
    Skoggins making as he pretended' and offers a sample
    of the imitation; see 'Gabriel Harvey's Maginalia',
    ed. G. C. Moore Smith (Stratford-upon-Avon, 1913),
    p. 154.
21 See 'The Collected Poems of Joseph Hall', ed.
    A. Davenport (Liverpool, 1949), p. 89, line 76.
22 Cf. Davenport, p. 252, n. 76, and the evidence of
    Skelton's influence cited there.
23 Meres's comments are conveniently reprinted in G. G.
    Smith, ed., 'Elizabethan Critical Essays' (Oxford,
    1904), II, p. 314.
24 Cf. J. A. S. McPeek, 'Catullus in Strange and Distant
    Britain', Harvard Studies in Comparative Literature,
    XV (Cambridge, Mass., 1939), pp. 61-9, for fuller
    details of the influences discussed in this paragraph.
25 The 'Revised Short Title Catalogue' (London, 1976)
    lists seven separate editions between 1531 and 1558.
    There were six separate editions of 'Philip Sparrow'
    and six of 'Why Come Ye Nat to Court' during the six-
    teenth century.
26 Nelson, p. 233, draws attention to the earlier
    appearance of Colin Clout as a character in 'The
    treatyse answerynge the boke of Berdes, Compyled
    by Collyn clowte' (1543).
27 See A. D. Deyermond, Skelton and the Epilogue to Mar-
    lowe's 'Dr. Faustus', 'Notes & Queries', CCVIII
    (1963), pp. 410-11, where the influence of 'The Gar-
    land of Laurel' is detected, and C. C. Seronsy, A
    Skeltonic Passage in Ben Jonson, 'Notes & Queries',
    CXCVIII (1953), p. 24, where the influence of 'Elynor
    Rumming' is suggested.
28 STC 18271, Sigs D 2-3 passim.
29 There are a number of allusions to a play entitled

'Scoggin and Skelton' (now apparently lost) during the
period 1600-1601; see 'Henslowe's Diary', ed. R. A.
Foakes and R. J. Rickert (Cambridge, 1961), pp. 138,
166, 167, 169.

30 See further on this point M. Pollet, 'John Skelton,
Poet of Tudor England' (London, 1971), pp. 152-4, to
which the rest of this paragraph is indebted.

31 'Summers Last Will and Testament' in 'The Works of
Thomas Nashe', ed. R. B. McKerrow (Oxford, reprinted
1958), III, p. 252. Nashe seems here to be echoing
the Prologue to Chaucer's 'Parson's Tale' where the
Parson talks disapprovingly of the 'rum, ram, ruf' of
northern alliterative writing.

32 I have followed the text in C. H. Herford and P. and
E. Simpson, eds, 'Ben Jonson', VII (Oxford, 1941), pp.
707-29.

33 Cf., for example, lines 369-80, 404-6.

34 Jonson also speaks of the poem in 'A Tale of a Tub'
(first published in 1640) (V, vii, 23-5):

The Worke-man Sir! the Artificer! I grant you.
So *Skelton*-Lawreat; was of *Elinour Rumming*
But she the subject of the Rout, and Tunning.

See 'Ben Jonson', III, ed. C. H. Herford and P. Simpson (Oxford, 1927), p. 85.

35 STC 4579; see the reprint edited with an introduction
by H. Neville Davies (Cambridge, 1976).

36 STC 4581; the work is reprinted in Mish, 'Short Fiction of the Seventeenth Century', pp. 118-91 (the
Skelton reference is on p. 120 of this edition).

37 Mention may also be made here of two works which
appear to be imitations of 'Elynour Rumming': 'Doctor
Double Ale' (n.d., STC 7071) and Richard West's 'News
from Bartholomew Fair' (1606), STC 25264).

38 Cf. 'The Poems of Michael Drayton', ed. J. W. Hebel
(Oxford, 1932), II, 360-1, 370.

39 For an attempt (in my view very unconvincing) to see
Skelton as a more serious influence in seventeenth-
century poetry, see S. Kandaswami, Skelton and the
Metaphysicals, in 'Critical Essays on English Litera-
ture Presented to Professor M. S. Duraiswami...' ed.
V. S. Seturaman (Madras, 1965), pp. 157-69. One pos-
sible minor indication of Skeltonic influence (not
noted by Kandaswami) is on Herrick; see, further,
Robert Graves, English Epigrams, 'Times Literary
Supplement', 19 July 1934, p. 511.

40 STC 22614; the picture and the verses are reproduced
in Dyce's edition, II, pp. 153-7.

41 The author was William Vaughan (1577-1641).
42 Page references in parentheses in the text are to the
    'Third Part of The Golden Fleece' (1626), STC 24609.
43 These lines do not appear in the first edition (1630).
44 See 'The Works of John Cleveland' (1687), pp. 306-7.
45 This contains two attempts at Skeltonics: 'The Awakened
    Child's Lamentation' (pp. 2-7) and 'Of Non by Nature'
    (p. 67).
46 ...we may gather that the *Old Testament, Christs
    Passion*, and the *Acts of the Apostles*, were the ordin-
    ary entertainment on the Stage, all *Europe* over, for
    an hundred year or two, of our greatest ignorance and
    darkness. But that in *England* we had been used to
    another sort of Plays in the beginnings of *H*. VIII.
    Reign may be seen from that of the *Laureat* on Cardinal
    woolsey:

            Like Mahound in a Play:
            No man dare him with say   ['Why Come Ye Nat to
                                            Court?', lines 594-5]

    ('The Critical Works of Thomas Rymer', ed. C. A.
    Zimansky (New Haven, 1956), pp. 129-30)
47 Before this, mention might be made of Swift's Skeltonic
    imitation 'Musa Clonsaghiana' written in 1717; see
    'The Poems of Jonathan Swift', ed, H. Williams, 2nd ed.
    (Oxford, 1958), III, p. 966. Swift wrote another
    Skeltonic in 1721, 'Copy of a Copy of Verses from
    Thomas Sheridan, Clerk, to George Nim-Dan-Dean' (ibid.,
    III, pp. 1019-20).
48 I. A. Gordon, 'John Skelton, Poet Laureate' (Melbourne,
    1943), p. 200.
49 The work was, in fact, written largely by Robert
    Shiels; the account of Skelton occurs in I, pp. 27-30.
50 See further on this point R. M. Baine, Warton,
    Collins and Skelton's 'Necromancer', 'Philological
    Quarterly', XLIX (1970), pp. 245-8.
51 'Gentleman's Magazine', XLVIII (1778), p. 270.
52 See 'The Poetical Works of William Wordsworth', ed.
    E. de Selincourt, 2nd ed. (Oxford, 1954), III, p. 18,
    sonnet xxii; this was first noted by Dyce in his edi-
    tion of Skelton, II, pp. 105-6.
53 See, for example, his letters to Dyce of 23 July 1831,
    21 July 1832, 4 December 1833 and his letter of thanks
    of 5 January 1844 to Dyce for a copy of his edition;
    'The Letters of William and Dorothy Wordsworth', ed.
    E. de Selincourt (Oxford, 1939), pp. 554, 630, 678,
    1196.
54 See the Preface to Dyce's 1843 edition, I, pp. *v-vi*;

Southey urges that 'an editor ... could not more worthily employ himself than by giving a good and complete
edition of [Skelton's] works'.

55 'Gentleman's Magazine', n.s. XXII (1844), p. 227.
56 See R. A. Davison, Melville's 'Mardi' and John Skelton,
'Emerson Society Quarterly', XLIII (1966), pp. 86-7.
57 This edition was published c. 1855 by Houghton Mifflin
of Boston, together with an edition of Donne; for details of this edition and its attribution to Lowell see
G. L. Keynes, 'A Bibliography of Dr. John Donne',
4th ed. (Oxford, 1973), p. 211.
58 'Essays About Men, Women and Books' (1894), p. 158.
59 Skelton Laureate, 'Gentleman's Magazine', CCLXXXIII
(1897), pp. 297-309.
60 Krumpholz's study was entitled 'Skelton und sein Morality play Magnyfycence' (Prosnitz, 1881). This was
followed by other scholarly studies including:
G. Schonenburg, 'Die Sprache Skeltons in seinem
kleineren Werken' (Marburg, 1888); J. Zupitza, Hand-
schriftliche Bruchstucke von Skeltons 'Why Come Ye
Not to Courte?', 'Archiv', LXXXV (1890), pp. 429-36;
A. Rey, 'Skelton's satirical poems...' (Stuttgart,
1899); A. Koelbing, 'Zur Characteristik Skeltons'
(Berne, 1904); A. Thummel, 'Studien uber Skelton'
(Leipzig, 1905); and F. Brie, Skelton Studien,
'Englische Studien', XXXVII (1907), pp. 1-86.
61 The Dating of Skelton's Satires, 'PMLA', 29 (1914),
pp. 499-516; The Poetry of Skelton, 'Romanic Review',
6 (1915), pp. 364-77; 'Speke Parrot': An Interpretation of Skelton's Satire, 'Modern Language Notes',
30 (1915), pp. 140-4; 'Early Tudor Poetry' (New York,
1920), passim.
62 In the 'Adelphi' article included in this collection
he states that he first read Skelton 'in 1915'. But
in 'Oxford Addresses on Poetry' (1962), p. 5, he
claims to have discovered Skelton 'by accident in
1916, while on short leave from the Somme trenches,
and on long leave from St. John's College'.
63 The poem occurs on pp. 6-8. Graves may have been
affected earlier in his poem 'Free Verse' included
in 'Over the Brazier' (1916), pp. 14-15, where Skeltonic influence has been detected by D. Day; see
'Swifter than Reason' (Chapel Hill, NC, 1963), p. 6.
64 For details see F. Higginson, 'A Bibliography of Robert
Graves' (Hamden, Conn., 1966), nos A 6, 7, 12, 14, 16,
23, 24, 25, 31, 48.
65 Cf. Graves's comments in the reprint of 'The Marmosite's Miscellany' issued by the Pharos Press (Victoria, BC, 1975).

66 'Woman's Leader', 18 June 1920, pp. 462-3; this
    article is signed 'FUZE'.
67 'Beastly' Skelton, 'Nation and Athenaeum', XXXVI
    (1925), pp. 614-15.
68 'Fortnightly Review', 125 (1926), p. 295. This com-
    ment was deleted when this essay was reprinted in
    'The Common Asphodel' (1949); see p. 53.
69 'John Skelton Laureate' (Augustan Books of English
    Poetry, 2nd series, no. 12).
70 I am only aware of two letters in the 'Times Literary
    Supplement': 19 July 1934, p. 511 (on Skelton and
    Herrick), and 28 May 1938, p. 368 (on the neglect of
    Skelton), between the early 1930s and late 1940s.
71 3rd ed. (1951), p. 451: 'The only two English poets
    who had the necessary learning, poetic talent, human-
    ity, dignity and independence of mind to be Chief
    Poets were John Skelton and Ben Jonson; both were
    worthy of the laurel that they wore.'
72 See his reply to Graves's review in 'Adelphi', n.s.
    III (1933-4), pp. 239-41.
73 Merie Skelton, 'Saturday Review', 14 January 1922,
    pp. 30-1.
74 The various studies by these scholars are most con-
    veniently collected in their subsequent books; see
    L. J. Lloyd, 'John Skelton' (Oxford, 1938); W. Nelson
    'John Skelton, Laureate' (New York, 1939); I. A.
    Gordon, 'John Skelton, Poet Laureate' (Melbourne,
    1943); and H. L. R. Edwards, 'Skelton' (London, 1949).
75 For example, he reviewed Henderson's edition of Skel-
    ton in 'Criterion', XI (1932), pp. 316-19; and a
    number of his early poems in 'Poems' (1928) and
    'Poems' (1930) seem to reflect Auden's study of
    Skelton's verse.
76 One possible exception is Stanley E. Fish's book (see
    below, n. 79).
77 See, for example: 'Phyllyp Sparowe': Titulus,
    'Studies in Philology', XLVII (1950), pp. 473-84; The
    'Buck' and the 'Fox' in Skelton's 'Why Come Ye Nat to
    Court?', 'Philological Quarterly', XXIX (1952), pp.
    61-4; Skelton's 'Colin Cloute': The Mask of 'Vox
    Populi', 'University of California Publications,
    English Studies', I (1950), pp. 17-26; Skelton's
    Uppon a Deedmans Hed': New Light on the Origin of the
    Skeltonic, 'Studies in Philology', L (1953), pp.
    101-9; The Voices of Dissonance: Patterns in Skelton's
    'Colyne Cloute', 'Huntington Library Quarterly', XXVI
    (1963), pp. 291-313; and Skelton's 'Magnyfycence':
    The Strategy of the 'Olde Sayde Sawe', 'Studies in
    Philology', LXIII (1966), pp. 99-125.

78   'John Skelton Poems', ed. R. S. Kinsman (Oxford, 1969),
     and R. S. Kinsman and T. Yonge, 'John Skelton: Canon
     and Census' (New York, 1967).
79   See M. Pollet, 'John Skelton' (Paris, 1962); Edvige
     Schulte, 'La Poesia di John Skelton' (Naples, 1963);
     and Stanley E. Fish, 'John Skelton's Poetry' (Cam-
     bridge, Mass., 1965).

Note on the Text

The materials in this volume follow the original texts
in most important respects. Occasionally, light punctuation has been added and contractions have been silently
expanded. Antiquated footnotes in the original have
generally been deleted; when this has been done it is
indicated in the headnote to the particular selection.
Obvious typographical errors have been silently corrected.
All references to Skelton's text are to 'The Poetical
Works of John Skelton', ed. Alexander Dyce (1843;
reprinted New York, AMS Press, 1965). It is a matter of
continuing regret that this edition has not yet been
superseded; but it is still the only available complete,
lineated edition. The prose translations from the Latin
are as literal as possible, with no claims to literary
style. For the translation of Whittinton (No. 7) I am
indebted to Mr William Fitzgerald of Princeton University.
Notes I have added have been given arabic numerals. The
authority for dates is generally the 'Dictionary of
National Biography'.

1. WILLIAM CAXTON ON SKELTON

c. 1490

William Caxton (1422?-91), from the prologue to the
'Eneydos' (STC 24796), his translation of Virgil's
'Aeneid', published c. 1490, A ii^{r-v}. Caxton was the first
English printer and publisher, as well as a prolific editor
and translator.

Thenne I praye alle theym that shall rede in this lytyl
treatys to holde me for excused for the translatynge of
hit. For I knowleche my selfe ignorant of connynge to
enpryse on me so hie and noble a werke / But I praye
mayster Iohn Skelton late created poete laureate in the
vnyuersite of oxenforde to ouersee and correcte this sayd
booke. And taddresse and expowne where as shalle be founde
faulte to theym that shall requyre it. For hym I knowe for
suffycyent to expowne and englysshe euery dyffyculte that
is therein / For he hath late translated the epystlys of
Tulle / and the boke of dyodorus syculus, and diuerse
other werkes oute of latyn in to englysshe not in rude
and olde language. but in polysshed and ornate termes
craftely. as he that hath redde vyrgyle / ouyde. tullye.
and all the other noble poetes and oratours / to me
vnknowen: And also he hath redde the ix. muses and
vnderstande theyr musicalle scyences and to whom of theym
eche scyence is appropred. I suppose he hath dronken of
Elycons well.

2. ERASMUS ON SKELTON, 'THAT INCOMPARABLE LIGHT AND ORNAMENT OF BRITISH LETTERS'

c. 1499

(a) From 'Opus Epistolarum Des. Erasmi Roterodami',
edited by P. S. Allen (Oxford, 1906), I, p. 241, letter
104. This letter is to Prince Henry, the future Henry
VIII, to whom Skelton was tutor at the time of writing.
The letter can be assigned to autumn 1499. The

translation is by F. M. Nichols, 'The Epistles of
Erasmus' (1901), I, p. 202.

Erasmus (d. 1536) was perhaps the most notable European
humanist of the early sixteenth century.

Et hec quidem interea tanquam ludicra munuscula tue
puericie dicauimus, vberiora largituri vbi tua virtus
vna cum etate accrescens vberiorem carminum materiam
suppeditabit. Ad quod equidem te adhortarer, nisi et
ipse iamdudum sponte tua velis remisque (vt aiunt)
eotenderes et domi haberes Skeltonum, vnum Brittanicarum
litterarum lumen ac decus, qui tua studia possit non
solum accendere sed etiam consummare.

(We have for the present dedicated these verses, like a
gift of playthings, to your childhood, and shall be ready
with more abundant offerings, when your virtues, growing
with your age, shall supply more abundant material for
poetry. I would add my exhortation to that end, were it
not that you are of your own accord already, as they say,
under way with all sails set, and have with you Skelton,
that incomparable light and ornament of British letters,
not only to kindle your studies, but bring them to a
happy conclusion.)

(b) From British Library MS Egerton 1651, ff. 6^v-7^r.
Headed 'Carmen Extemporale' ('Extemporary Song'), these
verses were presumably composed in the autumn of 1499
during Erasmus' visit to England.

Quid tibi facundum nostra in praeconia fontem
    Soluere collibuit,
Aeterna vates Skelton dignissime lauro
    Castalidumque decus?
Nos neque Pieridum celebrauimus antra sororum,
    Fonte nec Aonio
Ebibimus vatum ditantes ora liquores.
    At tibi Apollo chelyn
Auratam dedit, et vocalia plectra sorores;
    Inque tuis labiis

Dulcior Hyblaeo residet suadela liquore.
　　Se tibi Calliope
Infudit totam; tu carmine vincis olorem;
　　Cedit et ipse tibi
Vltro porrecta cithara Rhodopeius Orpheus.
　　Tu modulante lyra
Et mulcere feras et duras ducere quercus,
　　Tu potes et rapidos
Flexanimis fidibus fluuiorum sistere cursus,
　　Flectere saxa potes.
Graecia Maeonio quantum debedat Homero,
　　Mantua Virgilio,
Tantum Skeltoni iam se debere fatetur
　　Terra Britanna suo.
Primus in hanc Latio deduxit ab orbe Camoenas,
　　Primus hic edocuit
Exculte pureque loqui. Te principe Skelton
　　Anglia nil metuat
Vel cum Romanis versu certare poetis.
　　Viue valeque diu.

O eternal poet Skelton, most deserving of the laurel
crown and worthy of the Muses' favour, why does it please
you to pour out your charming fountain of eloquence for
our benefit. We do not celebrate in the caves of the
sister Muses, nor do we drink rich liquors from the lips
of poets by the Aonian fountain. (1) But Apollo gave you
his golden lyre, and the sisters (2) gave the words for
your songs. And sweet persuasion dwells on your lips
with sweet liquor. (3) Calliope (4) poured all her
talents upon you; you vanquish sense by your song; and
Orpheus of Thrace spontaneously yields up to you his
proferred lute. By the melody of your lyre you both
soothe wild beasts and bend sturdy oaks; you can cause
the swift torrent of rivers to stand still by your moving
words; you can make stones weep. As much as Greece owes
Lydian Homer, as much as Mantua owes to Virgil, so much
should the land of Britain now confess that it owes to
its Skelton. He first led away the Muses from their
Italian dwelling place into this country. Here he first
taught how to speak freely and purely. While you are its
principal poet, O Skelton, England need fear nothing, for
you are worthy to vie in versifying with Roman poets.
Long may you live in health.

Notes

1 Near mount Helicon, where the Muses were traditionally

held to dwell.
2 I.e. the Muses.
3 'Hyblaeo ... liquore': Hybla was a mountain in Sicily
   noted for its honey.
4 The chief of the Muses.

3. ALEXANDER BARCLAY ON 'PHILIP SPARROW'

1509

From 'The Ship of Fools' (STC 3545), printed by Pynson in
1509, Y iiiʳ. This is a translation by Alexander Barclay
(1475?-1552) of Sebastian Brandt's 'Narrenschiff', an
elaborate classification of fools and their various kinds
of folly. Barclay is the author of a number of other
verse works, including the first eclogues in English and
a 'Life of St. George'. This passage is from the section
of his work entitled 'A brefe addicion of the syngularyte
of some new Folys'.

Holde me excusyd: for why my wyll is gode
Men to induce vnto vertue and goodnes
I wryte no Iest ne tale of Robyn hode
Nor sawe no sparcles ne sede of vyciousnes
Wyse men loue vertue, wylde people wantones
It longeth nat to my scyence nor cunnynge
For Phylyp the Sparowe the Dirige to synge.

4. 'THE GREAT CHRONICLE' ON SKELTON AND HIS CONTEMPORARIES

c. 1510

From 'The Great Chronicle of London' (Guildhall Library
MS 3313), a history of London in verse and prose from
1189 to 1512, generally held to be the work of Robert
Fabian (d. 1513); as edited by A. H. Thomas and I. D.
Thornley (London, 1938), p. 361. The passage was probably

written c. 1510. The 'Cornysh' mentioned is the poet
William Cornish (d. 1524); 'mastyr moor' is St Thomas More
(1478-1535). The passage is an attack on John Baptist de
Grimaldis (the 'cursid Caytyff'), a henchman of Henry
VII's advisors, Empson and Dudley.

O most cursid Caytyff, what shuld I of the wryte
Or telle the particulers, of thy cursid lyffe
I trow If Skelton, or Cornysh wold endyte
Or mastyr moor, they myght not Inglysh Ryffe
Nor yit Chawcers, If he were now in lyffe
Cowde not In metyr, half thy shame spelle
Nor yit thy ffalshod, half declare or telle

5. HENRY BRADSHAW ON SKELTON AND OTHER SUPERIOR POETS

c. 1513

(a) From 'The Life of St. Werburge of Chester' by Henry
Bradshaw (d. 1513?), a Benedictine monk living in Chester
and posthumously printed by Richard Pynson in 1521 (STC
3506), S ii^r. The stanza is a variant of the 'modesty
topos' whereby the author contrasts his work with that of
other superior poets, in this instance Chaucer, John
Lydgate, Skelton and Alexander Barclay.

To all auncient poetes litell boke submytte the
Whilom flouryng in eloquence facundious
And to all other / whiche present nowe be
Fyrst to maister Chaucer / and Ludgate sentencious
Also to preignaunt Barkley / nowe beyng religious
To inuentiue Skelton and poet laureate
Praye them all of pardon both erly and late

(b) From Bradshaw's other posthumously published saint's
life, 'The Life of St. Radegunde', published by Pynson

c. 1521 (STC 3507), D iv. Once again, Bradshaw employs the modesty topos contrasting his capacities as poet with the same four poets as in No. 5a ('the monk of Bury' is Lydgate).

What memory or reason is sufficient
To remembre the myracles of this lady
What story can expresse or pen is conuenient
Playnly to discribe all the noble story
It were a plesaunt werke for the monk of Bury
For Chaucer or Skelton fathers of eloquens
Or for religious Barkeley to shewe theyr diligens

6. WILLIAM LILY ON SKELTON: 'NEITHER LEARNED, NOR A POET'

c. 1519

The text of these lines by the grammarian William Lily (1468?-1522) comes from British Library MS Harley 540, f. 57v. The translation is that made by bishop Thomas Fuller in 1662 (see below, No. 24).

Quid me Scheltone fronte sic aperta
Carnis vipereo potens veneno
Quid versus trutina meos iniqua
Libras. Dicere vera num licebit
Doctrina tibi dum parari famam
Et doctus fieri studes poeta:
Doctrinam nec habes nec es poeta

(With face so bold, and teeth so sharp
Of Viper's venome, why dost carp?
Why are my verses by thee weigh'd
In a false scale? May truth be said?
Whilst thou, to get the more esteem,
A learned Poet fain wouldst seem;
Skelton, thou art, let all men know it,
Neither learned, nor a poet.)

7. ROBERT WHITTINTON IN PRAISE OF SKELTON, THE 'LEARNED
POET'

1519

From Whittinton's poem 'In clarissimi Scheltonis
Louaniensis poeta: laudes epigramma' ('On the most famous
John Skelton, poet of Louvain: laudatory epigrams')
included in his 'Opusculum Roberti Whittintoni in
florentissima Oxoniensi achademia Laureati' (1519),
Sigs c iiii^v–viii, STC 25540.5. The work is a series of
laudatory poems addressed to such contemporary figures
as Henry VIII, Thomas More and Cardinal Wolsey.
   I have adopted Dyce's emendation of *Tum* for *Cum* in line
75. Whittinton's astrological preamble (lines 1–34) has
been omitted.
   Whittinton (fl. 1519) was the author of a number of
grammatical treatises.

Nubifer assurgit mons Pierus atque Cithaeron,   35
    Gryneumque nemus dehinc Heliconque sacer;
Inde et Parnasi bifidi secreta subimus,
    Tota ubi Mnemosynes sancta propago manet.
Turba pudica novem dulce hic cecinere sororum;
    Delius in medio plectra chelynque sonat: 40
Aurifluis laudat modulis monumenta suorum
    Vatum, quos dignos censet honore poli:
De quo certarunt Salamin, Cumae, vel Athenae,
    Smyrna, Chios, Colophon, primus Homerus erat;
Laudat et Orpheum, domuit qui voce leones,   45
    Eurydicen Stygiis qui rapuitque rogis;
Antiquum meminit Musaeum Eumolpide natum,
    Te nec Aristophanes Euripidesque tacet;
Vel canit illustrem genuit quem Teia tellus,
    Quemque fovit dulci Coa camena sinu;   50
Deinde cothurnatum celebrem dat laude Sophoclem,
    Et quam Lesbides pavit amore Phaon;
Aeschylus, Amphion, Thespis nec honore carebant,
    Pindarus, Alcaeus, quem tuleratque Paros;
Suat alii plures genuit quos terra Pelasga,   55
    Daphnaeum cecinit quos meruisse decus:
Tersa Latinorum dehinc multa poemata texit,
    Laude nec Argivis inferiora probat;
Insignem tollit ter vatem, cui dedit Andes
    Cunas urbs, clarum Parthenopaea taphum;   60
Blanda Corinna, tui Ponto religatus amore,

Sulmoni natus Naso secundus erat;
Inde nitore fluens lyricus genere Appulus ille
Qui Latiis primus mordica metra tulit;
Statius Aeacidem sequitur Thebaida pingens,   65
   Emathio hinc scribens praelia gesta solo;
Cui Verona parens hinc mollis scriptor amorum,
   Tu nec in obscuro, culte Tibulle, lates;
Haud reticendus erat cui patria Bilbilis, atque
   Persius hinc mordax crimina spurca notans;   70
Eximius pollet vel Seneca luce tragoedus,
   Comicus et Latii bellica praeda ducis;
Laudat et hinc alios quos saecula prisca fovebant;
   Hos omnes longum jam meminisse foret.
Tum Smintheus, paulo spirans, ait, ecce, sorores,   75
   Quae clausa oceano terra Britanna nitet!
Oxoniam claram Pataraea ut regna videtis,
   Aut Tenedos, Delos, qua mea fama viret:
Nonne fluunt istic nitidae ut Permessidos undae,
   Istic et Aoniae sunt juga visa mihi?   80
Alma fovet vates nobis haec terra ministros,
   Inter quos Schelton jure canendus adest:
Numina nostra colit; canit hic vel carmina cedro
   Digna, Palatinis et socianda sacris;
Grande decus nobis addunt sua scripta, linenda   85
   Auratis, digna ut posteritate, notis;
Laudiflua excurrit serie sua culta poesis,
   Certatim palmam lectaque verba petunt;
Ora lepore fluunt, sicuti dives fagus auro,
   Aut pressa Hyblaeis dulcia mella favis;   90
Rhetoricus sermo riguo fecundior horto,
   Pulchrior est multo puniceisque rosis,
Unda limpidior, Parioque politior albo,
   Splendidior vitro, candidorque nive,
Mitior Alcinois pomis, fragrantior ipso   95
   Thureque Pantheo, gratior et violis;
Vincit te, suavi Demonsthene, vincit Ulyxim
   Eloquio, atque senem quem tulit ipse Pylos;
Ad fera bella trahat verbis, nequiit quod Atrides
   Aut Brisis, rigidum te licet, Aeacides;   .   100
Tantum ejus verbis tribuit Suadela Venusque
   Et Charites, animos quolibet ille ut agat,
Vel Lacedaemonios quo Tyrtaeus pede claudo
   Pieriis vincens martia tela modis,
Magnus Alexander quo belliger actus ab illa   105
   Maeonii vatis grandisonante tuba;
Gratia tanta suis virtusque est diva camenis,
   Ut revocet manes ex Acheronte citos;
Leniat hic plectro vel pectora saeva leonum,
   Hic strepitu condat moenia vasta lyrae;   110

Omnimodos animi possit depellere morbos,
    Vel Niobes luctus Heliadumque truces;
Reprimat hic rabidi Saulis sedetque furores,
    Inter delphinas alter Arion erit;
Ire Cupidineos quovis hic cogat amores,   115
    Atque diu assuetos hic abolere queat;
Auspice me tripodas sentit, me inflante calores
    Concipit aethereos, mystica diva canit;
Stellarum cursus, naturam vasti et Olympi,
    Aeris et vires hic aperire potest,   120
Vel quid cunctiparens gremio tellus fovet almo,
    Gurgite quid teneat velivolumque mare;
Monstratur digito phoenice ut rarior uno,
    Ecce virum de quo splendida fama volat!
Ergo decus nostrum quo fulget honorque, sorores,   125
    Heroas laudes accumulate viro;
Laudes accumulent Satyri, juga densa Lycaei,
    Pindi, vel Rhodopes, Maenala quique colunt;
Ingeminent plausus Dryades facilesque Napaeae,
    Oreadum celebris turba et Hamadryadum;   130
Blandisonum vatem, vos Oceanitidesque atque
    Naiades, innumeris tollite praeconiis;
Aeterno vireat quo vos celebravit honore,
    Illius ac astris fama perennis eat:
Nunc maduere satis vestro, nunc prata liquore   135
    Flumina, Pierides, sistite, Phoebus ait.
Sat cecinisse tuum sit, mi Schelton, tibi laudi
    Haec Whitintonum: culte poeta, vale.

(From here we approach also the retreats of cleft
Parnassus, where all the holy progeny of Mnemosyne lives.
Here the chaste band of nine sisters sang and the Delian
(1) in their midst plays with plectrum and lyre. With
golden-flowing measures he praises the monuments of his
poets, those he thinks worthy of the honour of the
heavens. First was Homer, whose birthplace was contested
by Salamis, Cumae, Athens, Smyrna, Chias and Colophon.
And he praises Orpheus who with his voice tamed lions and
who snatched Eurydice from the pyres of the Styx. And he
calls to mind ancient Musaeus, son of Eumolpis, and is not
silent about you, Aristophanes, nor Euripides. Then he
sings of the famous poet born of Teian soil (2) and the
one whom the Coan Muse fondled in her lovely lap; (3) and
then buskined Sophocles is celebrated with praise and the
Lesbian whom Phaon fed with love. (4) Aeschylus, Amphion
and Thespis had their honour and Pindar, Alcaeus and the
poet born of Paros. (5) Several others born in Pelasga he
sang, that had observed the honour of Daphne's laurel.
Then he glorifies many neat poems of the Latins and judges

them to be not inferior to the Argives. Three times he
praises the poet to whom the city Andes was a cradle
and Parthenope a famous grave. (6) Naso, (7) born in
Sulmo was the second, bound by love of you, charming
Corinna, in Pontus. Then that brilliantly flowing lyric
poet, (8) Apulian by birth, who first brought the biting
metre to the Latins. Statius follows the Aeacid (9)
picturing the Thebais, then the one who writes of the
battles fought on Emathian soil. (10) And you, elegant
Tibullus, do not lie in obscurity, smooth writer of love
poetry whose birthplace was Verona. The one whose country
was Bilbilis (11) was not passed over; and then came biting
Persius marking dirty crimes. The excellent Seneca is
brilliant as tragedian, as the battle spoil of a Latin
general is as comedian. (12) After this he praises others
whom former ages cherished, but to call to mind all these
now would be tedious.

Then Apollo, with deeper breath, said, 'Behold sisters,
the land which shines surrounded by the ocean, Britain!
Famous Oxford you see, like the Pataraean kingdom, or
Tenedos, or Delos where my fame is strong. Do not the
waters there flow bright as those of Peressus, and do I
not see there the Aonian mountains? This land gently
nourishes the poets who are my attendants, among whom
Skelton is rightly to be celebrated. He cultivates my
godhead; he sings songs worthy of the cedar even, songs
to be added to the Palatine rites. His songs give us great
glory and should be overlaid with gold, as worthy of
posterity. His polished poetry runs in a chain flowing
with praise and the selected words seek the palm in
rivalry. His mouth flows with charm as the holy beech
does with gold, or the sweet honey pressed from Hyblaean
honeycombs. His rhetorical speech is more bountiful than
a watered garden, and much more beautiful even than purple
roses, more clear than a wave, more smooth than the white
of Parian marble, more brilliant than crystal and whiter
than snow, riper than the apples of Alcinous, more
fragrant than Thurean and Panthean perfume, and more
pleasing than violets. He conquers you, smooth Demosthenes, and you, Ulysses, in eloquence, as well as that
old man that Pylos bore. (13) He could persuade you to
war, stubborn Achilles, with his words, which Agamemnon
or Brisis could not; so much force has Persuasion and
Venus and the Graces given to his words, that he might
lead minds wherever he wants, either in the limping metre
in which Tyrtaeus led the Spartans (14) overcoming the
weapons of Mars with Pierian rhythms, or that in which
great Alexander, the warlike, was spurred on by that
great-sounding trumpet of the Maeonian poet. (15) There

is such charm and divine power in his Muses that he might
recall the shades, summoning them from Acheron. He could
calm with his plectrum even the savage breasts of lions,
or with the sound of his lyre build vast walls. He could
chase away all diseases of the mind, even the violent
griefs of Niobe or of the sisters of Phaethon. He could
check and calm the furies of raging Saul; among the
dolphins he will be another Arion. He could compel the
desires caused by Cupid to go anywhere, and he could
destroy those long ingrained. With me as interpreter, he
feels the tripod, with me fanning them he conceives
heavenly flames and sings holy mysteries. He can reveal
the courses of the stars, the nature of the deep and of
Olympus and the powers of the sky, or what the earth,
mother of all, nourishes in her gentle lap, or what the
sail-flown sea holds in its waters. He is pointed out as
one rarer than a single phoenix: behold the man whose
brilliant fame flies! Therefore, sisters, wherever our
glory and honour shines, heap up a hero's praise on this
man. Let the satyrs heap up praise, those who inhabit
the thick hills of Lycaeus, of Pindus, and Rhodope and
Maenalus. Let the Oryads and the friendly dell-nymphs,
the numerous crowd of Oreads and of Hamadryads heap up
praise. You, daughter of Oceanus and Naiads praise the
smooth-sounding poet with innumerable proclamations. Let
him flourish in the eternal honour with which he
celebrated you, and let his fame be perennial in the
stars. Now the fields have been soaked enough in your
water; stop your rivers, Pierides, says Phoebus. Let
these praises of you, Skelton, sung by your Whittinton,
suffice: learned poet, farewell.)

Notes

  1 Apollo.
  2 Anacreon.
  3 Possibly Simonides or Bacchylides.
  4 Sappho.
  5 Archilochus.
  6 Virgil.
  7 Ovid.
  8 Horace.
  9 I.e. Achilles in the 'Achilleis'.
 10 Lucan.
 11 Martial.
 12 Terence.
 13 Nestor.
 14 I.e. elegiac.
 15 Homer.

8. JOHN BALE ON THE LIFE OF SKELTON

1557

From the 'Scriptorum illustrium maioris Brytanniae' of
bishop John Bale (1495-1563). The text is from the Basle
edition of 1557, p. 651. Bale was a dramatist, controversialist and the author in this instance of a biographical
and bibliographical reference work containing the fullest
early biography and bibliography of Skelton. It
supplements the accounts of Skelton in Bale's two earlier
works, his 'Illustrium Maioris Britanniae Scriptorum'
(1548) and his 'Index Britanniae Scriptorum' (post 1548).
Bale bases his account on the collections of the antiquary
Edward Braynewode, who is otherwise unknown.

Ioannes Skeltonus, poeta laureatus, ac theologie professor,
parochus de Dyssa in Nordouolgiae comitatu, clarus &
facundus in utroque scribendi genere, prosa atque metro,
habebatur. facetijs in quotidiana inuentione plurimum
deditus fuit: non tamen omisit sub persona ridentis, ut in
Horatio Flacco, ueritatem fateri. Tam apte, amoene, ac
false, mordaciter tamen, quorundam facta in amoena carpere
nouit, ut alter uideretur Lucianus aut Democritus, ut ex
opusculis liquet. Sed neque in scripturis facris absque
omni iudicio erat, quamuis illud egregie dissimulauit. In
clero non ferenda mala uidebat, & magna & multa: quae
nonnunquam uiuis perstrinxit coloribus, ac scommatibus
non obscoenis. Cum quibusdam blateronibus fraterculis,
praecipue Dominicanis, bellum gerebat continuum. Sub
pseudopontifice Nordouicensi Ricardo Nixo, mulierem illam,
quam sibi secreto ob Antichristi metum desponsauerat, sub
concubinae titulo custodiebat. In ultimo tamen vitae
articulo super ea re interrogatus, respondit, se nusquam
illam in conscientia coram Deo, nisi pro uxore legitima
tenuisse. Ob literas quasdam in Cardinalem Vuolsium
inuectiuas, ad Vuestmonasteriense tandem asylum confugere,
pro uita seruanda coactus fuit: ubi nihilominus sub abbate
Islepo fauorem inuenit. De illo Erasmus in quadam
epistola, ad Henricum octauum regem, sic scribit:
Skeltonum, Brytannicarum literarum lumen ac decus, qui
tua studia possit non solum accendere, sed etiam
consummare: hunc domi habes &c iste uero edidit, partim
Anglice, partim Latine,

[A list of Skelton's works follows.]

(John Skelton, poet laureate and professor of theology,
was priest of Diss in the county of Norfolk and skilled
in both kinds of writing, verse and prose. He was much
given to the daily invention of satires. Nevertheless,
under the mask of laughter, he did not omit to utter truth,
as did Horatius Flaccus. (1) He knew how to speak about
various matters in a pleasant manner, so skilfully,
pleasantly, deceitfully, albeit bitingly, that he seemed
another Lucian (2) or Democritus, (3) as is clear from his
works. But he was not in full accord with Holy Scripture,
although he concealed the fact deftly. He saw many great
evil deeds being carried out among the clergy, which he
sometimes attacked with lively rhetoric and judicious
sneers. He continuously waged war on certain babbling
friars, especially the Dominicans. Under the false bishop
of Norwich, Richard Nix, he kept that woman (whom he had
secretly married for fear of Antichrist) under the title
of concubine. When, as he was dying, he was asked about
her, he replied that he had nothing on his conscience
before God concerning her, since she had been kept as a
true wife. Because of certain satiric verses against
cardinal Wolsey he was at last compelled to seek
sanctuary at Westminster to save his life; where, notwithstanding he found favour with abbot Islep.)

Notes

1 Horace (65-8 BC), the Roman poet and satirist.
2 A Greek rhetorician and satirist.
3 The Greek philosopher (c. 460-370 BC).

9. WILLIAM BULLEIN ON SKELTON'S SATIRES ON WOLSEY

1564

From 'A Dialogue against the Fever Pestilence' by
William Bullein (d. 1576), printed by John Kingston
in 1564 (STC 4036), Bvi^{r-v}. Bullein was a physician who
wrote a number of medical tracts and who also had, as will
be apparent, distinctive and idiosyncratic views on
literature. The work from which this extract comes also

includes observations on such poets as Chaucer, Gower,
Lydgate and Barclay.

Skelton satte in the corner of a Piller, with a Frostie
bitten face, frownyng, and is scant yet cleane cooled of
the hotte burnyng Cholour, kindeled against the cankered
Cardinall Wolsey; wrytyng many sharpe Disticons, with
bloudie penne against him, and sent them by the infernall
riuers *Styx, Flegiton,* and *Acheron* by the Feriman of hell
called *Charon*, to the saied Cardinall.

10. THOMAS CHURCHYARD IN PRAISE OF SKELTON

1568

This poem by the soldier and poet Thomas Churchyard
(1520?-1604) appears as a preface (A ii^v-A iiii^v) to the
edition of the 'Pithy, Pleasaunt and Profitable Works of
Maister Skelton, Poete Laureate', published in 1568
(STC 22608). The punctuation has been somewhat modernized.

> If slouth and tract of time
>   (That wears eche thing away)
> Should rust and canker worthy artes,
>   Good works would soen decay.
> If suche as present are
>   For goeth the people past,
> Our selus should soen in silence slepe,
>   And loes renom at last.
> No soyll nor land so rude
>   But some odd men can shoe:
> Than should the learned pas vnknowe,
>   Whoes pen & skill did floe?
> God sheeld our slouth wear sutch,
>   Or world so simple nowe,
> That knowledge scaept without reward,
>   Who sercheth vertue throwe,
> And paints forth vyce a right,
>   And blames abues of men,
> And shoes what lief desarues rebuke,

And who the prayes of pen.
You see howe forrayn realms
    Aduance their Poets all;
And ours are drowned in the dust,
    Or flong against the wall.
In Fraunce did Marrot (1) raigne;
    And neighbour thear vnto
Was Petrark, marching full with Dantte,
    Who erst did wonders do;
Among the noble Grekes
    Was Homere full of skill;
And where that Ouid norisht was
    The soyll did florish still
With letters hie of style;
    But Virgill wan the fraes,
And past them all for deep engyen,
    And made them all to gaes
Vpon the bookes he made:
    Thus eche of them, you see,
Wan prayse and fame, and honor had,
    Eche one in their degree.
I pray you, then, my friendes,
    Disdaine not for to vewe
The workes and sugred verses fine
    Of our raer poetes newe;
Whoes barborus language rued
    Perhaps ye may mislike;
But blame them not that ruedly playes
    If they the ball do strike,
Nor skorne not mother tunge,
    O babes of Englishe breed!
I haue of other language seen,
    And you at full may reed
Fine verses trimly wrought,
    And coutcht in comly sort;
But neuer I nor you I troe,
    In sentence plaine and short
Did yet beholde with eye,
    In any forraine tonge:
A higher verse a staetly[er] style,
    That may be read or song,
Than is this daye in deede
    Our englishe verse and ryme,
The grace wherof doth touch ye gods,
    And reatch the cloudes somtime.
Thorow earth and waters deepe
    The pen by skill doth passe,
And featly nyps the worldes abuse,
    And shoes vs in a glasse

The vertu and the vice
    Of eury wyght alyue:
The hony combe that bee doth make
    Is not so sweete in hyue
As are the golden leues
    That drops from poets head,
Which doth surmount our common talke
    As farre as dros doth lead:
The flowre is sifted cleane,
    The bran is cast aside,
And so good corne is knowen from chaffe,
    And each fine graine is spide.
Peers Plowman was full plaine,
    And Chausers spreet was great;
Earle Surry had a goodly vayne;
    Lord Vaus (2) the marke did beat,
And Phaer did hit the pricke
    In thinges he did translate,
And Edwards had a special gift;
    And diuers men of late
Hath helpt our Englishe toung,
    That first was baes and brute: -
Ohe, shall I leaue out Skeltons name,
    The blossome of my frute,
The tree wheron indeed
    My branchis all might groe?
Nay, Skelton wore the Lawrell wreath,
    And past in schoels, ye know;
A poet for his arte,
    Whoes iudgment suer was hie,
And had great practies of the pen,
    His works they will not lie;
His terms to taunts did lean,
    His talke was as he wraet,
Full quick of witte, right sharp of words,
    And skilfull of the staet;
Of reason riep and good,
    And to the haetfull mynd,
That did disdain his doings still,
    A skornar of his kynd;
Most pleasant euery way,
    As poets ought to be,
And seldom out of Princis grace,
    And great with eche degre.
Thus haue you heard at full
    What Skelton was in deed;
A further knowledge shall you haue,
    If you his bookes do reed.
I haue of meer good will

> Theas verses written heer,
> To honour vertue as I ought,
>   And make his fame apeer,
> That whan the Garland gay
>   Of lawrel leaues but laet:
> Small is my pain, great is his prayes,
>   That thus sutch honour gaet.

Notes

1   Clement Marot (1496-1544), a French sonneteer and
    pastoral poet.
2   Thomas Vaux (1510-56), poet.

11. JOHN GRANGE ON SKELTON'S 'RAGGED RYME'

1577

The 'Golden Aphroditis' of John Grange, a euphuistic
work in verse and prose dedicated to noble ladies, was
published in 1577 (STC 12174). This extract occurs on
N 4ʳ. Little is known about Grange himself.

For by what meanes could *Skelton* that Laureat poet, or
Erasmus that great and learned clarke have uttered their
mindes so well at large, as thorowe their clokes of mery
conceytes in wryting of toyes and foolish theames?
as *Skelton* did by 'Speake Parrot', 'Ware the hauke', 'The
Tunning of Elynour rumming', 'Why come ye not to the
Courte?' 'Phillip Sparrowe', and such like, yet what
greater sense of better matter can be, that is in this
ragged ryme contayned? or who would haue hearde his
fault so playnely tolde him if not in such a gibyng
sorte?

12. WILLIAME WEBBE ON SKELTON: 'A PLEASANT CONCEYTED FELLOWE'

1586

From 'A Discourse of English Poetry' by William Webbe (fl. 1586-91), published by John Charlewood in 1586 (STC 25172), C iii^v. Webbe was a friend of Spenser. His comments on Skelton occur during a survey of the history of English poetry, in which it becomes clear that his sympathies lie with more recent sixteenth-century poetry rather than with Skelton's.

Since these I knowe none other tyll the time of Skelton, who writ in the time of kyng *Henry* the eyght, who as indeede he obtayned the Lawrell Garland, so may I wyth good ryght yeelde him the title of a Poet: hee was doubtles a pleasant conceyted fellowe, and of a very sharpe wytte, exceeding bolde, and would nyppe to the very quicke where he once sette holde.

13. GEORGE PUTTENHAM ON SKELTON'S METRE

1589

Extracts from 'The Arte of English Poesie' by George Puttenham (1529?-90), published in 1589 (STC 20519). This was one of the most important Elizabethan treatises on the history and practise of poetry.

(a) Book I, Chapter xxxi: 'Who in any age haue bene the most commended writers in our English Poesie, and the Authors censure vpon them', V I i^v.

Skelton a sharpe Satirist, but with more rayling and scoffery then became a Poet Lawreat, such among the

Greekes were called *Pantomimi*, with vs Buffons, altogether
applying their wits to Scurrillities & other ridiculous
matters.

(b) From Book II, Chapter ix: 'Of concorde in long and
short measures, and by neare or farre distaunces, and
which of them is most commendable', L iiiiᵛ-M iʳ. Here
Puttenham launches his attack on Skelton's verse. The
works of the 'tauerne minstrels' with whom Skelton is compared are Chaucer's 'Tale of Sir Thopas', the romances
'Bevis of Hampton' (STC 1987-96) and 'Guy of Warwick'
(STC 12540-42) and the popular tale of 'Clymme of the
Clough and Adam Bell' (STC 1806-13).

Note also that rime or concorde is not commendably vsed
both in the end and middle of a verse, vnlesse it be in
toyes and trifling Poesies, for it sheweth a certaine
lightnesse either of the matter or of the makers head,
albeit these common rimers vse it much, for as I sayd
before, like as the Symphonie in a verse of great length,
is (as it were) lost by looking after him, and yet may
the meetre be very graue and stately: so on the other
side doth the ouer busie and too speedy returne of one
maner of tune, too much annoy & as it were glut the eare,
vnlesse it be in small & popular Musickes song by these
Cantabanqui vpon benches and barrels heads where they
haue none other audience then boys or countrey fellowes
that passe by them in the streete, or else by blind
harpers or such like tauerne minstrels that giue a fit of
mirth for a groat, & their matters being for the most
part stories of old time, as the tale of 'Sir Topas', the
reportes of 'Beuis of Southampton', 'Guy of Warwicke',
'Adam Bell, and Clymme of the Clough' & such other old
Romances or historicall rimes, made purposely for recrea-
tion of the comon people at Christmasse diners &
brideales, and in tauernes & alehouses and such other
places of base resort, also they be vsed in Carols and
rounds and such light or lasciuious Poemes, which are
commonly more commodiously vttered by these buffons or
vices in playes then by any other person. Such were the
rimes of *Skelton* (vsurping the name of a Poet Laureat)

being in deede but a rude rayling rimer & all his doings
ridiculous, he vsed both short distaunces and short
measures pleasing onely the popular eare: in our courtly
maker we banish them vtterly. Now also haue ye in euery
song or ditty concorde by compasse & concorde entertangled
and a mixt of both, what that is and how they be vsed
shalbe declared in the chapter of proportion by *scituation*.

14. GABRIEL HARVEY ON SKELTON, THE 'MADBRAYNED KNAVE'

c. 1573-80, 1592

(a) From an incomplete elegy on the poet George Gascoigne,
which Gascoigne meets various English poets in Hades.
Taken from 'The Letter-Book of Gabriel Harvey, A.D.
1573-80', edited by E. J. L. Scott (1884), p. 57.

...Acquayntaunce take of Chaucer first
    And then wuth Gower and Lydgate dine.

And cause thou art a merry mate
    Lo Scoggin where he lawghes aloane
And Skelton that same madbrayned knave
    Looke how he knawes a deade horse boane

(b) From Gabriel Harvey's 'Four Letters and Certaine
Sonnets' (1592), p. 7 (STC 12900). The work is primarily
an attack on Robert Greene and his followers, with whom
Skelton and his alter ego Scoggin are linked. They appear
later in the same work (pp. 12-13).

Salust, and *Clodius* learned of *Tully* to frame
artificiall Declamations, and partheticall Inuectives
against *Tully* himself, and other worthy members of that

State: if mother Hubbard in the vaine of *Chawcer*, happened
to tell one Canicular (1) tale; father *Elderton*, (2) and
his sonne *Greene*, in the vaine of *Skelton*, or *Scoggin*,
will counterfeitan an hundred dogged Fables, Libles,
Calumnies, Slaunders, Lies for the whetstone, what not,
and most currishly snarle and bite where they should most
kindly fawne and licke.

Notes

1 Literally 'to do with a dog'; cf. the punning reference
   to 'an hundred dogged Fables...'.
2 William Elderton (d. 1592?), an Elizabethan actor and
   ballad writer.

15. ARTHUR DENT ON SKELTON'S IMMORAL WORKS

c. 1590

From 'The Plaine Man's Pathway to Heaven', first published
in 1601 (STC 6626), a didactic work written earlier
(c. 1590) by the puritan Arthur Dent (d. 1607). The
extract is taken from pp. 408-9. 'Elynor Rumming' is
linked here with a number of popular and (by Dent's standards) immoral works: 'The Court of Venus', first
published c. 1538 (STC 24650); William Painter's 'The
Palace of Pleasure', which appeared in at least five
editions from 1565 (STC 19121-5); the enormously popular
'Bevis of Hampton', of which there are at least ten pre-
1640 editions (STC 1987-96); 'The Merry Jest of the Friar
and the Boy', first published c. 1580 and surviving in
five editions (STC 14522-4.3); 'Clem of the Clough, Adam
Bell...', extant in at least eight edition (STC 1806-13);
and 'The Pretie Conceit of John Splinters last will and
Testament' (STC 23102), published c. 1520. (I have been
unable to identify 'The odd tale of William, Richard and
Homfrey'.) All these works are condemned in the course of
the following dialogue, together with Skelton's poem, as
Catholic ploys to divert men from the proper study of the
Bible. For comparable lists of popular works involving
Skelton see the extracts from Puttenham (No. 13b) and
Drayton (No. 16).

Antile: ... If you will goe home with me, I can giue you a speedy remedy: for I haue many pleasant and merry bookes, which if you should heare them read, would soone remedy you of this melancholy.   I haue the Court of Venus, the Pallace of pleasure, Beuis of Southampton, Ellen of Rumming, The mery Jest of the Friar and the Boy: The pleasaunt story of Clem of the Clough, Adam Bell, and William of Cloudesley.   The Odde Tale of William, Richard, and Homfrey.   The pretie Conceit of John Splinters last will, and Testament: which al are excellent and singular bookes against hartquames: and to remove such dumpish-nesse, as I see you are now fallen into.

Asune: Youre vaine and friuolous bookes of Tales, Iests and lies, would more increase my griefe, & strike the print of sorrow deeper into my heart.

Phila: ... How came you by all these good bookes? I should haue saide, so much trashe, and rubbish....   They be goodly geare, trimme stuffe.   They are good to kindle a fire, or to scoure a hotte Oven withall.   And shal I tel you mine opinion of them?   I doo thus thinke, that they were deuised by the diuel: seene, and allowed by the Pope: Printed in hel: bound vp by Hobgoblin: and first published and dispearsed in Rome, Italy and Spaine.   And all to this ende, that thereby men might be kept from the reading of the Scriptures.

16. MICHAEL DRAYTON IN PRAISE OF SKELTON

c. 1600, 1606, 1619

(a) From the play 'The first part of the True Honorable Historie of the life of Sir John Oldcastle' (1600) by Michael Drayton (1563-1631), H 2ʳ (STC 18795). All the works alluded to were highly popular works: there were at least ten editions of 'Bevis of Hampton' up to 1640 (STC 1987-96), two of 'Owleglasse' (STC 10563-4), three of 'The Friar and the Boy' (STC 14522-4.3), and seven of 'Robin Hood' in its various forms (STC 13687-93). For comparable lists of popular works including Skelton see the extracts from Arthur Dent (No. 15) and Puttenham (No. 13b).

Enter the Sumner with bookes.

Bish. What bringst thou there? what? bookes of heresie.
Som. Yea my lord, heres not a latine booke,
No not so much as our ladies Psalter,
Heres the Bible, the testament, the Psalmes in meter,
The sickemans salve, the treasure of gladnesse,
And al in English, not so much but the Almanack's English.
Bish. Away with them, to'th fire with them Clun,
Now fie upon these upstart heretikes,
Al English, burne them, burne them quickly Clun.
Harp. But doe not Sumner as youle answere it, for I
have there English bookes my lord, that ile not part
with for your Bishoppricke, Bevis of Hampton, Owleglasse,
the Frier and the Boy, Ellen of Rumming, Robin hood,
and other such godly stories, which if ye burne, by this
flesh ile make ye drink their ashes in S. Margets ale.

exeunt.

(b) From Drayton's 'Poems Lyrick and Pastorall' (1606?),
B 2^v (STC 7217). The passage is essentially a defence of
the ode form and the various metrical forms which can be
employed in it.

To those that with despight
shall terme these Numbers slight,
tell them their iudgements blind,
much erring from the right,
tis a Noble kind.

Nor ist the verse doth make,
that giueth or doth take,
tis possible to clyme
to kindle or to slake,
although in *Skelton's* Ryme.

(c) From 'Poems by Michael Drayton Esquyer' (1619),

Iii 4ᵛ (STC 7222), 'To the Reader of his Pastorals'.

Master EDMUND SPENSER had done enough for the immortalitie
of his Name, had he only giuen vs his 'Shepheards
Kalender', a Master-piece if any. The 'Colin Clout' of
SKOGGAN, vnder King HENRY the Seuenth, is prettie; but
BARKLEY's 'Ship of Fooles' hath twentie wiser in it.

17. PIMLYCO, OR RUNNE RED-CAP' IN PRAISE OF 'ELYNOR RUMMING'

1609

From 'Pimlyco, or Runne Red-Cap' (1609) (STC 19936),
B 2-2ᵛ. This curious work is part Skeltonic imitation,
part direct quotation from 'Elynor Rumming' and part a
burlesque dream vision.

> ... By chance I found a Booke in *Ryme*,
> Writ in an age when few wryt well,
> (*Pans* Pipe (where none is) does excell.)
> O learned *Gower*! It was not thine,
> Nor *Chaucer*, (thou are more *Diuine*.)
> To *Lydgates* graue I should do wrong,
> To call him vp by such a Song.
> No, It was *One*, that (boue his *Fate*,)
> Would be Styl'd *Poet Laureate*;
> Much like to *Some* in these our daies,
> That (as bold *Prologues* do to *Playes*,)
> With *Garlonds* haue their *Fore-heads* bound,
> Yet onely empty Sculles are crownde:
> Or like to these (seeing others bye)
> Will sit so, tho their *Seate* they buy,
> And fill it vp with loathed Scorne,
> Fit *burdens* being by them not borne,
> But seeing their *Trappings* rich and gay,
> The *Sumpter-Horses* trudge away,
> Sweating themselues to death to beare them,
> When poore *Iades* (drawing the *Plough*) outweare them.

But all this while we haue forgot
Our *Poet*: tho I nam'de him not,
But only should his *Rymes* recite,
These (all would cry) did *Skelton* write.
I tournde some leaues and red them o're
And at last spyed his *Elynor*,
His *Elynor* whose fame spred saile,
All *England* through for Nappy Ale
Elynour Rumming warmde his wit
With Ale, and his *Rimes* paide for it.

But seeing thou takst the *Laureats* name
(*Skelton*) I iustly thee may blame,
Because thou leau'st the *Sacred Fount*,
For *Liquor* of so base account.
Yet (I remember) euen the *Prince*
Of Poesie, with his pen (long since)
Ledde to a fielde, the *Mice* and *Frogges*;
Others haue ball'd out bookes of *Dogges*:
Our diuine *Maro* (1) spent much oyle
About a *Gnat*. One keeps a coyle
With a poore *Flea* (*Naso*, (2) whose wit
Brought him by *Phoebus* side to wit.)
Since then these *Rare-ones* stack'd their strings,
From the hie-tuned acts of Kings
For notes so low, lesse is thy *Blame*,
For in their pardon stands thy *Name*.
Let's therefore lead our eyes astray,
And from our owne intended may,
Go backe to view thine *Hostesse* picture
Whome thus thou draw'st in liuely coloure

[Goes on to quote (B3-B4^V), lines 1-100 of 'Elynour
Rumming'; subsequently C1^V-C4 quotes lines 101-234,243-50.]

Notes

1 A reference to the poem 'Culex' sometimes attributed
   to Virgil.
2 A reference to the late medieval 'Carmen de Pulice'
   ascribed to Ovid.

18. NICHOLAS BRETON ON SKELTON'S 'RUFFLING RIMES'

1612

This passage occurs in 'Cornu-copiae or Pasquils Night Cap' (STC 3639), O 2^r, published in 1612 and attributed to the poet Nicholas Breton (1545?-1626?). This work is a comic poem, the chief theme of which is cuckoldry. There is a later brief allusion to Skelton on Q 3^r.

But as for Skelton with his Lawrel Crowne,
Whose ruffling rimes are emptie quite of marrow:
Or fond *Catullus*, which set grossely downe
The commendation of a sillie Sparrow:
    Because their lines are void of estimation,
    I passe them ouer without confutation.
    Much would the Cuckoe thinke herselfe impared,
    If shee with Philip Sparrow were compared

19. HUMPHREY KING ON SKELTON AND OTHER 'MERRY MEN'

1613

From Humphrey King's 'An Halfe-penny-worthe of Wit, in a Penny-worth of Paper. Or, the Hermit's Tale', published in 1613, p. 21 (STC 14973). The work is a homiletic dialogue in verse, part of which (pp. 16-21) is written in what is characterized as 'Skeltons rime'. The comparison between Skelton and Robin Hood was a frequent one in the sixteenth and early seventeenth centuries, cf., for example, Nos 3, 16.

But what meane I to runne so farre?
My foolish words may breed a skarre,
Let vs talke of *Robin Hoode*,
And little *Iohn* in merry Shirewood,
Of Poet *Skelton* with his pen,
And many other merry men,

Of May-game Lords, and Sommer Queenes,
With Milke-maides, dancing o're the Greenes....

20. WILLIAM BROWNE ON SKELTON

1614

'The Shepherd's Pipe', published in 1614 (STC 3917), is a
series of eclogues by William Browne (1591-1643?) and
various other poets. This passage is from the end of the
first eclogue, C 7^r, after Browne's modernization of
Thomas Hoccleve's 'Tale of Jonathas'. After the tale
proper there follows a pastoral dialogue between Willie
and Roget in which Willie compares Skelton unfavourably
with Browne's version of Hoccleve.

Happy surely was that swaine!
And he was not taught in vaine:
Many a one that prouder is,
Has not such a song as this;
And have garlands for their meed,
That but iarre as *Skeltons* reed.

21. HENRY PEACHAM ON SKELTON'S UNMERITED REPUTATION

1622

'The Compleat Gentleman' by Henry Peacham (1576?-1643?)
was published in 1622 (STC 19502). It is a treatise on
manners and gentlemanly conduct and includes a chapter
'Of poetrie' from which (p. 95) the following extract
comes.

Then followed *Harding*, and after him *Skelton*, a Poet
Laureate, for what desert I could neuer heare. If you

Skelton desire to see his vaine and learning, an Epitaph vpon King *Henry* the seauenth at *Westminster* will discover it.

22. 'A BANQUET OF JESTS' ON THE NEGLECT OF SKELTON

1639

From 'A Banquet of Jests', '5th impression' (1639) (STC 1370). This work is a collection of prose jests. The lines below come from the prefatory Printer to the Reader, A 5^V. They do not occur in the first edition of the work in 1630.

The coarser Cates, that might the feast disgrace,
Left out: And better serv'd in, in their place
Pasquel's conceits are poore, and *Scoggins* (1) dry.
Skeltons meere rime, once read, but now laid by.

Note

1 'Pasquil' and 'Scogan' were by this time names typifying vulgar, satiric verse.

23. JAMES HOWELL ON THE NEGLECT OF SKELTON

1655

From 'Epistolae Ho-Elianae', 3rd ed. (1655), by James Howell. The work is a collection of Howell's letters on various subjects.
    Howell (1594?-1666) was historiographer to Charles II.

Touching your Poet Laureat *Skelton*, I found him (at last,

as I told you before) skulking in *Duck-lane*, pitifully
totter'd and torn, and as the times are, I do not think
it worth the labour and cost to put him in better clothes,
for the Genius of the Age is quite another thing: yet ther
be som Lines of his, which I think will never be out of
date for their quaint sense; and with these I will close
this Letter, and salute you, as he did his friend with
these options:

> Salve plus decies quam sunt momenta dierum,
> Quot species generum, quot pes, quot nomina perum,
> Quot pratis flores, quot sunt et in orbe colores,
> Quot pisces, quot aves, quot sunt et in aequore naves,
> Quot volucrum Pennae, quot sunt tormenta Gebennae,
> Quot coeli stellae, Quot sunt miracula Thomae,
>   Quot sunt virtutes, tantas tibi mitto salutes. (1)

These were the wishes in times of yore of Jo. Skelton,
but now they are of   Your J.H.

Note

1   This Latin poem is attributed to Skelton, see Dyce, I,
    p. 177.

24. THOMAS FULLER'S BIOGRAPHY ON SKELTON

1662

From the 'Worthies of England' (1662), pp. 257-8, by
Thomas Fuller (1608-61), bishop and chaplain in extraordinary to Charles II. The 'Worthies' is a series of
lives of eminent Englishmen.

John Skelton is placed in this County, on a double
probability. First, because an ancient family of his
name is eminently known long fixed therein. Secondly,
because he was beneficed at *Dis*, a Market-town in *Norfolk*.
He usually styles himself (and that *Nemine contradicente*
[without contradiction], for ought I find) *the King's
Orator and Poet Laureat*. We need go no further for a

testimony of his *learning* than to *Erasmus*, styling him in
his letter to King *Henry* the eight, *Britannicarum
Literarum Lumen et Decus* [see No. 2a above].

Indeed he had *scholarship* enough, and *wit* too much;
seeing one saith truly of him, *Ejus sermo salsus in
mordacem, risus in opprobrium, jocus in amaritudinem.* (1)
Yet was his Satyrical *wit* unhappy to light on *three Noli
me tangere's* (2) *viz.*, the *rod* of a *Schoolmaster*, the
Couls of *Friars*, and the *Cap* of a *Cardinal*. The *first*
gave him a *lash*, the *second* deprived him of his *lively-
hood*, the *third* almost outed him of his life.

William Lilly was the School-master, whom he fell foul
with, though gaining nothing thereby, as may appear by his
return. And this I will do for *W. Lilly* (though often
beaten for his sake) endeavour to translate his answer;
[For text and translations see No. 6 above].

The *Dominican Friars* were the next he contested with,
whose viciousness lay pat enough for his hand; but such
foul Lubbers fell heavy on all which found fault with
them. These instigated *Nix* Bishop of *Norwich* to call him
to account for keeping a *Concubine*, which cost him (as it
seems) a suspension from his benefice.

But Cardinal Wolsey (*impar congressus* [unequal con-
test] betwixt a *poor Poet* and so *potent a Prelate*) being
inveighed against by his pen, and charged with *too much
truth*, so persecuted him that he was forced to take
Sanctuary at *Westminster*, where Abbot *Islip* used him with
much respect. In this restraint he died, *June* 21, 1529;
and is buried in Saint *Margaret's* chapel with this
Epitaph:

    J. Skeltonus Vates Pierius hic situs est.

    [J. Skelton, poet of the Muses, is buried here.]

The word *Vates* being *Poet* or *Prophet*, minds me of this
dying *Skelton's prediction*, foretelling the ruin of
Cardinal Wolsey. Surely, one unskilled in *prophecies*, if
well versed in *Solomon's Proverbs*, might have prognosti-
cated as much, that, *Pride goeth before a fall*.

We must not forget, how being charged by some on his
death-bed, for begetting many children on the aforesaid
Concubine, he protested that in his Conscience he kept
her in the notion of a wife, though such his *cowardliness*,
that he would rather confess adultery (then accounted but
a *venial* (than own *marriage*, esteemed a *capital crime* in
that age.

Notes

1 A misquotation from John Pits, 'Relationum Historicarum
   de Rebus Anglicis' (1619); the correct translation
   reads, 'his nimble speech was often turned into jest,
   his laughter into opprobrium, his mirth into bitterness.'
2 Literally 'do not touch me', i.e. prohibited topics.

25. EDWARD PHILLIPS ON SKELTON'S CURRENT OBSCURITY

1675

From Edward Phillips's 'Theatrum Poetarum' (1675),
pp. 115-16, a biographical list of English poets.
Phillips (1630-96?) was a prose writer and a cousin of
John Milton.

John Skelton, a jolly English Rimer, and I warrant ye
accounted a notable Poet, as Poetry went in those daies,
namely King *Edward* the fourth's Reign, when doubtless
good Poets were scarce; for however he had the good fortune to be chosen Poet Laureat methinks he hath a miserable loos, rambling style, and galloping measure of Verse;
so that no wonder he is so utterly forgotten at this present, when so many better Poets of not much later a date,
are wholly laid aside. His chief Works, as many as I
could collect out of an old printed Book, but imperfect
are his 'Philip Sparrow', 'Speak Parrot', 'The death of
Edward the fourth', 'A Treatise of the Scots', 'Ware the
Hawk', 'The tunning of Eleanor Rumpkin'; in many of which
following the humor of the ancientest of our modern Poets,
he takes a Poetical libertie of Satyrically gibing at the
vices and corruptions of the Clergy.

26. AN EIGHTEENTH-CENTURY CRITIC IN PRAISE OF 'ELYNOR
RUMMYNG'

1718

'To the Reader' in a reprint of 'The Tunning of Elynor
Rumming' (1718). The authorship of these prefatory
remarks is unknown.

A View of past Times is the most agreable Study of humane
Life. To unveil the former Ages, call back Time in his
Course, and with a contracted View prie thro' the Clouds
of Oblivion, and see Things that were before our Being, is
certainly the most Amusement, if as Martial tells us,

> ------ *hoc est*
> *Vivere bis, vita posse priore frui.* (1)

how additional a Happiness is it to enlarge and draw it
into the Ages that were before?
    This, Reader, is the Editor's Reason for publishing
this very antient Sketch of a Drinking Piece; and tho'
some of the Lines seem to be a little defac'd by Time,
yet the Strokes are so just and true, that an experienc'd
Painter might from hence form the most agreeable Variety
requisite in a Picture, to represent the mirth of those
Times. Here is a just and natural Description of those
merry Wassail Dayes, and of the Humours of our great
Grandames, which our Poet hath drawn with that Exactness,
that, as Mr. *Dryden* says of *Chaucer's* Characters, he
thought, when he read them himself, *to have seen them as
distinctly as if he had sup'd with them at the Tabard Inn
in Southwark,* so I may truly say, I see before me this
Variety of Gossips, as plainly as if I had dropt into the
Alehouse at *Leatherhead* and sate upon the Settle to view
their Gamball's.
    It may seem a Trifle to some to revive a Thing of this
Nature: The Subject, they say, is so low, and the Time so
long since, that it would be throwing away more to peruse
it. What have we to do to puzle our Brains with old out-
of fashion'd Trumpery, when we have since had ingenious
Poets in our own Times easily to be understood, and much
more diverting too.
    As for Those nice Curiosoes, who can tast nothing but
Deserts; whose chief Perfection is to discover the fine

Turn in a new Epilogue, and have so much Work upon their
Hands to damn moderns, that they have none to read them;
it is not to be expected, that they will either read or
can understand the Antients; neither was it for such
Sparks that this piece of Antiquity was reviv'd. But
Persons of an extensive Fancy and just Relish, who can
discover Nature in the lowest Scene of life, and receive
pleasure from the meanest Views; who prie into all the
Variety of Places and Humours at present, and think
nothing unworthy their Notice; and not only so, but with
a contracting Eye, survey the Times past, and live over
those Ages which were before their Birth; it is in Respect
to them, and for a Moment's Amusement that this merry old
Tale is reviv'd. The Subject is low, it's true; and so
is *Chaucer's Old Widow*; yet the Description of her Hovel
pleases as much in it's Way, as a more lofty Theme.

Note

1 From Martial's 'Epigrams', Book X, xxiii, 7-8: 'He
   lives twice who can find pleasure in bygone life.'

27. ALEXANDER POPE ON 'BEASTLY SKELTON'

1737

(a) From 'Imitations of Horace' by Alexander Pope (1688-
1744), originally published in 1737. The present text is
that of the Twickenham Edition, edited by John Butt, 2nd
ed. (London, 1953), pp. 196-7.

Authors, like Coins, grow dear as they grow old;
It is the rust we value, not the gold.
Chaucer's worst ribaldry is learn'd by rote,
And beastly Skelton Heads of Houses quote:

[Pope adds the following note on the phrase 'beastly
Skelton':]

Poet Laureat to Hen. 8. a Volume of whose Verses has been
lately reprinted, consisting almost wholly of Ribaldry,
Obscenity, and Billingsgate Language.

(b) From Joseph Spence's 'Observations, Anecdotes and
Characters of Books and Men', edited by J. M. Osborn
(Oxford, 1966), I, p. 180, no. 414. Spence's work was
first published in 1820. Spence himself (1699-1768) was
a famous anecdotist. He records this comment by Pope.

Skelton's poems are all low and bad; there's nothing in
them that's worth reading.

28. ELIZABETH COOPER IN PRAISE OF SKELTON

1737

From Elizabeth Cooper, 'The Muses Library' (1737),
pp. 48-9. Mrs Cooper was a dramatist as well as a critic.

The Restorer of Invention in *English* Poetry! was born of
an ancient Family in *Cumberland*, received his Education
at *Oxford*, and, afterwards, entring into Holy Orders, was
made Rector of Dysse in *Norfolk*, in the reign of *Henry* the
Eighth; tho', in my Opinion, He appear'd first in that of
Henry the Seventh, and may be said, to be the Growth of
that Time. Some bitter Satires on the Clergy, and particularly, his keen Reflections on Cardinal *Wolsey*, drew
on him so severe Prosecutions, that he was oblig'd to fly
for Sanctuary to *Westminster*, under the Protection of
Islip the Abbot; where He dy'd in the Year 1529. It
appears, by his Poem, intitled, 'The Crown of Laurel',
that his Performances were very numerous, tho so few of
Them remain: In these is a very rich Vein of Wit, Humour,
and Poetry, tho' much debas'd by the Rust of the Age He
liv'd in. - His Satirs are remarkably broad, open, and
ill-bred; the Verse cramp'd by a very short Measure, and
incumber'd with such a Profusion of Rhimes, as makes the
Poet almost as ridiculous, as Those he endeavours to
expose. - In his more serious Pieces, He is not guilty of
this Absurdity; and confines himself to a regular Stanza,
according to the then reigning Mode. His 'Bouge of
Court', is, in my Opinion, a Poem of great Merit: it
abounds with Wit, and Imagination, and argues him well

vers'd in Human Nature, and the Manners of that insinuat-
ing Place. The Allegorical Characters are finely
describ'd, and as well sustain'd; The Fabrick of the
Whole, I believe, entirely his own, and, not improbably,
may have the Honour to be a Hint, even to the inimitable
Spencer; But, as his Poems have been lately reprinted, I
shall only annex the Prologue and submit this Conjecture
to the Correction of better Judges.

How, or by whose Interest He was made Laureat, or
whether 'twas a Title He assum'd himself, I cannot learn.
- Neither is his Principal Patron any where nam'd; but, if
his Poem of the 'Crown of Lawrell', before mention'd, has
any Covert-meaning, He had the Honour to have the Ladies
for his Friends, and the Countess of *Surrey*, the Lady
Elizabeth Howard, and many others united their Services
in his Favour.

[Quotes first 126 lines of 'Bouge of Court'.]

29. SAMUEL JOHNSON ON SKELTON

1755

From A History of the Language included in 'A Dictionary
of the English Language' (1755), I, p. 9, by Samuel Johnson (1709-84), the poet, critic and lexicographer.

At the same time with Sir *Thomas More* lived *Skelton*, the
poet laureate of *Henry* VIII. from whose works it seems
proper to insert a few stanzas, though he cannot be said
to have attained great elegance of language.

[Quotes lines 1-34 of the 'Bouge of Court'.]

30. THOMAS WARTON ON SKELTON

1778

From Thomas Warton, 'The History of English Poetry'
(1778), II, pp. 336-63. Warton (1728-90) was a poet and
critic. In reprinting his essay his original footnotes
have been deleted as have various excurses.

Most of the poems of John Skelton were written in the
reign of king Henry the eighth. But as he was laureated
at Oxford about the year 1489, I consider him as belonging
to the fifteenth century.

Skelton, having studied in both our universities, was
promoted to the rectory of Diss in Norfolk. But for his
buffooneries in the pulpit, and his satirical ballads
against the mendicants, he was severely censured, and
perhaps suspended by Nykke his diocesan, a rigid bishop
of Norwich, from exercising the duties of the sacerdotal
function. Wood says, he was also punished by the bishop
for 'having been guilty *of certain crimes*, AS MOST POETS
are.' But these persecutions only served to quicken his
ludicrous disposition, and to exasperate the acrimony
of his satire. As his sermons could be no longer a
vehicle for his abuse, he vented his ridicule in rhyming
libels. At length, daring to attack the dignity of
cardinal Wolsey, he was closely pursued by the officers
of that powerful minister; and, taking shelter in the
sanctuary of Westminster abbey, was kindly entertained
and protected by abbot Islip, to the day of his death.
He died, and was buried in the neighbouring church of
saint Margaret, in the year 1529.

Skelton was patronised by Henry Algernon Percy, the
fifth earl of Northumberland, who deserves particular
notice here; as he loved literature at a time when many
of the nobility of England could hardly read or write
their names, and was the general patron of such genius
as his age produced. He encouraged Skelton, almost the
only professed poet of the reign of Henry the seventh,
to write an elegy on the death of his father, which is
yet extant.... But Skelton hardly deserved such a
patronage.

It is in vain to apologise for the coarseness,
obscenity, and scurrility of Skelton, by saying that his
poetry is tinctured with the manners of his age. Skelton

would have been a writer without decorum at any period.
The manners of Chaucer's age were undoubtedly more rough
and unpolished than those of the reign of Henry the
seventh. Yet Chaucer, a poet abounding in humour, and
often employed in describing the vices and follies of the
world, writes with a degree of delicacy, when compared
with Skelton. That Skelton's manner is gross and
illiberal, was the opinion of his contemporaries; at
least of those critics who lived but a few years afterwards, and while his poems yet continued in vogue.
Puttenham, the author of the 'Arte of English Poesie',
published in the year 1589, speaking of the species of
short metre used in the minstrel-romances, for the convenience of being sung to the harp at feasts, and in
CAROLS and ROUNDS, 'and such other light or lascivious
poems which are commonly more commodiously uttered by
those buffoons or Vices in playes than by any other
person,' and in which the sudden return of the rhyme
fatigues the ear, immediately subjoins: 'Such were the
rimes of Skelton, being indeed but a rude rayling rimer,
and all his doings ridiculous; he used both short distaunces and short measures, pleasing only the popular
care.' And Meres, in his 'Palladis Tamia', or 'Wit's
Treasury', published in 1598. 'Skelton applied his wit
to skurilities and ridiculous matters: such among the
Greekes were called *pantomimi*, with us buffoons.'
    Skelton's characteristic vein of humour is capricious
and grotesque. If his whimsical extravagancies ever move
our laughter, at the same time they shock our sensibility.
His festive levities are not only vulgar and indelicate,
but frequently want truth and propriety. His subjects are
often as ridiculous as his metre; but he sometimes debases
his matter by his versification. On the whole, his genius
seems better suited to low burlesque, than to liberal and
manly satire. It is supposed by Caxton, that he improved
our language; but he sometimes affects obscurity, and
sometimes adopts the most familiar phraseology of the
common people.
    He thus describes, in the 'Boke of Colin Cloute', the
pompous houses of the clergy.

[Quotes lines 936-58, 962-70, 974-81.]

    These lines are in the best manner of his petty
measure: which is made still more disgusting by the
repetition of the rhymes....
    In the poem' Why Come Ye Not to the Court', he thus
satirises cardinal Wolsey, not without some tincture of
humour.

[Quotes lines 181-194, 200-4, 210-19, 222-3.]

The poem called the 'Bouge of Court', or the 'Rewards
of a Court', is in the manner of a pageaunt, consisting of
seven personifications. Here our author, in adopting the
more grave and stately movement of the seven lined stanza,
has shewn himself not always incapable of exhibiting
allegorical imagery with spirit and dignity. But his
comic vein predominates. RYOTT is thus forcibly and
humorously pictured.

[Quotes lines 344-64.]

There is also merit in the delineation of DISSIMULATION,
in the same poem,: and it is not unlike Ariosto's manner in
imagining these allegorical personages.

[Quotes lines 428-37.] ...

In the 'Crowne of Lawrell' our author attempts the
higher poetry: but he cannot long support the tone of
solemn description. These are some of the most ornamented
and poetical stanzas. He is describing a garden belonging
to the superb palace of FAME.

[Quotes lines 652-63, 665-72, 674-90.]
Our author supposes, that in the wall surrounding the
palace of FAME were a thousand gates, new and old, for the
entrance and egress of all nations. One of the gates is
called ANGLIA, on which stood a leopard. There is some
boldness and animation in the figure and attitude of this
ferocious animal.

[Quotes lines 589-95.]

Skelton, in the course of his allegory, supposes that the
poets laureate, or learned men, of all nations, were
assembled before Pallas. This groupe shews the authors,
both antient and modern, then in vogue. Some of them are
quaintly characterised. They are, first, - Olde Quintil-
ian, not with his Institutes of eloquence, but with his
Declamations: Theocritus, with his bucolicall relacions:
Hesiod, the Icononucar: Homer, the freshe historiar: The
prince of eloquence, Cicero: Sallust, who wrote both the
history of Catiline and Jugurth: Ovid, enshryned with the
Musys nyne: Lucan: Statius, writer of Achilleidos: Persius,
with problems diffuse: Virgil, Juvenal, Livy: Ennius, who
wrote of marciall warre: Aulus Gellius, that noble
historiar: Horace, with his New Poetry: Maister Terence,

the famous comicar, with Plautus: Seneca, the tragedian:
Boethius: Maximian, *with his madde dities bow dotyng age
wolde jape with young foly*: Boccacio, *with his volumes
grete*: Quintus Curtius: Macrobius, who treated of
Scipion's dreame: Poggius Florentinus, with many a *mad
tale:* a friar of France *syr* Gaguine, who frowned on me
full angrily: Plutarch and Petrarch, two *famous clarkes*:
Lucilius, Valerius Maximus, Propertius, Pisander, and
Vincentius Bellovacensis, who wrote the 'Speculum
Historiale'. The catalogue is closed by Gower, Chaucer,
and Lydgate, who first adorned the English language: in
allusion to which part of their characters, their apparel
is said to shine beyond the power of description, and
their tabards to be studded with diamonds and rubies.
That only these three English poets are here mentioned,
may be considered as a proof, that only these three were
yet thought to deserve the name.

No writer is more unequal than Skelton. In the midst
of a page of the most wretched ribaldry, we sometimes are
surprized with three or four nervous and manly lines, like
these.

[Quotes 'Garland of Laurel', lines 192-4.]

Skelton's modulation in the octave stanza is rough and
inharmonious. The following are the smoothest lines in
the poem before us; which yet do not equal the liquid
melody of Lydgate, whom he here manifestly attempts to
imitate.

[Quotes 'Garland of Laurel', lines 533-36.]

The following little ode deserves notice; at least as
a specimen of the structure and phraseology of a love-
sonnet about the close of the fifteenth century.

[Quotes 'Garland of Laurel', 906-25: 'To Maistress
Margary Wentworth'.]

For the same reason this stanza in a sonnet to
Maistress Margaret Hussey deserves notice.

[Quotes 'Garland of Laurel', lines 1004-7.]

As do the following flowery lyrics, in a sonnet addressed
to *Maistress Isabell Pennel*.

[Quotes 'Garland of Laurel', lines 985-92.]

But Skelton most commonly appears to have mistaken his
genius, and to write in a forced character, except when he
is indulging his native vein of satire and jocularity, in
the short minstrel-metre abovementioned: which he mars by
a multiplied repetition of rhymes, arbitrary abbreviations
of the verse, cant expressions, hard and founding words
newly-coined, and patches of Latin and French. This
anomalous and motley code of versification is, I believe,
supposed to be peculiar to our author. I am not, however,
quite certain that it originated with Skelton....
    We must, however, acknowledge, that Skelton, notwith-
standing his scurrility, was a classical scholar; and in
that capacity, he was tutor to prince Henry, afterwards
king Henry the eighth: at whose accession to the throne,
he was appointed the royal orator. He is styled by
Erasmus, 'Britannicarum literarum decus et lumen.' His
Latin elegiacs are pure, and often unmixed with the monastic phraseology; and they prove, that if his natural
propensity to the ridiculous had not more frequently
seduced him to follow the whimsies of Walter Mapes (1)
and Golias, (2) than to copy the elegancies of Ovid, he
would have appeared among the first writers of Latin
poetry in England at the general restoration of literature. Skelton could not avoid acting as a buffoon in any
language, or any character.
    I cannot quit Skelton, of whom I yet fear too much has
been already said, without restoring to the public notice
a play, or MORALITY, written by him, not recited in any
catalogue of his works, or annals of English typography;
and, I believe, at present totally unknown to the antiquarians in this sort of literature. It is, 'The
NIGRAMANSIR, a morall ENTERLUDE and a pithie written by
Maister SKELTON laureate and plaid before the king and
other estatys at Woodstoke on Palme Sunday'. It was
printed by Wynkin de Worde in a thin quarto, in the year
1504. It must have been presented before king Henry the
seventh, at the royal manor or palace, at Woodstock in
Oxfordshire, now destroyed. The characters are a Necromancer, or conjurer, the devil, a notary public, Simonie,
and Philargyria, or Avarice. It is partly a satire on
some abuses in the church; yet not without a due regard
to decency, and an apparent respect for the dignity of the
audience. The story, or plot, is the tryal of SIMONY and
AVARICE: the devil is the judge, and the notary public
acts as an assessor or scribe. The prisoners, as we may
suppose, are found guilty, and ordered into hell
immediately. There is no sort of propriety in calling
this play the Necromancer: for the only business and use
of this character, is to open the subject in a long

prologue, to evoke the devil, and summon the court. The
devil kicks the necromancer, for waking him so soon in the
morning: a proof, that this drama was performed in the
morning, perhaps in the chapel of the palace. A variety
of measures, with shreds of Latin and French, is used:
but the devil speaks in the octave stanza. One of the
stage-directions is, *Enter Balsebub with a Berde.* To
make him both frightful and ridiculous, the devil was
most commonly introduced on the stage, wearing a visard
with an immense beard. Philargyria quotes Seneca and
saint Austin: and Simony offers the devil a bribe. The
devil rejects her offer with much indignation: and swears
by the *foule Eumenides*, and the hoary beard of Charon,
that she shal be well fried and roasted in the unfathom-
able sulphur of Cocytus, together with Mahomet, Pontius
Pilate, the traitor Judas, and king Herod. The last
scene is closed with a view of hell and a dance between
the devil and the necromancer. The dance ended, the devil
trips up the necromancer's heels, and disappears in fire
and smoke. Great must have been the edification and
entertainment which king Henry the seventh and his court
derived from the exhibition of so elegant and rational a
drama! The royal taste for dramatic representation seems
to have suffered a very rapid transition: for in the year
1520, *a goodlie comedie of Plautus* was played before king
Henry the eighth at Greenwich....

Notes

1 A medieval English satiric poet.
2 A general name for medieval Latin satiric verse.

31. PHILIP NEVE ON SKELTON: 'A RUDE AND SCURRILOUS
RHYMER'

1789

From 'Cursory Remarks on Some of the Ancient English
Poets...' (1789), p. 10.

John Skelton, a rude and scurrilous rhymer of the reign of

Henry VIII. is mentioned here, only as his gross style and
measures reflect back some honor to *Chaucer*, by a comparison: and he seems further remarkable, as he had sufficient
confidence to satirize *Wolsey*, in the plenitude of his
power. *Puttenham* ... calls him 'a rude rayling rhymer and
all his doings ridiculous.' Yet he was this for want of
taste, not learning; as his scholarship excited a high
encomium from *Erasmus*.

Though neither the manner, nor versification of *Skelton*,
could recommend his poems, the justness of his satire
rendered them popular. *Wolsey's* profligacy, arrogance,
and oppressions were so excessive, that it required a very
ingenious poet to invent a charge against him, that would
not have application: and the generality of the court,
constrained through fear, to flatter a man they secretly
detested, were gratified in the boldness of one, who,
without hesitation or reserve, dared utter their common
sentiment.

32. ROBERT SOUTHEY ON SKELTON'S GENIUS

1814

From an unsigned review by Southey in the 'Quarterly
Review', XI (1814), pp. 484-5, of Chalmers's 1810 reprint
of the 1736 edition of Skelton. Southey (1774-1843) was a
prolific poet and man of letters.

Mr. Chalmers has done well in including Skelton, but he
has merely reprinted the imperfect and careless edition of
1736. 'It yet remains,' he says, 'to explain his obscurities, translate his vulgarisms, and point his verses. The
task would require much time and labour, with perhaps no
very inviting promise of recompense.' Let the reader
judge whether this be a sufficient excuse for an editor
who makes Skelton speak

  Of Tristem and King Marke
  And all the whole warke
  Of bele I sold his wife! (p. 294) ['Philip Sparrow',
                                        lines 641-3]

and who, rather than venture upon any emendation of a
grossly corrupted text, has printed all the comic and
satirical poems, and most of the others, without any
punctuation whatever! Considering the manner in which
works of this kind are *got up* in England, it would
certainly have been too much to expect that the writings
of so difficult an author should be elaborately eluci-
dated; yet surely some kind of glossary ought to have been
annexed, and those pieces should have been added which
Ritson indicated, and which have come to light since
Ritson's death. Mr. Chalmers has some sense of Skelton's
power, but when he ventures upon delivering a critical
opinion, he produces only a tissue of inconsistencies,
one sentence contradicting another. He tells us that
there is occasionally much sound sense and much just
satire on the conduct of the clergy, and presently adds,
that if his vein of humour had been directed to subjects
of legitimate satire, he might have been more worthy of a
placé in this collection. Did it never occur to him that
Skelton's buffooneries, like the ribaldry of Rabelais,(1)
were thrown out as a tub for the whale, and that unless he
had thus written for the coarsest palates, he could not
possibly have poured forth such bitter and undaunted
satire in such perilous times? Well did he say of himself -

> Though my rime be ragged,
> Tattered and jagged,
> Rudely rain-beaten
> Rusty and moth-eaten,
> If ye take well therewith
> It hath in it some pith.   ['Colin Clout', lines 53-8]

So much pith indeed, that an editor who should be com-
petent to the task, could not more worthily himself than
by giving a good and complete edition of his works. The
power, the strangeness, the volubility of his language,
the audacity of his satire, and the perfect originality
of his manner, render Skelton one of the most extraordinary writers of any age or country.

Note

1 François Rabelais (1494?-1554), author of the satires
   'Gargantua' and 'Pontagruel'.

33. WILLIAM GIFFORD IN PRAISE OF SKELTON

1816

From 'The Works of Ben Jonson', edited by William Gifford
(1816), VIII, p. 77. Gifford (1756-1826) was a satirist,
editor and scholar. This passage is from his annotation
of Jonson's masque 'The Fortunate Isles'.

Jonson was evidently fond of Skelton, and frequently
imitates his short titupping style, which is not his best.
I know Skelton only by the modern edition of his works,
dated 1736. But from this stupid publication I can easily
discover that he was no ordinary man. Why Warton and the
writers of his school rail at him so vehemently, I know
not; he was perhaps the best scholar of his day, and
displays, on many occasions, strong powers of description,
and a vein of poetry that shines through all the rubbish
which ignorance has spread over it. He flew at high game,
and therefore occasionally called in the aid of vulgar
ribaldry to mask the direct attack of his satire. This
was seen centuries ago, and yet we are now instituting a
process against him for rudeness and indelicacy!

[Goes on to quote Grange - see above No. 11.]

34. THOMAS CAMPBELL ON SKELTON'S BUFFOONERY

1819

From Thomas Campbell's 'Specimens of the British Poets'
(1819), I, pp. 101-3. Campbell (1777-1844) is best known
as a poet. The original footnotes have been deleted.

John Skelton, who was the rival and contemporary of
Barklay, was laureate to the University of Oxford, and
tutor to the prince, afterwards Henry VIII. Erasmus must
have been a bad judge of English poetry, or must have

alluded only to the learning of Skelton, when in one of
his letters he pronounces him 'Britannicarum literarum
lumen et decus.' There is certainly a vehemence and
vivacity in Skelton which was worthy of being guided by
a better taste; and the objects of his satire bespeak
some degree of public spirit. But his eccentricity in
attempts at humour is at once vulgar and flippant; and
his style is almost a texture of slang phrases, patched
with shreds of French and Latin. We are told, indeed,
in a periodical work of the present day, (1) that his
manner is to be excused, because it was assumed for 'the
nonce,' and was suited to the taste of his contemporaries.
But it is surely a poor apology for the satirist of any
age to say that he stooped to humour its vilest taste, and
could not ridicule vice and folly without degrading himself to buffoonery.

Note

1 A reference to Southey's 'Quarterly Review' article -
see No. 32 above.

35. EZEKIEL SANFORD ON SKELTON'S LIFE AND WORKS

1819

From Ezekiel Sanford's 'The Works of the British Poets'
(Philadelphia, 1819), I, pp. 259-61).
    Sanford (1796-1822) was an American historian. The
selection from Skelton which accompanies this introduction
appears to be the first American publication of any of
Skelton's works.

JOHN SKELTON, an eccentric satyrist, was born towards the
close of the fifteenth century. The two universities
dispute the honour of his education; but neither seems
to have established a very strong title. The poet-
laureateship was then a degree of the universities.
Caxton says, our author was made laureate at Oxford; and
Mr. Malone tells us, that he wore the laurel publicly at
Cambridge.

In 1507, we find him curate of Trompington, and rector
of Diss in Norfolk. But he is supposed to have added
little dignity to his calling. His pulpit, it is said,
became a theatre, and he, a buffoon. It was the business
of his life to lampoon Lilly, the grammarian, cardinal
Wolsey, the Scots, and the mendicant friars. There is no
doubt, that the clergy were then sufficiently corrupt;
but it was not for a man, who kept a concubine, to accuse
the immorality of others; and the whole tenor of Skelton's
life shows him to have been ignorant of the wholesome doctrine, that reform, like charity, should begin at home.

Wolsey, at last, thought his satires worthy of notice,
and ordered him to be apprehended. He took refuge in
Westminster abbey; and was protected by Islip, the abbot,
till his death in June, 1529. He was buried in St.
Margaret's church-yard; and the inscription in his tomb
is: -

J. SCELTONUS Vates Pierius hic setus est.
Animam egit 21 Juno An. Dom. MDXXIX.

Erasmus, in a letter to Henry VIII., called Skelton
Brittanicarum literarum decus et lumen. The praise may
have been just in his own day; but, at present, Skelton is
far from being considered as the light, or the ornament,
of British literature. He is, however, the father of
English *Macaronics*; a species of poetry, which consists
chiefly in interweaving Latin phrases with his native
language. It was his ambition to be grotesque and droll;
and the devices, to which he resorted for this purpose,
gained him the epithet of the 'inventive Skelton.' His
inventions are, indeed, entitled to the praise of originality. He first hunts up all the words, in Latin and
English, which will chime with each other; and, having
then set them down in a string, or tacked them to the
end of as many short phrases, imagines that he has been
writing poetry. Sense and prosody are entirely abandoned;
and he has sometimes even given us lines which consist
altogether of the nine digits. His poems are generally
long; and, as all his fire goes out, while he is in search
of rhymes, they are excessively monotonous and dull. For
a specimen of his best manner, we extract the exordium to
the 'Boke of Colin Clout'. The reader will see how one
rhyme after another seduces him from the sense, till at
last he loses sight of it altogether.

[Quotes lines 1-37.]

36. THE 'RETROSPECTIVE REVIEW' IN PRAISE OF SKELTON

1822

From the 'Retrospective Review', VI (1822), p. 353. These anonymous comments follow a selection of Skelton's works included in this journal.

This is certainly a sufficient specimen of this extraordinary versifier - both as to matter and manner. The talents of John Skelton are easily estimated. With strong sense, a vein of humour, and some imagination, he had a wonderful command of the English language. His rhymes are interminable, and often spun out beyond the sense in the wantonness of power. In judging of this old poet, we must always recollect the state of poetry in his time and the taste of the age, which being taken into the account, we cannot help considering Skelton as an ornament of his own time, and a benefactor to those which came after him. Let him be compared to a fine old building, which once glittered in a wanton lavishment of ornament, and revelled in the profusion of its apartments, and in the number of its winding passages, is now grown unfit for habitation, and only remains as a model of the architecture of past times and a fit subject for the reverence and the researches of the antiquarian.

37. WILLIAM WORDSWORTH ON SKELTON: 'A DEMON IN POINT OF GENIUS'

1823, 1833

From 'The Letters of William and Dorothy Wordsworth', edited by E. de Selincourt (Oxford, 1939), pp. 129, 638.
    Wordsworth (1770-1850) appears to have had a high regard regard for Skelton.

(a) Wordsworth to Allan Cunningham, the Scottish poet,

23 November 1823.   He is discussing northern English poet
poets.

The list of English border poets is not so distinguished,
but Langhorne (1) was a native of Westmoreland, and Brown
the author of the 'Estimate of Manners and Principles',
etc., - a poet as his letter on the vale of Keswick,
with the accompanying verses, shows - was born in
Cumberland. (2)   So also was Skelton, a demon in point of
genius; and Tickell (3) in later times, whose style is
superior in chastity to Pope's, his contemporary.

(b) Wordsworth to Alexander Dyce, the editor of Skelton,
7 January 1833, referring to his then projected edition.

Sincerely do I congratulate you upon having made such progress with Skelton, a Writer deserving of far greater
attention than his works have hitherto received.   Your
Edition will be very serviceable, and may be the occasion
of calling out illustrations perhaps of particular
passages from others, beyond what your own Reading, though
so extensive, has supplied.

Notes

1   John Langhorne (1735-79), an eighteenth-century minor
    poet.
2   John Brown (1715-66); his 'Estimate of Manners and
    Principles of the Times' was published in 1757.
3   Thomas Tickell (1686-1740), a minor poet.

38. SAMUEL TAYLOR COLERIDGE ON 'PHILIP SPARROW'

1827, 1836

(a) From 'Specimens of the Table Talk of the late Samuel
Taylor Coleridge' (1835), I, pp. 59-60. The entry is
dated 12 March 1827.

For an instance of Shakespeare's power *in minimis*, I
generally quote James Gurney's character in *King John*.
How individual and comical he is with the four words
allowed to his dramatic life! And pray look at Skelton's
'Richard [sic] Sparrow' also!

(b) From 'The Literary Remains of Samuel Taylor
Coleridge', edited by Henry N. Coleridge (1836), II,
p. 163.
   Coleridge is commenting on a proposed emendation to
Shakespeare's 'King John' (I, i, 232) by the editor of
Shakespeare, William Warburton (1698-1779).

Theobald (1) adopts Warburton's conjecture of 'spare me'.
   O true Warburton! and the *sancta simpicitas* of honest
dull Theobald's faith in him! Nothing can be more lively
or characteristic than 'Philip? Sparrow!' Had Warburton
read old Skelton's 'Philip Sparrow', an exquisite and
original poem, and, no doubt popular in Shakespeare's
time, even Warburton would, scarcely have made so deep a
plunge into the *bathetic* as to have deathified 'sparrow'
into 'spare me'!

Note

1   Lewis Theobald (1688-1744), editor of Shakespeare.

39. HENRY HALLAM ON SKELTON: 'CERTAINLY NOT A POET'

1837

From Henry Hallam's 'Introduction to the Literature of
Europe in the Fifteenth, Sixteenth and Seventeenth
Centuries' (1837), I, p. 313.
     Hallam (1777-1859) was chiefly notable as an historian.
His footnotes have been deleted from this selection.

The strange writer, whom we have just mentioned, seems to
fall well enough within this decad; though his poetical
life was long, if it be true that he received the laureate
crown at Oxford in 1483, and was also the author of a
libel on Sir Thomas More, ascribed to him by Ellis, which
alluding to the Nun of Kent, could hardly be written
before 1533. (1) But though this piece is somewhat in
Skelton's manner, we find it said that he died in 1529,
and it is probably the work of an imitator. Skelton is
certainly not a poet, unless some degree of comic humour,
and a torrent-like volubility of words in doggrel rhyme,
can make one; but this uncommon fertility, in a language
so little copious as ours was at that time, bespeaks a
mind of some original vigour. Few English writers come
nearer in this respect to Rabelais, whom Skelton preceded.
His attempts in serious poetry are utterly contemptible,
but the satirical lines on Cardinal Wolsey were probably
not ineffective. It is impossible to determine whether
they were written before 1520. Though these are better
known than any poem of Skelton's, his dirge on Philip
Sparrow is the most comic and imaginative.

Note
1 See George Ellis, 'Specimens of the Early English
   Poets' (1790), II; the poem there credited to Skelton
   is not by him.

40. ISAAC D'ISRAELI ON SKELTON'S GENIUS

1840

From Isaac D'Israeli's essay Skelton, in his 'Amenities of
Literature', 2nd ed. (1842), pp. 69-82.   D'Israeli (1766-
1848) was a noted scholar and critic.   A few of his
excurses and most of his footnotes have been deleted in
the present selection.

At a period when satire had not yet assumed any legitimate
form, a singular genius appeared in Skelton.   His satire
is peculiar, but it is stamped by vigorous originality.
The fertility of his conceptions in his satirical or his
humorous vein is thrown out in a style created by himself.
The Skeltonical short verse, contracted into five or six,
and even four syllables, is wild and airy.   In the quick-
returning rhymes, the playfulness of the diction, and the
pungency of new words, usually ludicrous, often expressive, and sometimes felicitous, there is a stirring spirit
which will be best felt in an audible reading.   The velo-
city of his verse has a carol of its own.   The chimes ring
in the ear, and the thoughts are flung about like corusca-
tions.   But the magic of the poet is confined to his
spell; at his first step out of it he falls to the earth
never to recover himself.   Skelton is a great creator only
when he writes what baffles imitation, for it is his fate,
when touching more solemn strains, to betray no quality of
a poet - inert in imagination and naked in diction.   Whenever his muse plunges into the long measure of heroic
verse, she is drowned in no Heliconian stream.   Skelton
seems himself aware of his miserable fate, and repeatedly,
with great truth, if not with some modesty, complains of

> Mine homely rudeness and dryness.   ['Upon the death ...
>   of Northumberland,
>   line 13]

But when he returns to his own manner and his own rhyme,
when he riots in the wantonness of his prodigal genius,
irresistible and daring, the poet was not unconscious of
his faculty; and truly he tells, -

> Though my rime be ragged,
> Tattered and jagged,

Rudely rain-beaten,
Rusty, moth-eaten,
If ye take well therewith,
It hath in it some pith.   ['Colin Clout', lines 53-8]

Whether Skelton really adopted the measures of the old
tavern-minstrelsy used by harpers, who gave 'a fit of
mirth for a groat,' or 'carols for Christmas,' or
'lascivious poems for bride-ales,' as Puttenham, the
arch-critic of Elizabeth's reign, supposes; or whether in
Skelton's introduction of alternate Latin lines among his
verses he caught the Macaronic caprice of the Italians, as
Warton suggests; the Skeltonical style remains his own undisputed possession. He is a poet who has left his name
to his own verse - a verse, airy but pungent, so admirably
adapted for the popular ear that it has been frequently
copied and has led some eminent critics into singular
misconceptions. The minstrel tune of the Skeltonical
rhyme is easily caught, but the invention of style and
'the pith' mock these imitators. The facility of doggrel
merely of itself could not have yielded the exuberance of
his humour and the mordacity of his satire.
    This singular writer has suffered the mischance of
being too original for some of his critics; they looked
on the surface, and did not always suspect the depths they
glided over: the legitimate taste of others has revolted
against the mixture of the ludicrous and the invective.
A taste for humour is a rarer faculty than most persons
imagine; where it is not indigenous, not art of man can
plant it. There is no substitute for such a volatile
existence, and where even it exists in a limited degree,
we cannot enlarge its capacity for reception....
    Puttenham was the first critic who prized Skelton
cheaply; the artificial and courtly critic of Elizabeth's
reign could not rightly estimate such a wild and irregular
genius. The critic's fastidious ear listens to nothing
but the jar of rude rhymes, while the courtier's delicacy
shrinks from the nerve of appalling satire 'Such,' says
this critic, 'are the rhymes of Skelton, usurping the
name of a Poet Laureat, being indeed but a rude rayling
rhimer, and all his doings ridiculous - pleasing only the
popular ear.' This affected critic never suspected 'the
pith' of 'the ridiculous;' the grotesque humour covering
the dread invective which shook a Wolsey under his canopy.
Another Elizabethan critic, the obsequious Meres, re-
echoes the dictum. These opinions perhaps prejudiced the
historian of our poetry, who seems to have appreciated
them as the echoes of the poet's contemporaries. Yet we
know how highly his contemporaries prized him, notwith-

standing the host whom he provoked. One poetical brother*
distinguishes him as 'the Inventive Skelton,' and we find
the following full-length portrait of him by another**:-

A poet for his art,
    Whose judgment sure was high,
And had great practise of the pen,
    His works they will not lie'
His termes to taunts did leane,
    His talk was as he wrate,
Full quick of wit, right sharpe of wordes,
    And skilful of the state;

And to the hateful minde,
    That did disdaine his doings still,
A scorner of his kinde.

When Dr. Johnson observed that 'Skelton cannot be said
to have attained great elegance of language,' he tried
Skelton by a test of criticism at which Skelton would have
laughed, and 'jangled and wrangled.' Warton has also censured him for adopting 'the familiar phraseology of the
common people.' The learned editor of Johnson's Dictionary corrects both our critics. 'If Skelton did not
attain great elegance of language, he however possessed
great knowledge of it. From his works may be drawn an
abundance of terms which were then in use among the vulgar
as well as the learned, and which no other writer of his
time so obviously (and often so wittily) illustrated.'(1)
Skelton seems to have been fully aware of the condition of
our vernacular idiom when he wrote, for he has thus described it:

[Quotes 'Philip Sparrow', lines 774-83.]

It was obviously his design to be as great a creator
of words as he was of ideas. Many of his mintage would
have given strength to our idiom. Caxton, as a contemporary, is some authority that Skelton improved the
language.
Let not the reader imagine that Skelton was only 'a
rude rayling rhimer.' Skelton was the tutor of Henry the
Eighth; and one who knew him well describes him, as -

Seldom out of prince's grace.

 * Henry Bradshaw [see No. 5 above].
** Thomas Churchyard [see No. 10 above].

Erasmus distinguished him 'as the light and ornament of British letters;' and one, he addresses the royal pupil, 'who can not only excite your studies, but complete them.' Warton attests his classical attainments: 'Had not his propensity to the ridiculous induced him to follow the whimsies of Walter Mapes, Skelton would have appeared among the first writers of Latin poetry in England.' Skelton chose to be himself; and this is what the generality of his critics have not taken in their view.

Skelton was an ecclesiastic who was evidently among those who had adopted the principles of reformation before the Reformation. With equal levity and scorn he struck at the friars from his pulpit or in his ballad, he ridiculed the Romish ritual, and he took unto himself that wife who was to be called a concubine. To the same feelings we may also ascribe the declamatory invective against Cardinal Wolsey, from whose terrible arm he flew into the sanctuary of Westminster, where he remained protected by Abbot Islip until his death, which took place in 1529, but a few short months before the fall of Wolsey. It is supposed that the king did not wholly dislike the levelling of the greatness of his overgrown minister; and it is remarkable that one of the charges subsequently brought by the council in 1529 against Wolsey - his imperious carriage at the council-board - is precisely one of the accusations of out poet, only divested of rhyme; whence perhaps we may infer that Skelton was an organ of the rising party.

'Why come you not to Court?' - that daring state-picture of an omnipotent minister - and 'The Boke of Colin Clout,' where the poet pretends only to relate what the people talk about the luxurious clergy, and seems to be half the reformer, are the most original satires in the language....

In 'The Crown of Lawrell' Skelton has himself furnished a catalogue of his numerous writings, the greater number of which have not come down to us. Literary productions were at that day printed on loose sheets, or in small pamphlets, which the winds seem to have scattered. We learn there of his graver labours. He composed the 'Speculum Principis' for his royal pupil -

To bear in hand, therein to read,   [lines 1229-30]

and he translated Diodorus Siculus -

Six volumes engrossed, it doth contain.   [line 1502]

To have composed a manual for the education of a prince,

and to have persevered through a laborious version, are
sufficient evidence that the learned Skelton had his
studious days as well as his hours of caustic jocularity.
He appears to have written various pieces for the court
entertainment; but for us exists only an account of the
interlude of the 'Nigraminsir,' in the pages of Warton,
and a single copy of the goodly interlude of 'Magnificence,' in the Garrick collection. If we accept his
abstract personations merely as the names, and not the
qualities of the dramatic personages, 'Magnificence'
approaches to the true vein of comedy.
     Skelton was, however, probably more gratified by his
own Skeltonical style, moulding it with the wantonness of
power on whatever theme, comic or serious. In a poem
remarkable for its elegant playfulness, a very graceful
maiden, whose loveliness the poet has touched with the
most vivid colouring, grieving over the fate of her
sparrow from its feline foe, chants a dirige, a pater-
noster, and an Ave Maria for its soul, and the souls of
all sparrows. In this discursive poem, which glides from
object to object, in the vast abundance of fancy, a
general mourning of all the birds in the air, and many
allusions to the old romances, 'Philip Sparrow,' for
its elegance, may be placed by the side of Lesbia's Bird,
and, for its playfulness, by the Ver Vert of Gresset.
     But Skelton was never more vivid than in his Alewife,
and all

     The mad mummyng
     Of Elynour Rummyng, -   [lines 620-1]

a piece which has been more frequently reprinted than any
of his works. It remains a morsel of poignant relish for
the antiquary, still enamoured of the portrait of this
grisly dame of Leatherhead, where her name and her domi-
cile still exist. Such is the immortality a poet can
bestow. 'The Tunning of Elynoure Rummyng' is a
remarkable production of the GROTESQUE, or the low burlesque; the humour as low as you please, but as strong as
you can imagine....
     The latest edition of Skelton was published in the days
of Pope, which occasioned some strictures in conversation
from the great poet. The laureated poet of Henry the
Eighth is styled 'beastly;' probably Pope alluded to this
minute portrait of 'Elynoure Rummynge' and her crowd of
customers. Beastliness should have been a delicate subject for censure from Pope. But surely Pope had never
read Skelton; for could that great poet have passed by the
playful graces of 'Philip Sparrow' only to remember the

broad gossips of 'Elynoure Rummyng?'

The amazing contrast of these two poems is the most
certain evidence of the extent of the genius of the poet;
he who with copious fondness dwelt on a picture which
rivals the gracefulness of Albano, could with equal com-
pleteness give us the drunken gossipers of an Ostade. It
is true that in the one we are more than delighted, but
in the impartiality of philosophical criticism, we mist
award that none but the most original genius could produce
both. It is this which entitles our bard to be styled the
'Inventive Skelton.'

But are personal satires and libels of the day deserving the attention of posterity? I answer, that for
posterity there are no satires nor libels. We are concerned only with human nature. When the satirical is
placed by the side of the historical character, they
reflect a mutual light. We become more intimately
acquainted with the great Cardinal, by laying together
the satire of the mendacious Skelton with the domestic
eulogy of the gentle Cavendish. The interest which
posterity takes is different from that of contemporaries;
our vision is more complete; they witnessed the beginnings, but we behold the ends. We are no longer deceived
by hyperbolical exaggeration, or inflamed by unsparing
invective; the ideal personage of the satirist is compared
with the real one of the historian, and we touch only
delicate truths. What Wolsey was we know, but how he was
known to his own times, and to the people, we can only
gather from the private satirist; corrected by the
passionless arbiter of another age, the satirist becomes
the useful historian of the man.

The extraordinary combination in the genius of Skelton
was that of two most opposite and potent faculties - the
hyperbolical ludicrous masking the invective. He acts the
character of a buffoon; he talks the language of drollery;
he even mints a coinage of his own, to deepen the colours
of his extravagance - and all this was for the people!
But his hand conceals a poniard; his rapid gestures only
strike the deeper into his victim, and we find that the
Tragedy of the State has been acted while we were only
lookers-on before a stage erected for the popular gaze.

Note

1 The passage occurs in 'A Dictionary of the English
   Language' ... [edited by] H. J. Todd (London, 1818),
   I, pp. cv-cvi.

41. ELIZABETH BARRETT BROWNING IN PRAISE OF SKELTON

1842

From The Book of the Poets, in the 'Athenaeum', 11 June
1842, p. 521, by Elizabeth Barrett Browning (1806-61), the
poetess.

Skelton 'floats double, swan and shadow,' as poet laureate
of the University of Oxford, and 'royal orator' of Henry
VII. He presents a strange specimen of a court-poet, and
if, as Erasmus says, 'Britannicarum literarum lumen' at the
same time, - the light is a pitchy torchlight, wild and
rough. Yet we do not despise Skelton: despise him? it
were easier to hate. The man is very strong; he triumphs,
foams, is rabid, in the sense of strength; he mesmerizes
our souls with the sense of strength - it is easy to
despise a wild beast in a forest, as John Skelton, poet
laureate. He is as like a wild beast, as a poet laureate
can be. In his wonderful dominion over language, he tears
it, as with teeth and paws, ravenously, savagely:
devastating rather than creating, dominant rather for
liberty than for dignity. It is the very sans-culottism
of eloquence; the oratory of a Silenus drunk with anger
only. Mark him as the satyr of poets! fear him as the
Juvenal of satyrs! and watch him with his rugged, rapid,
picturesque savageness, his 'breathless rhymes,' to use
the fit phrase of the satirist Hall, (1) or -

> His rhymes all ragged,
> Tattered, and jagged,   ['Colin Clout', lines 53-4]

to use his own, climbing the high trees of Delphi, and
pelting from thence his victim underneath, whether priest
or cardinal, with rough-rinded apples! And then ask,
could he write otherwise than so? The answer is this
opening to his poem of the 'Bouge of Court,' and the
impression inevitable, of the serious sense of beauty and
harmony to which it gives evidence

[Quotes lines 1-6.]
;

but our last word of Skelton must be, that we do not doubt
his influence for good upon our language. He was a writer
singularly fitted for beating out the knots of the

cordage, and straining the lengths to extension; a rough
worker at rough work. Strong, rough Skelton! We can no
more deride him than my good lord cardinal could.

Note

1 Joseph Hall in 'Virgidemiarium' (1598), VI, i, line 76.

42. AGNES STRICKLAND ON SKELTON: 'THIS RIBALD AND ILL-
LIVING WRETCH'

1842

From 'The Lives of the Queens of England' (1842), IV,
pp. 103-4, by the historian Agnes Strickland (1796-1874).
This extract is from her life of Katharine of Aragon.

Skelton the poet laureate of Henry VIII.'s court,
composed verses of the fall of the Scottish monarch. (1)
    In part of this poem he thus addresses the deceased
king in allusion to the absence of Henry.

[Quotes lines 143-50.]

    He then breaks into the most vulgar taunts on the
unconscious hero, 'who laid cold in his clay' abusing him
as 'Jemmy the Scot' with a degree of virulence which would
have disgusted any mind less coarse than that of his
master. The beautiful lyric, called the 'Flowers of the
Forest,' in which Scotland bewailed her loss of Flodden,
forms a noble contrast to this lampoon. But the laureated
bard of Henry knew well his sovereign's taste, for it is
affirmed that Skelton had been tutor to Henry in some
department of his education. How probable it is that the
corruption imparted by this ribald and ill-living wretch
laid the foundation for his royal pupil's gravest crimes.

Note

1 King James, killed at Flodden in 1513; the poem is

Skelton's 'Against the Scottes' (printed in Dyce, I, pp. 182-8).

43. THE 'QUARTERLY REVIEW' on DYCE'S EDITION OF SKELTON

1844

This review of Dyce's edition of Skelton appeared in the 'Quarterly Review', LXXIII (March 1844), pp. 510-36. The review is unsigned and its authorship cannot be determined. All the original footnotes have been deleted, as well as small portions of the text.

We opened these volumes with the fear of Pope's well-known couplet before our eyes -

Chaucer's worst ribaldry is learned by rote,
And beastly Skelton Heads of Houses quote.

But on such subjects our much-loved Pope was not always just, and sometimes extremely rash. His own purity is not unexceptionable. The worst passages in Chaucer's bold impersonation of the manners of his time are decent in comparison with a certain shameless imitation of his style; and modest under-graduates might be as much per-plexed by some lines of Pope, from the lips of those models of dignified propriety, the Heads of Houses, as by the worst parts of Skelton. Skelton, especially in his gay and frolicsome mood, is no doubt occasionally indeli-cate, but with none of that deep-seated licentiousness which taints some periods of our literature: and the Laureate of those days may fairly be allowed some indul-gence for the manners of his time, when, to judge from the letters of Henry VIII, to Anne Boleyn, there was no very fine sense of propriety even among the highest of the land. Skelton is frequently coarse, as satirists usually are, who, in assailing the coarse vices of a corrupt court and a corrupt clergy, take the privilege of plain-speaking; his invective, especially against his personal enemies, is utterly unscrupulous; he discharges at their unfortunate heads any weapon which may come to hand. When he gets among ale-wives and their crew, his language

is that of the ale-house bench: and his wit is not very
reverent of sacred things, and mingles them up with the
strangest buffoonery. Still as to the gross epithet which
Pope has associated with his name, he deserves it far less
than Pope's dear bosom-friend. There is more 'beastliness' in a page of Swift than in these two volumes of
Skelton. The most offensive allusions are in his libel
against Wolsey. But even these, disgusting as they are,
are of perpetual recurrence in the writer of Queen Anne's
court. There is, in truth, a very whimsical analogy between these two clerical personages. Skelton's resem-
blance to Swift is not, it must be owned, in the best and
strongest of the Dean's points. His prose is insufferable;
a mass of pedantic affectation: and altogether he is as
far below the inimitable humour, the exquisite pleasantry,
the grave, and apparently unconscious, satire of Swift,
as incapable of his unrivalled idiomatic English. Still -
though Skelton throughout is not less immeasurably
inferior to Swift in wit than in uncleanliness - in his
verse there is the same inexhaustible command of doggrel,
the same profusion of quaint and incongruous imagery; the
same utter want of self-respect or of regard for his
station or order; the same rude and at times rabid satire;
the same delight in abusing the vices of the court, within
the precincts of which he was only solicitous to find a
comfortable post; the same propensity to flatter great
men, and, when disappointed of their favour, to turn upon
them with the fiercest bitterness of invective. Finally,
Skelton, like Swift, notwithstanding his contempt in many
respects not merely for professional dignity, but even for
decency, was an acceptable guest in the houses of the
great, and, it should seem, even of the virtuous. It is
an odd further coincidence that Islip, abbot of Westminster, should have been the protector of Skelton against
the wrath of Wolsey, and that Atterbury, the dean of that
church, should have been among Swift's most intimate
friends.

Skelton must fill a very considerable place in every
history of our literature. As a poet, he cannot, in our
judgment, be ranked high; yet, with the exception of the
love-sonnets of Surrey and Wyatt, he is the only English
verse-writer between Chaucer and the days of Elizabeth
who is _alive_. Students of early poetry may find passages
worthy of quotation in the long and weary allegories of
Gower; and we cannot refuse our admiration to those powerful stanzas which the fine and discriminating eye of Gray
discovered in the vast epics of Lydgate; Barclay's 'Ship
of Fools' contains much well worthy of preservation: yet
Skelton, however deficient in the higher qualifications of

a poet, is the link which connects the genuine English
vernacular poetry, that of Chaucer's more humorous vein,
and Piers Ploughman, with the Elizabethan dramatists. The
racy humour, the living description of English manners,
the idiomatic language, which is only obscure from its
perpetual allusions to obsolete customs and forgotten
circumstances, from its frequent cant phrases, its
snatches and burthens of popular songs, the very *vulgar*
tongue of the times, abound far more in Skelton than in
any of the intermediate race of poets. We are thankful,
therefore, to Mr. Dyce for this new and complete edition
of his works; which as the single pieces were extremely
rare, even the earlier bad and imperfect edition by no
means of common occurrence, was wanting to fill up the
cycle of our earlier poets. For though Skelton has been
interred in that vast cemetery of English poets,
Chalmers's Collection, the disagreeable form of that book,
to say nothing of its inaccuracy, was not likely to awaken
the notice of ordinary readers. Mr. Dyce, to whom our
older literature owes a great debt of gratitude, has
brought to his task those best qualifications of an
editor, industry, accuracy, and good sense. Nor does he
injure his author by that excessive demand on the
admiration of the reader, which is so apt to excite disappointment and distaste. We shall hope to preserve the
same equable and impartial tone; for in our opinion
Skelton has not been very happily defended by his
admirers, and admirers he has had of no inconsiderable
name; nor do we think him to deserve that contemptuous
censure which he has met from others. In his serious
vein he is in general very bad, laboured, pedantic, and
dull; and the spirit, we must admit, is often very offensive where - we must not say the poetry - the verse is the
best. But, besides this, these volumes are so full of
curious matter relating to the popular manners, habits,
feelings, and even the historic events of his time, that
even his broadest and most railing rhymes are both amusing
and instructive.

John Skelton's birth is fixed about 1460 (we should
incline to a somewhat later date), the year before the
accession of Edward IV. The place of his birth is not
certain; but there is some reason for believing him a
native of Norwich. Cambridge and Oxford contend for his
education. Antony Wood assumes that he was of Oxford
because he attained the dignity of laureateship there:-

> At Oxforthe the universyte
> Avaunsid I was to that degree;

By hole consent of theyr senate
I was made Poete laureate.   ['Against Garnesche',
                                      lines 81-4]

But elsewhere Skelton himself distinctly owns Cambridge as
his 'Gentle Parent;' and Warton cites two entries from the
university registers at Cambridge, by which Skelton is
admitted to his *ad eundem* laureateship in his own university. This double dignity was enhanced by the royal
permission to wear some decoration, of which Skelton was
obviously very proud; he says, 'a king to me mine habit
gave;' and in another passage he speaks of 'the kynge's
colours, white and grene,' which he had the permission to
wear. This appears to have been a court-dress, probably
not an ordinary one, on which, as is clear from a third
poem, the name of the Muse Calliope was embroidered in
gold letters. Though not, we presume, by this decoration
actually recognised as laureate of the court, it is clear
that the crown recognised the privilege of the universities to create laureates, and ratified by royal favour
this solemn academical judgment. We know not whether
the right to wear the royal livery of white and green,
with its embroidered decoration, belongs to the royal
laureateship; or whether it was commuted for the more
inspiring allowance of the butt of sack; but we recommend
our excellent friend Mr. Wordsworth to look to it.
  Lest, however, those grave and learned bodies, the
universities of the land, should be suspected of having
lavished their honours on a poet, whose later strains
were far from strictly academical in tone or taste, it
must be observed that Skelton, in the earlier part of his
life, seems to have been known only as a laborious and
accomplished scholar; as a translator of Greek and Latin
authors, and of some French writings of a sober and
religious cast; and all of his early poetry which survives
is grave, serious, and solemn. He speaks of a translation
of Cicero's Familiar Epistles, and of the History of
Diodorus Siculus. He is entreated by Caxton, in the
preface to his Boke of Eneydos (a prose romance founded
on Virgil's poem) to revise that work; he is there named
as one of the most finished scholars of the time; as
having translated not merely the works mentioned above,
'but diverse other works oute of Latyn into Englysshe, not
in rude and olde language, but in polished and ornate
termes craftely, as he that hath redde Vyrgyle, Ovyde,
Tullye, and all the other noble poetes and oratours to me
unknowen.' As a man of learning and as a poet Skelton had
more than an English reputation. The university of
Louvain added her testimony to those of Oxford and

Cambridge; and Skelton might boast a triple laureateship, one of which three crowns he received *e transmarinis partibus*. Mr. Dyce has printed a pedantic effusion of the day, in which the author, a certain Robert Whittington, addresses Skelton as the poet of Louvain. After a long enumeration of all the Greek and Latin poets, Whittington recommends Apollo and the Muses to visit England, to look especially to Oxford, immortalised by Skelton, whose verses would be held worthy by posterity.

But Skelton's merits promoted him to still greater honours; honours which might have been expected to lead to high preferment, especially in the church. He was appointed tutor to Prince Henry, afterwards King Henry VIII., designed, as is well known, during the life-time of his brother Arthur, for an ecclesiastic; and, no doubt, intended by his prudent and wealth-loving father to enjoy the dignity and revenues of the see of Canterbury. It is in this character that Skelton is named by no less authority than Erasmus as a distinguished scholar, as an apt interpreter of the sacred poets, and even an instructor in theology - 'donec haberes Skeltonum, unum Britannicarum literarum lumen et decus,'

>   Jam puer Henricus, genitoris nomine laetus,
>   Monstrante *fontes* vate Skeltono *sacres*,
>   Palladias teneris mediatatur ab unguibus artes
>   [See Dyce, I, xxiii]

All, unquestionably, that is extant of Skelton's early poetry answers to the propriety, if not dignity of character, which might be expected in the Laureate of three Universities, and the instructor of a prince destined for the ecclesiastical order. However of no great merit as poetry, his serious as well as his satirical pieces have an historical value; they chiefly relate to events of the day; and though this interest belongs more to the satires, still in periods of history so eventful, yet so imperfectly known, we cannot read without some curiosity contemporary elegies on such persons as Edward IV. and Margaret, Countess of Richmond. In his earliest poem, on the death of Edward IV, (A.D. 1483, our poet, if born in 1460, was twenty-three years old), Skelton indulges in the habit, in which in his comic pieces he afterwards ran riot, of interspersing Latin among his English verses. No doubt there was some disposition to display his scholarship; but, in fact, as we find in all quarters, even in the popular songs, it was a general custom. It might originate from, or be justified by, the usage of the time, during which, in vernacular religious writings or sermons,

the texts were usually in Latin, and the ecclesiastical
law, where it condescended to English, quoted its authorities in the original. To us there is something striking
in the solemn Latin burthen with which each stanza of his
Elegy on Edward IV. closes; and altogether there is, we
think, not only more truth and simplicity but more of the
deeper feeling of poetry in the language which he makes
Edward utter, than is to be found in the later serious
verses of Skelton.

[Quotes lines 61-72.]

The second poem has likewise some curious historical
matter. It is an Elegy on the Death of Northumberland,
Lord Lieutenant of Yorkshire, who was murdered in an in-
surrection of the Commons, while engaged in levying a
subsidy for Henry VII. Bishop Percy, who reprinted this
poem, from hereditary interest, observes that the reader
'will see a striking picture of the state and magnificence
kept up by our ancient nobility during the feudal times.'
The great Earl is described as having among his household
retainers knights, squires, and even barons (see v. 32,
183, &c.); but they all seem to have been on the Commons'
side, perhaps being equally impatient of the taxation
with the rest of the people. Skelton attributes the death
of Northumberland to their treachery.

[Quotes lines 73-7, 92-8.]

So far the Laureate seems to have maintained the
sedate tone and bearing which might become his station
and his accomplishments as a scholar: a sudden change now
comes over his character, his genius, and, it should seem,
his fortune. He appears to discover where his real
strength lies (for if Skelton had continued a grave and
serious poet, we believe Mr. Dyce would scarcely have
thought him worth his labour); he breaks out at once in
his light, frolicsome, or bitterly satirical vein; he does
not entirely abandon his more stately form of verse and
his intricate stanza (he reserves that for high and solemn
occasions); but runs riot in an easy inimitable doggrel,
as it should seem entirely his own, and in which he
appears inexhaustible. His jingling rhymes, as far as we
know the pronunciation of the day, and admitting an accent
on final syllables with us unaccentuated, are in general
remarkably correct, and always ready at his command;
images the most fantastic and incongruous crowd upon him
so fast that he can scarcely set them in their places;
his classical lore furnishes him with allusions, mingled

up, in the most grotesque manner, with the *slang* of the
day. Southey charitably suggested that Skelton's
'buffooneries, like those of Rabelais, were thrown out
as a tub to the whale; for unless Skelton had written thus
for the coarsest palates, he could not have poured forth
his bitter and undaunted satire in such perilous time.'
We very much doubt whether the free indulgence of broad
and grotesque humour was so secondary, even in Rabelais,
to more serious objects; in Skelton we cannot but think
that it was the genuine love of fun, the reckless enjoyment of rude, farcical, and bitter merriment, which was
the inspiration of his careless rhymes. It is true that
in Wolsey he flew at high game: but - long before his
poetic onslaught on the Cardinal, and even before his more
mature and deliberate satire on the clergy - while he
could scarcely need concealment for deeper or more dangerous opinions, he had already given loose to this saturna-
lian lawlessness of language and metre, and to all his
joyous scurrility. Though less rancorous, perhaps, his
verses against Garnesche and against the Scots are not
less full of buffoonery than those against the Bishops or
the Cardinal. The truth is, that Skelton's serious language is an acquired, a stiff, and artificial dialect; the
vulgar is his mother tongue; he is not at ease till free
from all restraint; he is rarely happy except when he is
at least light and jovial, if not pouring forth all his
unchecked volubility of abuse.

From all that is extant, it would appear that this
change came over Skelton when we might least expect it -
about the time when he entered into the Church. This took
place in 1498; and we find him very soon rector of Diss,
in Norfolk. He seems never to have attained any higher
preferment. In truth, we cannot much wonder at this. It
must have been, we presume, during his residence in his
Norfolk parsonage, that he wrote the 'Boke of Phylipp
Sparrowe.' This is known to have appeared before 1508, at
which time it is scornfully mentioned by a rival poet.
Coleridge has called 'Phylipp Sparrowe' an exquisite and
original poem; and certainly, for its ease and playfulness, its quaintness, and, in a certain sense, its delicacy, its mirthful and dancing measure, the lightness
with which we read it off till we are out of breath, and
the amusing variety of strangely-assorted imagery, it is,
for its time, a most extraordinary work. Prior is hardly
lighter; and, in the fertility of his gaiety, Skelton may
almost make up for his want of that grace and elegance,
that happy harmony of thought and language which belongs
to a more refined period of letters.

But this poem is not less curious as illustrative of

clerical and conventual manners. The damsel, of whom the
Sparrowe celebrated by our clerical Catullus was the
delight, was, we will presume with Mr. Dyce, only a lay
boarder, not a professed votary or noviciate, among the
black nuns at Carowe, a small convent near Norwich. We
presume that the priestly character of our poet made the
courtier and the laureate to be thought a *safe* guest in
this holy community. We only hope that he was not the
father confessor of the fair Joanna Scroope, on whose
personal charms, as well as on the doleful loss of her
favourite, he indulges in rather ardent raptures; and as
Skelton constantly asserts the propriety of his own conduct, and the purity as well as the loveliness of his
Norfolk Lesbia, we are bound to believe him.

The poets, and indeed the priests and monks of those
days, allowed themselves liberties, which to modern eyes
seem strangely irreverent, with the services of the Church.
The 'Dirige,' or dirge, over the 'Sparrowe' begins, and is
constantly interlarded, with Latin lines and musical notes
from the chaunts for the dead: it is, in short, a parody
on the whole service.

[Quotes lines 1-12.]

And so the bereaved mistress goes on, for 1260 lines, to
express her sorrow.

[Quotes lines 23-7.]

It is difficult, by a few extracts, to give a notion of
a poem, the peculiar character of which is the wild profusion of all sorts of thoughts and images, more like the
ribands out of a conjuror's mouth at a fair than anything
else. But it is curious how like the idiomatic English of
Skelton's day was to that of our own. We give the following lines in modern spelling, merely noting the obsolete
words:

It was so pretty a fool,
It would sit on a stool,
And learned after my school.

It had a velvet cap,
And would sit on my lap;
Sometimes would he gasp
When he saw a wasp.
A fly or a gnat,
He would fly at that;
And prettily he would pant

When he saw an ant.
And seek after small worms,
And sometimes white-bread crumbs;
And many times and oft,
Between my breasts soft,
It would lie and rest:
It was so propre and prest.
Lord, how he would pry
After the butterfly!
Lord, how he would hop
After the grasshop!
And when I said Phip, Phip,
Then he would leap and skip,   ·
And take me by the lip. (1)

A little further on, our poet becomes much too *Prior-
ish*, not without a touch of Swift. The privileged bird
was even admitted into the young lady's chamber, and
there, among his other amusements -

[Quotes lines 179-82.]

We are to suppose, we presume, that in these were the
usual inhabitants of a lady's couch. We must compensate
for this impropriety by the following pretty lines, too
characteristic to be passed over.

[Quotes 'Philip Sparrow', lines 210-41.]

We are then off to Noah's ark - never was such a sparrow since those days - and by and bye 200 lines of all
the birds in the air coming to the funeral, with their
various offices.

[Quotes lines 386-402, 550-5, 569-70.]

If Chaucer be the father of English poetry, Skelton is
the father of English doggrel; and while we study the
wisdom of our ancestors, it is not amiss - at least, not
unamusing - to know something of their nonsense. If our
readers are not content with this, they will find many
hundred more lines, to say nothing of four hundred
besides in commendation of the lovely mistress of Philip
Sparrow. The poem ends with these Latin lines.

[Quotes lines 1261-7.]

All this Skelton protests (and it seems that Phylipp
Sparrowe had excited envy, and given some offence) was

innocent gaiety, a relaxation, as he says above, from his
graver toils. But, after all, we fear that the rector of
Diss was altogether out of his element as a country
parson. 'Antony Wood,' (2) says Mr. Dyce, 'affirms that
at Diss and in the diocese Skelton was esteemed more fit
for the stage than the pew or pulpit.' It is at least
certain that anecdotes of the irregularity of his life, of
his buffoonery as a preacher, &c. &c. were current long
after his decease, and gave rise to that amusement of the
vulgar and entitled 'The Merie Tales of Skelton.' As he
spared nobody, he got into a quarrel with the neighbouring
Dominican friars, whom he had made the objects of some
satire. At their instigation he was charged before his
diocesan with living with a concubine, but whom he had
secretly married. The fact seems to have been notorious:
he had several children by this woman, and is said to have
reproached himself on his death-bed for his cowardice in
not openly avowing his marriage. The Bishop of Norwich
was, in the hard words of Mr. Dyce, 'the bloody-minded
and impure' Richard Nyke, or Nix. The bishop may have
been, according to the strong and, we fear, just language
of the Protestant writers, a cruel and not irreproachable
man; but, in this case, he could not refuse to take cognizance of such a charge. What excuse Skelton may have
found before a higher tribunal, we presume not to say, if,
as we will charitably suppose, he was really married; but
either way he was guilty of an offence against the discipline of his Church, and suspension from his clerical
functions, which appears to have been his punishment, was
certainly no harsh sentence. Yet Bishop Nyke cannot have
kept a very watchful eye over his diocese, if such proceedings as Skelton remonstrates against in his extraordinary poem, 'Ware the Hawke,' went on without
ecclesiastical censure. It appears that some neighbouring
clergyman was accustomed to amuse himself with flying his
hawks in Skelton's church. Why Skelton did not summarily
eject, instead of lampooning, the irreverent intruder does
not appear. If we remember right, it is in a note to Mr.
Hallam's 'Middle Ages' that we find a papal exemption to
the clergy of Berks from maintaining the archdeacon's
hawks when he was on his visitation. But we cannot discover from the poem what superior authority this ungentle
falconer had over the parson of Diss, unless it might be
during Skelton's suspension. We cannot quote all the
circumstances of this disgusting profanation - two
stanzas will be quite enough, and these we are obliged
to mutilate: Skelton lays it on with more than his usual
profusion of Latin, we presume because he was satirizing
a clerical adversary.

[Quotes 'Ware the Hawke', lines 278-98.]

Among the graver labours to which Skelton alludes during
his residence, we are unable to reckon with certainty any
of the more serious or even devotional writings which
appear in his works, or are recounted in the long and
rather ostentatious list of his compositions in the 'Garlande of Laurel.' How and at what period he became
acquainted with Elynour Rummin, the ale-wife of Leatherhead, in Surrey, there is hardly a conjecture. This is
the coarsest, but not the least clever, of Skelton's
poems. It is a low picture of the lowest life - Dutch in
its grotesque minuteness: yet, even in the description of
the fat hostess herself, and one or two other passages, we
know not that we can justly make any stronger animadversion
than that they are very Swiftish. But it will further show
how little (of course excepting cant words) the genuine
vulgar tongue and, we may add perhaps, vulgar life is
altered since the time of Henry VIII. Take the general
concourse of her female customers to Elynour Rummin, un-
controlled by any temperance societies.

[Quotes 'Elynour Rumming', lines 244-308.]

During all this period Skelton's relations to the court
are, unfortunately, rather obscure. He is said by Churchyard to have been 'seldom out of princes' grace.' Mr.
Dyce has found a suspicious entry, in which one John
Skelton was committed to prison by the Court of Requests;
but whether this was our poet (who by that time was certainly in orders), or even of what offence the said John
Skelton was guilty, there is nothing to show. But there
is one of his poems which appears to us to bear internal
evidence of having been written at this period. 'The
Bowge of Court' - literally, the Bouche, the allowance of
meat and drink for the retainers - which Warton has rendered the 'Rewards of a Court.' The scene of this poem is
laid in Harwich Harbour, where Skelton, in his allegoric
character, goes on board the stately vessel, bound for the
court. Now we apprehend that in those days the easiest,
and perhaps the most expeditious, way for the parson of
Diss to find his way to London would have been to run down
to Harwich, and there embark. During one of these jour-
neys, after the poetic fashion of the day, he may have
idealised his ship, and impersonated the false friends and
open enemies who may already have crossed his path, and
thwarted his hopes of advancement; he may have essayed for
once to make his satire take a higher and more serious
form. The poet is slumbering at mine host's house called

Power's Key, at Harwich Harbour, when he sees his vision.

[Quotes 'Bouge of Court', lines 36-42.]

The owner of this bark is the Lady Saunce-pere (sans peer): the royal chaffre (merchant), a lady likewise, is Favour; with Daunger, her chief-gentlewoman. Skelton (anticipating M. de Custine) embarks under the modest impersonation of Drede, or Timidity; and is successively accosted by Favel (cajolery), Suspecte (suspicion), Harry Hafter (we cannot interpret this better than by Roguery), Disdayne, Ryotte, Dyssimular, and Subtylte. 'Mr. Gifford describes this poem as a very severe satire, full of strong painting, and excellent poetry. The courtiers of Harry must have winced at it.' Even if Skelton intended those abstract personages to represent his old friends or foes of the court, we cannot think that the courtiers of that day would be quite so sensitive. If Skelton had con-tented himself with representing the vices of the clergy in these cold impersonations, or dressing up Wolsey as an allegory of pride, he would not have needed to seek asylum in Westminster Abbey. There is, however, much vigour, and, we should suppose, originality in some of his concep-tions. The reader may probably remember the striking pic-ture of *Riot* quoted by Warton: it is, perhaps, the best of the gallery.
    This Interlude and the 'Morality of Magnificence' con-tain no doubt on the whole the best of Skelton's serious poetry; but the best of that only proves more plainly that his strength lies in a lower region: his Pegasus is not equal to the stately amble, or even processional march; it is a wild, rugged colt, full of fire and of vigor, and not a little vicious, as the phrase is; kicking out on all sides, and delighting in splashing up the dirt on every one he passes. His whole value is, as a vulgar vernacular poet, addressing the people in the language of the people.
    Notwithstanding his own poetic warning, Skelton was still a hanger-on upon this treacherous and dissembling court; but it is difficult to make out his position or the estimation in which he was held. Mr. Dyce has first pub-lished certain poems against Garnesche, full of the most rabid abuse; each of which, Skelton declares, was written by the 'commandment of the king.' Garnesche, however, by the appointments which he held on several occasions of important trust as well as of state ceremony, seems to have stood high in royal favour - he was gentleman usher to Henry VIII., and received the honour of knighthood. It may have been one of Bluff King Hal's coarse amusements to encourage this poetical fray in which Garnesche, it should

seem, was the challenger. Yet, if Skelton had not in a
great degree lost his self-respect, even Harry would hardly
have shown such little respect to his old tutor (Skelton
takes care to boast in these verses of the intimate relation in which he had stood to majesty) as graciously to
command him to undertake this war of gross personal abuse.
It was but a sorry occupation for a laureate, though one
in which Skelton evidently delighted, to keep the field
against all comers, and combat *a l'outrance* in good set
Billingsgate. Such literary duels were not uncommon even
in later and better days of our literature; but we do not
know that they were waged, as it were, in the presence
and expressly for the amusement of the sovereign. Some
kings, it must be acknowledged, have whimsical notions of
fun; but when one Martin Luther ventured to Skeltonise
even against the sacred person and controversial erudition
of the royal polemic, probably he did not think it quite
so diverting.

But there was another piece of Skelton's coarsest
abuse, which we trust Henry was not so ungenerous as to
approve - though perhaps Skelton might think it no
inappropriate nor unacceptable flattery if he should turn
those weapons of foul words, which he had wielded so
successfully against his own adversaries, and in which
royalty had condescended to find amusement, upon the
enemies of the king. The laureate, after the battle of
Flodden, thought it incumbent upon him to take the field
against the Scots. And this is the chivalrous and
Christian tone in which he speaks of the gallant king who
had died fighting valiantly.

[Quotes 'Against the Scottes', lines 91-3, 146-52, 164-7.]

...During all this time, Skelton, whatever his position
at court, was an acceptable guest at the castle-palaces of
the great nobles, and even in some of the wealthy religious
foundations. His 'Garland of Laurel' was written at
Sheriff Hutton Castle; and some of the most gentle and
high-born ladies of the land did not disdain his complimentary verses. He mentions in that poem the wealthy
college of the Bonhommes of Ashridge, near Berkhampstead,
as a place where he was a frequent visitor.
The poems against the Scots belong more properly to
that class of Skelton's writings in which lies his main
strength, and for which alone he has much claim on the
notice of posterity, his political satire. His 'Colin
Cloute,' and 'Why come ye not to Court?' - the former a
general satire against the clergy, the latter a most
vehement libel on the all-powerful Wolsey - are the

cleverest and most remarkable specimens of this peculiar
vein. Skelton, indeed, had no great right to throw stones
at the clergy, or to pelt them as he does with such sharp
and dangerous missiles: and the indignation which, as all
satirists pretend, inspired our laureate's verse, even
against Wolsey, was not a high, disinterested, and
intrepid aversion to his pride, his avarice, or his licentiousness. Unfortunately, there is a dedication to the
full-blown Wolsey, crammed with the most fulsome Latin
superlatives, expressing the poet's humblest deference for
'the super-illustrious legate - the most magnificent and
worthy prince of priests - the most equitable distributor
of justice' - and, moreover, the 'most excellent patron'
of his work. Still more unfortunately, another of his
poems, the 'Garland of Laurel,' closes with an envoy to
the king and to the most *honorificate* cardinal - from one
line of which we are forced to conclude that the source
of Skelton's ultimate ire was neither less nor more than
a disappointment touching a fat prebend.

[Quotes 'Garland of Laurel', lines 1589-91.]

The parson of Diss, in short, seems to have much resembled
Byron's court Poet,

> Who being unpensioned wrote a satire,
> And boasted that he could not flatter.

Nor was Skelton (with all respect for Mr. D'Israeli
be it said) in any proper sense a Reformer: his opinions
upon doctrine, as far as they appear, were those of his
Church. The poem set forth with this adulatory dedication
to Wolsey is a furious invective against the new teachers,
who were springing up in the University of Cambdrige; and
the 'horryble heresy of these young heretykes, that stynke
unbrent,' is the denial of worship to the Virgin Mary.

[Quotes from 'A Replycacion...', lines 73-91.]

This was the difference between Skelton and Roy, (3)
the other celebrated satirist of Wolsey: Roy was a
Reformer, an assistant, not altogether it should seem
an unexceptionable assistant, of Tyndale in his translation
of the Bible; and it was the burning of these Bibles which
excited Roy's violent indignation against the Cardinal.
Yet for this very reason Skelton's picture of the
clergy, and of the great Cardinal, is the more curious,
and, in some respects, more trustworthy, for, at least, it
is not darkened by theological hatred; this Skelton

reserved most piously for heretics. Much allowance must
in justice be made for the personal character and feelings
of Skelton; for the natural scurrility of the man, his
envy in the one case, his disappointment in the other; but
the libels of one age, fairly considered, become valuable
historical evidence to posterity - often, as to manners
and the opinions of the time, the best that can be
attained. Skelton, in truth, was but the last echo of
that voice, which had long been arraigning to the popular
ear the inordinate wealth, the pride, the carelessness,
the licence, the secular habits and feelings, and some of
the more glaring superstitions of the clergy. Since the
time of Wickliffe and the Lollards, no doubt this was
mingled with much secret repugnance to some, at least, of
the doctrines of the Church. But the dogmatic Reformers
would have made their way much more slowly without these
allies, who by no means shared their religious opinions,
but confined themselves to lampooning the vices both of
the secular and regular clergy. This politico-religious
satire had long been at work, first in Latin, and afterwards in the rude vernacular tongues of Europe. Only
occasionally, as we have said, and partially, but by no
means generally connected with the Wickliffite or Hussite
doctrines, it was a kind of spontaneous remonstrance
against frauds and follies too palpable to the common
sense of mankind; against the glaring disagreement of the
lives of multitudes among both the monks and clergy, not
only with the gospel, and the examples of worth and
purity which had shone even on the worst ages of the
Church, but even with the positive regulations of their
own Canon-law. These songs were to the popular mind,
what Erasmus was to the more learned world; and in the
spirit at least, though neither in the tone nor taste of
that scholar's attacks upon the monastic system, and the
manners of the clergy, Skelton might shelter himself
under his 'great and much injured name,' with whose praise
he had been honoured at the commencement of his literary
career....
   Colyn Cloute is a kind of rustic impersonation of
popular discontent. But Skelton himself lurks within the
disguise.

[Quotes lines 53-8.]

   And so he goes rattling on with his quick-recurring
rhymes, all in the plain vernacular idiom; here and there
only a word betraying, by its false rhyme when thrown into
modern spelling, that the pronunciation was somewhat
different from our one.

[Quotes lines 115-41, 147-51.]

One of the most remarkable things to be traced throughout these popular satirical songs, is the veneration for
the memory of Thomas-a-Becket. The invasion on the royal
power, the spiritual usurpation of this bold ecclesiastic
seem entirely forgotten; he is the severe disciplinarian
of the clergy, the martyr and the saint of popular reverence. Even in Skelton this traditionary feeling has not
died away. Speaking of some of the gentler bishops, he
says

[Quotes lines 168-74.]

This sounds like a quotation from some older song - it
may be a hymn. Out poet then falls on the bishops' want
of care in admitting unlearned persons to holy orders. He
might have remembered that learning was no sure guarantee
for priestly propriety, or even decency; but it is a
curious picture.

[Quotes lines 228-9, 236-9, 272-8, 287-90, 257-61.]

Here Skelton again comes under his own lash. It would
require a firm and delicate hand to trace out the evidence
we have of the extent to which actual marriage prevailed
among the English clergy even after the time of Innocent
III....
The pomp, the state, and the dress of the bishops next
come under the sarcastic notice of Colyn Cloute.

[Quotes lines 303-14.]

The extortions and oppressions of the poor, by 'sum-
mons and citations, and excommunications,' are not forgotten; nor do the regular clergy fare much better in his
hands. They are charged with leaving their cloisters,
and wandering about the world. The abbesses and prior-
esses are said to be as little inclined to the total
seclusion required by their order; and alas! when abroad
they are rather too much disposed 'to cast up their black
veils.' The religious houses are accused of great neglect
in their services, and with the wanton dilapidation of
their buildings.

[Quotes lines 408-17, 419-35.]

And these lines can scarcely refer to the monasteries
which were forcibly suppressed by Wolsey before the

Reformation. It is a distinct accusation of culpable
negligence.

There is a curious passage on the pride with which the
clergy, many of them of the lowest birth, treated the
nobility of the land. No doubt the ruin of the old feudal
baronage of England during the civil wars, and the depres-
sion of the few who held their estates comparatively
undiminished under the iron policy of Henry VII., showed
the wealth of the higher Churchmen in more disproportionate and invidious grandeur. The Church property, also,
no doubt, suffered in these devastating wars, but it must
have been more secure against confiscation. If, in the
confusion of the times, it was exposed to forcible or
fraudulent alienation; it would, on the other hand, from
its greater security, the facility of acquisition where so
much property was, as it were, cast loose, and from the
greater solicitude of men involved in the crimes and
miseries of civil war to purchase peace with heaven by
lavish donations or bequests to the Church, notwithstanding
the statute of Mortmain, accumulate very largely. If we
are to believe Skelton, the temporal peers were not disposed to contest this contemptuous superiority asserted by
the ecclesiastic.

[Quotes lines 610-28.]

After the clergy and nobility we have the four orders of
fryers - and the coarse sequel fits well with this flatter-
ing prelude. We must rather, however, make room for the
style and furniture of the episcopal palaces. We
recommend this passage to Mr. Pugin, for the next edition
of his 'Contrasts between the Episcopal Residences of the
Olden Time with those of the Present Day.' Drawing-
rooms with pianofortes, and even work-tables, perhaps
even nurseries themselves, may find some excuse.

[Quotes lines 936-81.]

Even in 'Colin Cloute,' Skelton ventured to assail,
though rather more covertly, the despotic Wolsey. No one,
however high his rank, could obtain a hearing of the king
without the leave, or without the presence, of the Presi-
dent.

[Quotes lines 1047-50.]

Throughout, however, Skelton protests his attachment to
the good clergy and to Holy Church; his design was the
amendment of the prevailing vices and irregularities.

[Quotes lines 1097-107, 1119-20, 1123-30.]

We cannot leave 'Colyn Cloute,' without the following
amusing description of the summary proceedings to which he
exposed himself by his rash rhymes, which were only circulated in manuscript he says himself that he could not get
them printed.

[Quotes lines 1163-72, 1175-6, 1184-91.]

These were, no doubt, the most popular churches in the
City; St. Mary was in Bishopsgate ward; the Austin friars
in Broad Street ward; St. Thomas of Acre near the great
conduit in Cheape.

But in audacity, in bitterness, in coarseness, and in
scurrility, the 'Colyn Cloute' is far surpassed by the
'Why come ye not to Court?' - while in rude cleverness,
in volubility of abuse, in the homely but vigorous abundance of images and allusions, the latter poem is in no
degree inferior. The whole is a fierce invective against
Wolsey; and though the Prime Ministers of England have
usually come in for their full share of virulent personal
invective, both in prose and verse, yet we question
whether in his utmost height of unpopularity any minister
was ever more recklessly assailed, or in language more
galling, than by this satire against the all-powerful
Cardinal. To have written, and, though no doubt unpub-
lished, to have allowed such a poem to transpire even
among friends, shows such extraordinary courage as almost
to require a higher motive in our laureate than the mere
disappointment about his coveted prebend. It is still
more extraordinary that Wolsey, armed with such enormous
ecclesiastical power, should have allowed a sanctuary to
protect so pestilent a libeller; or that an abbot of
Westminster, of so high a character as Islip, should
either, in the assertion of the privileges of his church,
or, as is intimated, from some secret favour towards
Skelton, have dared or desired to protect him from pro-
secution. It might seem as if Wolsey, if he had really
seen the poem, knew that it was but the expression of a
dangerous but wide-spread popular sentiment; the Cardinal
might be struck with some of its terrible truths - his
supercilious treatment of the nobility, his usurpation of
the royal power, his presumption upon the blind, but perhaps precarious, favour of the King; and he might think it
prudent, as he had failed in arresting and crushing him by
a sudden act of authority, not to attribute too much
importance to the insolent poet, or to give unnecessary
publicity to that which was yet lurking in secret.

We may add here that Skelton died in sanctuary, at
Westminster, and was buried in the adjoining church of
St. Margaret.

As few readers, perhaps, will encounter 1250 lines of
antiquated libel against a minister who lived some centuries ago, they may yet be obliged to us for selecting
some passages, which may show how such things were written
in the time of Henry VIII. Skelton first takes a sort of
view of the Cardinal's foreign politics as regards Spain,
France, and Scotland; he is charged with receiving bribes
from France, with whom England, in alliance with the
Emperor, was at war. Our laureate vaunts the prowess of
the 'good Erle of Surrey,' who had abated the courage of
the French, and made them take to their fortified cities,
like 'foxes in their dens, and urchins (hedgehogs) in a
stone wall,' and even a more unseemly illustration.

[Quotes 'Why Come Ye Nat to Court?', lines 166-99.]

A great deal more follows (we shall give presently a
graphic passage) on his insolent overbearing of the nobility, and likewise of the judges in the courts of law.
There is a sort of slyness in the few lines about Hampton
COurt.

[Quotes lines 398-412.]

He soon, however, gets more personal; there is not a
vice, bad passion, or iniquity, which he does not charge
upon the Cardinal - ambition, avarice, pride, sloth,
incontinence (and on this point we must acknowledge that
here and there he deserves Pope's epithet). Of course he
does not forget his humble origin.

[Quotes lines 488-91.]

He is contemptuous on the Cardinal's want of learning.
A thought may have crossed the mind of Skelton that the
gentleman's son of Norwich, whose scholarship had been
rewarded by three universities and admired by Erasmus,
might have aspired to as high distinction as the butcher's
boy of Ipswich. Wolsey, he says, was neither Doctor of
Divinity nor of Law, but a poor Master of Arts. He was
ignorant of everything - letters, policy, astronomy.

[Quotes lines 517-26.]

If Wolsey was indeed less learned than became his station, he deserved the greater honour for his magnificent

encouragement of learning. Whatever other heads of houses
may do, the dean of Christ Church should abstain from
quoting Skelton, for better reasons than that assigned by
Pope.

[Quotes lines 582-99, 612-35.]

    There is great boldness yet some tact in the verses on
the influence of the Cardinal over the king; while he
exposes the weakness, he respects the royal dignity.

[Quotes lines 654-9, 666-79.]

He attributes this influence to sorcery, and tells the
famous old story of the bewitchment of Charlemagne, on
which Southey wrote a ballad. He adds very significantly
the case of Cardinal Balue (see 'Quentin Durward'), (4)
who, though advanced to the dignity of a cardinal by the
influence of Louis XI., according to our poet

[Quotes lines 734-40.]

Skelton is wrong in his history, as the French cardinal
only suffered a long imprisonment; but he points his moral
in these words.

[Quotes lines 743-6.]

Afterwards, however, he is not quite so merciful in his
wishes for the fate of his enemy. After a long passage on
the impoverishment of the people by his rapacious extortions

[Quotes lines 966-84, 986-93.]

    If our readers' historic ideal of Wolsey be disturbed
by these rude rhymes, which we have thus copiously
extracted both for their intrinsic singularity, and for
the extraordinary fact that such things were ventured in
such days, we would send them to refresh their memory with
the Wolsey of Shakespeare; let them take the honest
chronicle of Griffith, which extorts the admission of its
justice even from the injured Catherine, and they will
have, we are persuaded, not merely the noblest poetic
impersonation, but the most fair and impartial historic
estimate of this great man.
    As to Skelton's more general satire on the church and
clergy, we have heard so much lately of the iniquities of
the Reformation, the crimes and weaknesses of those who

were concerned in it, that it may not be unseasonable to
show something of the other side of the picture. Let us
know what it was which was reformed by the Reformation.
It must, of course, be remembered that Skelton's is a
satire, the satire of a rude, bitter, and disappointed man;
still his verse was the popular expression of a strong
popular feeling, much darkened and exaggerated, no doubt,
as the popular feeling, especially of an ignorant people,
usually is - but with much truth - with more truth, we
fear, than that poetic view of the past with which young
minds are of late years so enamoured. This imaginative
retrospect hardly deigns to see anything but stately
cathedrals rising, abbeys and cloisters in their holy
seclusion; will hear only the fine anthems and choral
services; and will take cognizance of only such saintly
and apostolic men, as have never been wanting to the
Christian Church in its most unenlightened and unchristian
days. Nothing can be more delightful than thus to trace
out and to hold up for the admiration which is their due
these hidden treasures of divine grace, of holiness,
humanity, and love; far more so than to rake up obscure
and forgotten libels; but even the latter is a service to
which the severe lover of truth (of truth at every cost
and at every sacrifice, even of personal inclination and
poetic enjoyment) must occasionally submit; for it is only
by the due imbalance, the impartial comparison of these
conflicting materials - by the calm and dispassionate
hearing of every testimony that judicial history can sum
up its solemn sentence; so only can we obtain, we will not
merely say the philosophy, but even the religion, of
history.

Notes

1 'Philip Sparrow', lines 122-7, 134-40.
2 Anthony à Wood, 'Athenae Oxonienses' (1691-2), column
   20.
3 William Roy (fl. 1527), co-author of the satiric poem
   'Rede Me and Be Not Wroth', first published in 1526.
4 A novel by Sir Walter Scott.

44. HIPPOLYTE TAINE ON SKELTON THE 'CLOWN'

1863

From Hippolyte Taine's 'Histoire de la littérature
anglaise' (1863), first translated into English in 1871
as 'The History of English Literature'. This extract is
from this translation, p. 139.
    Taine (1828-93) was a French philosopher, critic and
historian. One footnote has been deleted from this
selection.

At the end of all this mouldy talk, and amid the disgust
which they have conceived for each other, a clown, a
tavern Triboulet, (1) composer of little jeering and
macaronic verses, Skelton makes his appearance, a virulent pamphleteer, who, jumbling together French, English,
Latin phrases, with slang, and fashionable words, invented
words, intermingled with short rhymes, fabricates a sort
of literary mud, with which he bespatters Wolsey and the
bishops. Style, metre, rhyme, language, art of every kind,
is at an end; beneath the vain parade of official style
there is only a heap of rubbish. Yet, as he says

[Quotes 'Colin Clout', lines 53-8.]

It is full of political animus, sensual liveliness,
English and popular instincts; it lives. It is a coarse
life, still elementary, swarming with ignoble vermin, like
that which appears in a great decomposing body. It is life,
nevertheless, with its two great features which it is
destined to display: the hatred of the ecclesiastical hierarchy, which is the Reformation; the return to the senses
and to natural life, which is the Renaissance.

Note

1 The court fool in Victor Hugo's drama of 'Le Roi
   s'amuse'.

45. 'DUBLIN UNIVERSITY MAGAZINE' ON SKELTON

1866

This unsigned article titled A Satirical Laureate of
the Sixteenth Century appeared in the 'Dublin University Magazine', LXVIII (1866), pp. 601-18. It has not
proved possible to determine its authorship. The
original footnotes have been deleted.

Swift sat in Rabelais' easy chair; but there is another
English satirist whose pantagruelistic tendencies were
still more evident, who was a contemporary of the French
humorist, and whose virulent attacks against the corruptions of the Church do not yield in coarseness and energy
to Luther's diatribes. John Skelton, Laureate, was the
link between Chaucer and Surrey, Wolsey and Cranmer - the
representative of the reformatory spirit of the first part
of the sixteenth century. He wrote powerful invectives
against the Church while Luther was still macerating himself in a convent cell; and he was an important agent in
bringing about the English Reformation.
In Germany a monk stood against principalities and
powers; but in England the evolution of the great change
was still more curious and interesting. As Piers Ploughman had prophesied, the Crown alone could conquer the
Church. And now was seen a young prince whose chief
characteristic was an inexorable will; and it was by
coming into collision with that will that the great
hierarchy, which had cursed royal kings, was to fall, or
to be absorbed by the crown. The King himself, had not in
the early part of his reign, discerned the approach of
this consumation, which More had foreseen; but he had
often been offended by the pride and power of Churchmen,
and was, accordingly, not inimical to attacks on the
clergy. Without perceiving the results that would
accrue from popularising a contempt of the hierarchy, he
fostered Skelton's vigorous satire. Monarch and poet were
tacitly allied together against Wolsey; and by this action
against the common enemy, unconscious and intermittent
though it often was, the one built up the Church of England, the other imprinted to England satire the political
character which it retained in Butler, Dryden, Swift.
Before Skelton the clergy had not been attacked in
England under such stirring circumstances, or in so

merciless a fashion. Like other sublunary things, satire
has its periods of evolution. It exists wherever there is
a dead body, but, like the eagles, it flies down upon it
in circles, the earliest of which are wide and circuitous;
the fell swoop, the destroying attack, do not occur suddenly. It was thus with English satire. Directed chiefly
against the Church, its attacks were at first timid and
indirect. Piers Ploughman veiled his invectives under the
mask of allegory. Chaucer is caustic, but courtly and
moderate; he seems rather to reflect calmly the general
opinion of his times than to attempt raising a tempest of
his own. Lyndsay is too general, and his satire is but a
feeble echo of Wycklyffe. There is an advance in William
Roy's attack on Wolsey, in which invective is directed
against the cardinal himself, and not merely the clergy in
general; but literary talent is absent from that production, which is the offspring of misanthropical common
sense rather than of poetical inspiration. In Skelton the
satire of the age reaches its acme, and after him disappears. He raised it to intense poetry, melting and
modelling it with the fire of his original genius. Rich
with the knowledge of the ancients, zealous for the
improvement of his own language, admitted at court, he had
all the opportunities required for observing and portray-
ing his age, and his aquafortis has left an indelible
caricature of the great priest of the time.

Of himself scarcely any record remains; and his authentic portrait is not to be found. What fate attends inven-
tors and fathers of arts, Homer, Piers Ploughman, Chaucer,
Skelton, Shakespeare, that their persons should have this
tendency to disappear from history? Is it because these
men were too great to foster an egotistical fame; or that
there is a law of compensation, a Nemesis in history,
which orders that the sublimer a man's work the more in-
definite shall his person remain? Skelton's mind may be
studied in his writings, but information respecting his
private life can only be reconstructed by means of scattered allusions. Born about 1460, educated at Cambridge,
where he most probably took his M.A. degree in 1484, he
began his poetical career by writing on the death of
Edward IV.; a 'Balade of the Mustard Tarte' is also
ascribed to that early period of his literary life. He
bewailed the death of the Earl of Northumberland, a
liberal and lettered nobleman, slain by an infuriated mob,
which the poet thus apostrophizes -

[Quotes 'The ... Dethe ... of the Erle of Northumberland',
lines 50-6.]

In 1490 Skelton probably corrected Caxton's version of
the Aeneid; for the old printer, in the preface to his
book, desires the assistance of 'Mayster John Skelton,
late created poete laureate in the Vnyversite of Oxenforde.' In this preface Caxton alludes to Skelton's
classical learning, which so much transcended his own;
the Laureate had translated 'Tulle' and Diodorus Siculus.
Cambridge too made Skelton a laureate; the laureateship
was then a university degree, and not a dignity corres-
ponding to that of the modern poet laureate. There exists
however, a document declaring Skelton Poet Laureate to
Henry VIII.; and it is not improbable that the king should
have created a royal laureateship. If so, the distinction
was most likely honorary as well as honorable, for there
is not a maravedi of evidence to show that a salary was
attached to it. Henry was fond of being surrounded with
literary men, especially if they humored his jovial
character; besides, he must have liked to associated with
Skelton, who had been his tutor, and have given him
'drynke of the sugryd well of Elicony's waters crystal-
lyne, aqueintyng hym with the Musys Nyne.' In an ode to
Prince Henry, when the boy was nine years old, Erasmus
congratulates him on having in his house that 'Skelton,
who is the luminary and honour of British literature.'
No one was fitter than Erasmus to appreciate Skelton's wit
and learning; his testimony is therefore especially valuable to confute the laureate's detractors; but, as
Goldsmith has observed, great men generally understand
and praise one another, while inferior writers endeavour
to bring others down to their own level.
   Skelton's appointment as tutor to a prince shows the
esteem in which he must have been held by society in
general as well as by Erasmus. The pupil himself not a
little contributes to the master's credit; for in after-
life Henry proved to be imbued with real learning, and a
fervent love of literature. He was vividly interested in
the efforts made to improve the English language; he
assembled artists and learned men around him. That
strength of will, which was his characteristic, grasped
the sweets of knowledge as eagerly as those of pleasure
and power. Before students of history join in the ridicule and hostility which have been directed against that
great king, they must investigate his titles to the
gratitude of posterity. It must never be forgotten that
he made England the arbiter of Europe, and founded the
Anglican Church; he also greatly contributed to the edification of English letters. Skelton, whom Henry must
have greatly respected as his former teacher, doubtless
often conversed with the king on literary subjects and

amused the merry monarch with satirical productions. The
laureate's other associates at court, are Thynne, clerk of
the royal kitchen, whom the king promised to protect in
his attacks against the clergy; Sir Thomas Elyot, whose
endeavours were notable in the work of creating a vernacular style; Parker, Surrey, Wyatt, literary favourites of
the king; gentle Sir Thomas More, who was not without
considerable pantagruelistic tendencies, who perhaps
loved staying at home to read and dream, and examine his
shells, his minerals, his Indian ape, his fox, and other
animals, much better than coming to court, but was as it
were compelled to yield to imperious Henry's will; Lily,
the grammarian; most likely Dunbar, the Scottish poet,
who often visited England; and officious Garnesche, the
usher, who carried the Princess Mary through the surf on
landing in France, and against whom the malicious monarch
directed the shafts of the Laureate's satire. The pompous
cardinal himself condescended to patronise Skelton, who
probably did not object to be on good terms with the great
man, at least while that dignitary was basking in the sunshine of royal favour.

Skelton was therefore a court poet; a man of learning
and repute in his day, and not, as some seem to have
thought, a poor, obscure priest, envious of Wolsey's
splendour. Skelton had indeed taken orders in 1498, and
held the title of Rector of Diss in Norfolk; but in those
times clerical residence was not very rigidly enforced, and
and it is not likely that the poet, generally in favour at
court, would willingly have buried himself alive in the
Norfolk parsonage. He doubtless preferred residing near
the court, where he could observe the ways of the world,
become as versed in the knowledge of men as he was in that
of the ancient writers, and find materials for his satirical rhymes. Gifted with a sensitive and fervid temperament, he must have liked the excitement of society; and he
must have felt that the best manner of improving the language - and this culture seems to have been the chief purpose of his life - was to imprint upon it the tints of that
passion which springs from intercourse with the world, as
the Geyser from the boiling lake. He knew that pedantry,
coldness, affectation, were the defacement and ruin of
tongues. From his musings over the decline of Greek and
Roman letters, he must have learnt the great lesson that
a real sentiment and not cold rhetoric is the vital prin-
ciple of literature. He accordingly fired his mind with
passion from the burning pile of the world, but with the
passion of philosophers, which is satire, or rather the
complex combination of sentiments of which satire is the
effect. From the days of the Hebrew prophets, and the time

when Juvenal thundered forth his invectives, to the bitter
accents of Byron, and the mad Circean carnival of
Shelley's irony, sublime discontent and satire has been
the characteristic of the greatest men; and those who have
never played the Quixote have not ascended to the highest
degree among the immortal hierarchy.

Not being a stranger to the manners of the days when
Henry VII. was king, Skelton must have been interested in
observing the changes brought about by a new generation.
That love for wealth and apparel which Andrew Borde, some
years afterwards so shrewdly noted as being characteristic
of the English, was, during the reign of Henry VIII., no
longer repressed by the terroristic regimen of collectors.
Under the late King, poverty and and avarice had spread
far and wide throughout the realm. But now a golden age,
in the literal sense, had dawned; luxury, as well as
learning, was revived, and was displayed with almost
oriental profuseness. Gold and silver, pearls of great
price came from the coffers where they had been concealed,
and sparkled on the breasts of ladies, on the vesture of
noblemen. Clothiers, gold-beaters, weavers, had full
employment. More bound his Utopian convicts in golden
fetters. The adventure of the Field of the Cloth of Gold
was but the climax of the pomp and pride of the time.
Never were king and queen more brilliant than Henry VIII.
and Catherine of Aragon. The festivities of their marriage lasted six months. They were but the royal gems of
a parterre in which the white and green of Tudor mingled
with the violet and miniver-purpled gowns of the Knights
of the Bath, the crimson velvet robes of dukes set with
pearls, and the lettice-edged scarlet trains of courtly
beauties. Imagine the King and a dozen other maskers
coming to Wolsey's palace disguised as shepherds, with
clothes of fine cloth of gold and crimson satin, with
beards of fine gold or silver wire, every hair of which
sparkled in the glare of torches borne by satin-clothed
attendants. Attracted by the lustre of royal splendour,
literary men came forth, as, when the sun rises, crabs
crawl from their beds of sand. Odes and dedications
abounded. Mars, Jupiter, Hercules, were once more pitilessly dragged from their Olympus to do duty as 'proper-
ties' in the laudatory compositions of the age. Morus was
bold enough to compare the new era with the preceding
reign, and to rejoice that a happier time was come, when
the people of England no longer stood in dread of spies and
tax-gatherers, when the merchant again launched his vessel
on the waters, and illiberal strong boxes no longer with-
held the riches of the land. As Skelton's position
enabled him to enjoy many social privileges, we can fancy

him visiting the court, and greeting the Countess of
Surrey, by whom he was patronised, and perhaps even the
queen and maids of honour, according to that custom which
so delighted Erasmus. He enters the presence-chamber, or
is warned by the officer's trumpet to approach a supper-
table covered with quaint devices of churches, castles,
beasts, birds, fowls, and personages. Turning from the
splendour of the court, he casts a somewhat cynical eye on
the pomps and vanities of Wolsey, that modern Eutropius
who would at the last have no Chrysostom to intercede for
him; Skelton satirically marks the gorgeous vestments of
the cardinalship, the torches, and the banquets, and the
plaudits of the crowd, and the flatteries of courtiers;
and what a poem on 'Mutabilitie' the old philosopher might
have written had he lived to see what he foretold - the
fall of this energetic priest - Wolsey's death in the
quiet abbey, when his prestige had departed, and the
velvet-clothed gentlemen, and the yeoman of the barge,
and the pure wine ever flowing, and the crooks, and the
heralds, and the cross-bearers, and the horses, and the
pleasures devised for the King's consolation, had vanished
away like unsubstantial dreams.

Although Skelton was not to see this consummation, he
in the meanwhile contributed to it. His friend William
Thynne, clerk of the royal kitchen, and himself not very
friendly to the bishops, is said to have prompted the
Laureate to attack Wolsey. Such satire was by no means un-
uncongenial to Henry. His fiery spirit could not but feel
the curb of the Church; like a young horse under a rider,
he had a disagreeable sense of restraint. In vain had
Wolsey endeavoured to tame him - now by enjoining the
prince to read nineteen folios of Aquinas, then by making
him go through a course of boisterous pleasure. The
King's powerful organization was not to be subdued in
either way. Wolsey, whose nose denotes more energy than
meditative power, seems not to have understood that
Henry's will was to be courted and complied with at all
hazards; had he determined to retain Henry's favour at any
price, at any risk of alienating the Pope, he probably
would not have fallen; but not being satisfied with the
height he had reached, he, like so many other great men,
was at last conquered by fate. The beginnings of the end
were, as in all other matters, slow and gradual. In Skelton's first attack, entitled 'Colin Cloute,' the allusions
to Wolsey are few and delicate. That satire is directed
against the clergy in general; Skelton's indignation rises
against the luxury, pride, and ignorance of priests and
monks. He tears the mask away wich such violence as
almost to flay the faces of his victims. To read this

poem is to evoke from the catacombs of the past, from the
vaults of ruined convents and abbeys, a motley multitude
of monks, Cistercians, Virginians, Benedictines; to see
them burying their sensual faces in cups of hypocras, or
discussing the masterpieces of the cooks, or consecrating
the decaying bones of macerated saints in shrines radiant
with pearls and precious stones, or winding through vil-
lages and cities to conciliate the people and arrogate
sacerdotal privileges. An ill-concealed spirit of anta-
gonism was diffused among the people; women, butchers,
servants, apprentices, carpenters would read forbidden
translations of the Scriptures, and scoff at Papistical
ordinances. The general discontent converges in 'Colin
Cloute;' in which no charge which could be laid on a
graceless clerical corporation is forgotten; neither the
ignorance which is unable to construe gospel and epistle,
nor the neglect of midnight masses, the traffic in mitres,
the yoke of citations and excommunications laid on the
poor, the wearing singular garments of russet and hair.
The satirist inveighs against the disputations, conten-
tions, and heresies that corrode the Church; some members
of which are tainted by Lutheran doctrines, or Wyckliffian
errors, or Hussian, Arian, Pelagean tendencies. Skelton
also refers to the political obnoxiousness of the clergy,
in a passage which must have reflected the feelings of
many a haughty nobleman, and perhaps of the King himself.

[Quotes 'Colin Clout', lines 595-7, 613-14, 629-31.]

All those invectives are hurled in short lines of five or
six syllables, rhyming in couplets, triplets, quartets,
falling and rattling down like hailstones in a storm;
merciless, abrupt, and copious, the words strike and re-
bound till they take away the breath; wit flashes like
lightning through that storm in which the thunder of
indignation booms. Skelton's attempt to translate his
passion into a vernacular form involves a struggle with
an imperfect language; he fully appreciates the nature of
the conflict, and acknowledges that he has not achieved so
consummate a triumph as he would have wished.

[Quotes lines 53-8.]

Rugged as his language is, it can reflect the various
moods of his valiant mind. Towards the end of the poem
he relents, and declares that he decries no good bishop,
no good priest, no good canon; and he concludes with a
metaphor, in which he expresses his aspiration towards
rest -

[Quotes lines 1253-60.]

The somewhat mournful opening of the poem shows that he
had a sense of the uselessness of casting too much truth
abroad on the world -

[Quotes lines 1-5, 13-14.]

Cockneys who steam down the Thames, and captains who
anchor off Erith, will be glad to recollect that Skelton
wrote his 'Colin Cloute' in that town, while he was on a
visit at his friend Thynne's father's 'howse.'
    In 'Why come ye not to court?' the Laureate threw off
all restraint. Wolsey is personally attacked in that
virulent satire, in which series of vituperative enumerations succeed one another like the waves of snakes in some
serpents' cave, or after the Ophidian adventure in Pande-
monium. Had the old rector - for he must have been nearly
sixty when he wrote this - been soured by lack of promotion, or is the virulence of his language to be ascribed
to the tone of satire in that age? As it is, the verse
flows on like a rill of Tartarus, the fluid of which is
molten metal, and evolves clouds of stifling vapours. The
images arise like malicious imps attendant on furies; and
all this rout of horrors is directed against the hapless
Cardinal with the science of a Prospero waving his wand
for the punishment of some obscene slave. Feature after
feature, Skelton flays and dissects his antagonist's
character; he shows that its primary element is an iron
will, on which he insists with emphatic repetition:

[Quotes 'Why Come Ye Nat to Court?' lines 102-4.]

That will has brought Wolsey pomp and pride; he keeps himself in luxury and sensuality; he affects to rule the
roast, to usurp speech at council, to mar all things in
the 'Chamber of Starres.' Noblemen and barons cower before
before the imperious priest, as sheep before a 'bocher's
dogge'

[Quotes lines 304-8.]

And it is a fact that in that age many noblemen were
unable to sign their name.
    Wolsey is also charged with ruling the King by craft
and subtlety; laws melt like snow before the Cardinal's
will, bland is his breath of flattery. Probably instituting in his mind a comparison between his own career and
that of Wolsey, the Laureate asks what was this upstart?

No doctor of divinity, no doctor of law, but a puny master
of arts whom the King thought fit to endow with prelacy; a
man who certainly knew the humanities, but was ignorant of
the sciences, philology, philosophy, astronomy -

[Quotes lines 517-19.]

Does this reproach intimate that Skelton himself was con-
versant with those writers? did he suffer from the comparison between his acquirements and the lack of promotion
he had to bear? did he remember the days when, more than
any other man at court, he influenced the mind of Henry?
did he chafe at being supplanted by this upstart Cardinal?
To crown his grievances, had Wolsey's credit brought the
author of 'Colin Cloute' into disfavour at court? He
warns the King respecting the consequences of having so
powerful a rival:-

[Quotes lines 582, 584-7.]

A gentle hint is thrown, intimating that the King must be
bewitched to have such a favourite as Wolsey. Petrarch
tells how Charlemagne was bewitched in a like fashion; but
still further extending his researches on this point, the
horrified Laureate finds it recorded in Gaguin that King
Louis of France elevated a poor man, by name Balua, to
splendour, to chancellorship, to cardinalship; until

[Quotes lines 734-7.]

Scarcely, however, has he uttered this significant warning, than he repents of so cruel an allusion:

[Quotes lines 743-6.]

He hints, however, at the existence of some real danger,
by comparing the Cardinal to a mouse fearlessly dwelling
in a cat's ear; and he indulges in an aspiration to the
effect that Henry may retain a sound zoological knowledge:-

[Quotes lines 769-74.]

Again recurring to examples of traitors' deaths, he
alludes to the punishment of Master Mewtas, the King's
French secretary, who had informed the French king of
Henry's designs:-

[Quotes lines 792-3.]

That secretary has, it seems, taken his

> pasport to pas
>   To the devyll, Sir Sathanas,
>   To Pluto and Syr Belyall.   [lines 800, 802-3]

Notwithstanding the manifold details given respecting the
Cardinal, Skelton does not intend to leave that 'matter
mysticall' completely aside.

[Quotes lines 823-8.]

Towards the end of the poem, he bemoans the sad state of
the country:-

[Quotes lines 1021-4, 1027-37.]

He concludes with explaining how he came to write this
satire:-

[Quotes lines 1199-202, 1205-8, 1222.]

Such is this extraordinary production, in which the indignation of a fine mind is clothed in such power, invention,
and copiousness of diction. There is no better type of
satire; Skelton's metre is all his own; the words spring
from line to line like so many monkeys, pointing, grin-
ning, chattering, howling, biting. The similes have that
pitiless pungency which Butler afterwards evinced. The
whole is breathless and fierce as a panther's attack.
In 'Colin Cloute' there were but generalities; here the
personality lends piquancy to the poem.
    This great satire is a most valuable illustration of
that period of Henry VIII.'s reign, which preceded the
Reformation; it is the best poetical expression of the
sentiments that then pervaded the minds of men - the
pride of the Saxon fermenting against the haughty demeanor
of Church dignitaries, the rebellion of the northern
spirit against the dominion of a foreign hierarchy. Roy,
Lindsay, declaim against the corruptions of the clergy;
but in these writers the political element is not salient,
as it is in Skelton's invective. The latter echoes the
grievances of the court as well as those of the people;
he complains that the Cardinal threatens to checkmate the
King. The colours of Skelton's picture show his antagonist's character with more vividness than any chronicle.
Pride and ambition were Wolsey's chief attributes; and
although when viewed apart from other traits, the proportion of them which has been laid to his charge may appear

exaggerated, the relations of other writers can furnish
an equilibrium and compensation to the estimate of
Wolsey's character; but it is not the less certain that
Skelton's portrait of him is indispensable for a correct
view of the Cardinal. Skelton's defects are those of
reformers - a propensity to half truths, a violent
adherence to one side of the question; but with the short-
comings of satirists he also had their virtues - the
power and justice which differentiate a satire, however
harsh, from a libel, the writings of Juvenal from those
of Dennis. Good satire is, in earnest natures, the product of a strong sense of justice rather than an overflow
of animal spirits; it is therefore essentially practical;
and such was Skelton's invective. Before him, Piers
Ploughman had cautiously given vent to his feelings in
allegorical poems; Chaucer's caustic wit had ridiculed
monks without any other purpose than to give the artistic
representation of a class and furnish matter for boisterous merriment. Lindsay inveighs against the clergy in a
far less vigorous and original manner than the Rector of
Diss, his long cadences, more like a lamentation than a
scourge, flows like tears which course one another down
the cheeks. But in Skelton's writings English satire
first bears the new characteristic which it has since
presented, without making artistic effect his chief
object; he devotes his energies to most powerfully
impressing a practical purpose on the reader's mind; in
this respect he resembles Luther, who, like him, uses
popular invective with a sternly destructive end.
    Indignation and loathing against corrupt things are
the sentiments which Skeltonic satire fosters; in the
same manner did Swift write his withering invectives on
mankind, and Pope defend taste against the assaults of
Grub-street writers. English satire is a conflagration,
and not merely the lambent lightning flashes of a summer
evening; it is differentiated by this characteristic from
the satire of other countries. Folengo, whose poems have
been erroneously considered as having influenced Skelton,
ridicules monks without any earnestness, with the bantering indolence of a cook; so varied, unceasing, and pur-
poseless is his laughter, that it very nearly wastes
itself, becomes pithless and injures the satirical effect,
as too numerous dishes impair, instead of consolidating,
the nutritive powers. Rabelais, although presenting a
similarity to Cocceius and Skelton, with respect to some
characteristics of style, such as copiousness of language
and long enumerations, is differentiated from the English
satirist by his allegorical method of ridicule; for
though his symbolical narratives, which he compares to a

'medullary bone,' convey a pithful and important meaning,
he is far from personally denouncing ecclesiastical
dignitaries; he is playful, and not burning with a sombre
earnestness of purpose; his laughter, partaking of artis-
tical rather than of practical irony, throws its bril-
liancy over the whole circle of human affairs. Skelton
concentrates the rays of his irony on one point - the
clergy and the cardinal are ever before him; he finally
takes the latter as the type of the class and pitilessly
analyses him, dissects him, as a microscopist some noxious
insect. His satire has all the accuracy of a scientific
study; he is not, like Rabelais, obliged to disguise himself for fear of being burned; the King is predisposed in
his favour, if not exactly on his side. Skelton gives in
his writings a reflection of the political wants of the
age - the destruction of a power which stood in obnoxious
rivalry to the Crown. He appeals to the people, prepares
them for the Reformation which Henry was to accomplish;
his writings are what Hudibras would have been had that
poem been written before the downfall of the Puritans.
Hence his denunciations of the grievances of the time -
'So myche nobyll prechyng, and so lytell amendment' - 'so
lytell care for the comyn weall, and so myche nede' - 'so
myche pride of prelattes, so cruell and so kene.' ['Speak
Parrot', lines 445, 466, 468.] His indignation strings
grievance after grievance together, like the beads on a
chaplet; he enumerates the crossings and blessings performed by the clergy, the poverty of the people, the
taxes, the wasteful banqueting, the hatred that prevails
against the Church, the abundance of beggars, the boldness of vagabonds. He is too earnest for indulging in
sceptical or frolicsome laughter. His copiousness of
words is not intended to heighten buffoonery, but to
strengthen the expression, present it under all its
facets, with all available resources; he recruits words as
a captain does men, in order to aggravate his attack; his
clearness strikes like a sword, while the brilliant poly-
gonal mirror of Rabelais merely reflects surrounding
things. Skelton's similes are not rollicking and
sprightly, like those of the French author, but fierce and
abusive; he calls Wolsey -

      So fatte a maggott, bred of a flesshe flye;
  Was never such a ffylty gorgon, nor such
      an epicure,
  Syns Dewcalyon's flodde, I make the feste
      and sure.   ['Speak Parrot', lines 502-4]

Whenever he uses fable, as when he makes a parrot declaim

against the evils of the age, it is to lend more variety
to his denunciations, and not to disguise them. So cir-
cumstantial is he, that were it not for the variety of his
imagery and the purpose running through his writings, he
would have remained as realistic as Lydgate; and it is by
this characteristic that he is linked to the middle ages.
Like other branches of literature, satire has its periods
of growth; it is at first cradled in myths and allegories; it then passes into the minuteness and detail of the
chronicle; and at last some powerful idea is implanted
into it, pervades it, links it to some great movement,
organises it into a living form, which, however, like a
hamadryad, may present some traces of the past. This
latter stage, which, considered relatively to modern
times, is but the first phase, is exhibited in Skelton's
verse. As the fabric of civilization becomes more complicated, satirical writing becomes more refined, embraces
more relations of social life, is impregnated with subtler
thought, reflects more shifting and delicate hues of mind;
this aspect it presents in Dryden, Pope, and Addison. But
it is with satire as with poetry; although its processes
may become more refined and complicated in highly civil-
ized ages, its substratum, its essence is rather clouded
than really improved by such refinement, as the highly-
polished man of mature age has lost the freshness of
youth. Pope's invective is to that of Skelton, what his
translation of Homer is to the original. Swift's 'Gulliver,' the most profound work which the eighteenth century
has produced, may be considered as a by no means
unsuccessful attempt to revive the old pungency of satire;
it is a pre-Raphaelite picture; and when Pope compared
Swift to Rabelais, he could not more pointedly have hinted
how closely Gulliver's coarseness, realism, and allegorical meaning approximate him to the old satirical creations. Skelton, compared with which even Butler is highly
artificial, is a well of undefiled English satire in all
is freshness. To him invective was an element of opposition and of popular instruction; he strove to rouse the
passions of men by curt denunciations in the common dialect; his blows are at once vigorous, trenchant, and
embarrassed, like those of a young soldier, still incum-
bered with armour. Skelton's satire was a most perfect
expression of that wild age in which the stern will of the
royal Comus presided over a riot of gushing wealth, portly
Churchmen, whose fondness for wine was noted by Erasmus;
dull barons whose great banquets included such delicacies
as peacocks, seals, and porpoises. The people too had
their revellings, for in all ages of irony, reformation,
destruction, a thirst for the good things of this world

pervades the children of men; the higher motives of human
action, faith, enthusiasm, or even some noble supersti-
tion, having disappeared, the senses gain the upper hand,
whether from a reaction against previous abstinence, or
the direct influence of new tendencies, or both causes
united. When, in the fifteenth century, irony prevailed
in Italy, Pulci expressed, as his great aspiration, a
desire to enjoy good game, good wine, and a soft couch;
Teofilo Folengo revelled in visions of culinary dainties.
At the period of the Reformation, libations were as widely
indulged in throughout Germany, as theological discussions; and Piccolomini was aghast at the strenuous pota-
tions of the land. The conversaziones of the eighteenth
century in France, assumed the forms of suppers, where
champagne sparkled as well as wit; and when the crash had
come, a liberal distribution of sausages was a prominent
characteristic of the Feast of Reason. The roystering
tendencies of the sixteenth century in merry England are
reflected in Skelton's 'Tunning of Elynoure Rumming.'
Before Rabelais' epic to wine-drinkers, and the creation
of Sancho Panza, this curious poem gives a humorous picture
of the sensual element of modern times. It presents the
portrait of the queen of ale-wives, the idealization of
the glories of beer. Redolent with the fumes of hops,
and Saxon all over, like the immortal beverage quaffed by
the heroes of the Walhalla, it is the epic of pot life;
real as a picture of Teniers, it exhibits the forms of
existence and scenes of the ale-house, the tapsters,
the potboys, the ringing of the metal, and the over-
flowing of the cups. Here the peasant, if Wolsey's taxes
have left him a penny, can have a full quart of ale, can
steep his lips in the bitter froth of a sterling and un-
adulterated beverage, such as that described by a writer
who added some lines to the opening of the poem -

    Full Winchester gage
    We had in that age;
    The Dutchman's strong beere
    Was not hopt over heere
    To us 'twas unknowne. (1)

This imitator also declared that there was no smoking in
the tavern - Raleigh and his Virginian weed not having yet
made their appearance; but notwithstanding this intercala-
tion, there is no doubt that 'Elynoure Rumming' was written by Skelton. When the court was kept at Nonsuch, Skelton and other courtiers used to come to this ale-house
for refreshment after fishing in the Mole; hence his
delineation of the celebrated dame, some of whose

descendants' names were to be seen in parish registers
as late as the first part of the eighteenth century.
(Dyce). That licensed victualler's appearance seems not
to have been very inviting -

[Quotes lines 17-19, 27-8, 31-3.]

Her dress consists of a russet gown and mantle of Lincoln
green; on Sundays she makes herself fine with 'her kyrtel
Brystow red,' and a head-dress composed of a -

> Whym wham,
> Knit with a trym tram,
> Upon her brayne pan
> Like an Egyptian.   [lines 75-8]

Although her ordinary occupation is that of brewing and
dispensing beer; it must be owned that she may not be
innocent of witchcraft -

> She is a tonnish gyb;
> The dewyll and she be syb.   [lines 99-100]

Her more legitimate business, however, is to dispense
'noppy ale,' -

[Quotes lines 104-8.]

Slatternly girls also come to fetch beer

[Quotes lines 123-30.]

Some of the customers have no cash, and bring honey,
spoons, shoes, stockings, in exchange for beer. Some
timorous people, probably teetotal backsliders, come in
at the back door -

> Over the hedge and the pale
> And all for the good ale.   [lines 264-5]

Some thirsty women bring wedding rings, or a husband's
cap, or instruments of labour, hatchets, spinning-wheels,
needles, thimbles, which they recklessly pawn for ale.

[Quotes lines 301-6.]

In this manner does Elynour's house become a store of mis-
cellaneous articles - skeins of thread, flitches of bacon,
frying-pans, walnuts, apples, pears, puddings, sausages.

The satirist exposes the pathological results of some of
the customers' habits -

[Quotes lines 480-5.]

Nor were surgical diseases unknown to the frequenters
of the tavern; there was an old lady who -

Had broken her shyn
At the threshold coming in ...
She yelled like a calfe.   [lines 494-5, 500]

But the most comical figure among all these customers is
that of the prudish, affected woman -

[Quotes lines 582-5.]

She rises from the table, calls the hostess apart, and explains in a confidential manner that she has not a groat
wherewith to pay; but she settles the account by giving up
her amber beads. At last the poet exclaims:-

My fingers ytche,
I have written to mytche
Of this mad mummynge
Of Elynoure Rummynge.   [lines 618-21]

Notwithstanding its humour, this satire is a bitter
exposition of human weakness. It is, in its way, and in a
lower sphere, almost as sardonic as the invectives of
Swift and Juvenal. There is in it none of the boisterous
gaiety of Rabelais. With the French satirist, drinking is
associated with reckless jollity, if not with pleasure and
knowledge; here it is a vice, productive of squalor and
wretchedness, it has no attractive side, and all its
sombre colours are displayed. Here again we see the
character of English satire - always practical, and moral
when not political; severe and straightforward, without
any halo of illusive sprightliness around it. Pope ridiculing the poverty and dulness of Grub street writers,
Swift hurling burning missiles from the depths of his
troubled heart, are as different from Voltaire as Skelton
is from Rabelais. Stern, pitiless, almost despairing
reproof on one side, inexhaustible levity on the other -
concentrated bitterness, diffusive merriment - such are
the contrasts presented by the satirists of the two
greatest nations in the world; the Germans and Italians
respectively present analogous general characteristics,
diversified only by secondary tints. Luther too was

earnest and destructive, while Folengo was sceptical and
light-hearted. 'Elynoure Rumming' is the saddest of
Skelton's works; there is no relenting, no hope in it, as
in the poems against the clergy, to the end the scene
remains a 'mad mummynge,' the wretched actors of which
sacrifice everything to their sensuality. Like Hogarth's
'Progress,' it pictures infatuated man under the sway of
passion, recklessly sacrificing his all to morbid propensities. The frailties of human beings have ever been the
theme of satirists and cynics, and Skelton was one of the
most earnest of these; his view of the world pained him,
and made him misanthropical. His invectives against the
clergy are not to be ascribed to mere envy and disappointment; it is easy to see they were a natural product of his
disposition, for what could disappointed interest have to
do with a satire like 'Elynour Rumming'? This poem only
shows what cynicism, what sorrowful pity this old laureate's character contained. His frankness of expression
well recalls his rich, sturdy, generous nature; his writings well represent the general character of his age. He
stands alone in his time, as every great satirist usually
does. Is it Swift, or Addison, or Pope, who will tell us
most about the eighteenth century? In the same manner we
glean more from Skelton than from More, who was a dreamer
and ascetic, as well as a humorist; or from the inferior
writers of the age, Heywood, Barclay; of from the polished
and artificial Wyatt and Surrey.

   Even in Skelton's time, began the transitionary period
which was to prepare the way for the Shakespearean epoch;
Wyatt and Surrey produced polished imitations of Italian
poetry. Skelton forms an intermediate figure between
those writers and the 'barbaric pearl and gold' of Lydgate, and some of his poems give a foreshadow of that
Italian revival, under which the English language was to
rise to its first perfection; he could doubtless have
borne an important part in this great movement, had he not
sacrificed poetry to political irony; like Swift, he was
essentially a pamphleteer, and his writings enjoyed a
widespread popularity. On the other hand, he incurred the
contempt of some Elizabethan critics.

   But even Puttenham, Meres, and in our age Hallam, who
have depreciated Skelton's rude rhymes, could scarcely
have objected to the graceful 'Boke of Philip Sparrow.'
In this exquisite poem appears the best side of his character, his love for nature and the beautiful, his delicate
sensitiveness, his genial humour. The language of this
poem is quite different from that of Skelton's satirical
writings; it flows easily, without unnatural contortions,
like a brook which mirrors the flowers of a garden.

Nothing can be more graceful than the subject; as birds
have ever excited much sympathy among human beings, the
death of a bird is one of the most humorsome and melancholy themes which a poet can choose. Catullus wrote a
sonnet upon it. The middle ages indulged in graceful
imaginings on the relations between birds and men. A
legend of the time describes an island tenanted by monks,
in which birds joined the pious worshippers in singing the
praises of God. St. Guthlac was said to have lived with
swallows, who nested in his cell. Assisi was wont to
preach the gospel to birds and butterflies, called swallows his sisters, taught a locust to sing hymns, and persuaded birds to fast on Fridays. But the winged tribes
were seldom chosen to be the heroes of verse; and in the
great Fox Satires of the thirteenth century, the actors
were chiefly quadrupeds. The 'Boke of Sparrow' is not
then derived from the literature of the middle ages; it
is an original work, in which irony and burlesque have
given place to humour and gentleness. It is a dirge for
the soul of Philip Sparrow, who had been slain by one
Gyb, a cat. After wishing the departed soul immunity from
the attacks of Pluto, the Furies, and Cerberus, the poet
invokes the aid of philosophy as an alleviation of his
grief.

[Quotes 'Philip Sparrow', lines 98-107.]

   After describing at length the various habits and
capabilities of the deceased bird, he apostrophises the
murderous cat in this wise -

[Quotes lines 282-91, 309-10.]

He then gives a long enumeration of birds, whom he con-
vokes to the funeral ceremony -

[Quotes lines 387-8, 392-405, 420-1.]

And so on for nearly a hundred lines. Among those sum-
moned to the obsequies is the phoenix -

   The byrds of Araby
   That potencially
   May never dye.   [lines 513-15]

The funeral ceremonies being concluded, the poet sheds his
last tear over the grave -

[Quotes lines 587-93.]

The state of the English language precludes its being
used 'to write ornatly,' so that the epitaph is composed
in Latin -

[Quotes lines 826-9.]

Follows a 'commendacion,' in which Skelton's verse assumes
erotic tendencies; he becomes a doughty knight and defen-
der of womankind -

[Quotes lines 977-83.]

He then mentions his 'maistres' with some enthusiasm -

[Quotes lines 998-1001, 1031-2, 1041-58.]

   The bird is forgotten in all these gallantries, until
the end of the poem, when 'here foloweth an adycion made
by Maister Skelton' against his critics. In those verses
he complains of the attacks made on the 'Boke,' and argues
that the critical 'commendation' is not out of place, in-
asmuch as it was intended to assuage the grief consequent
on the Sparrow's interment; and he conjures the bird -

[Quotes lines 1324-7, 1330-6, 1367-70.]

And he concludes with wishing his detractors -

   No worse than is contayned.
   In verses two or thre
   That followe as ye may se:
   Luride, cur, livor, volucris pia funera
      damnas?
   Talia te rapiant rapiunt quae fata vo-
      lucrem!
   Et tamen invidia mors tibi continua.   [lines 1376-82]

From which it appears that in those times laureates were
wont to reply somewhat vigorously to their reviewers.
   Coleridge characterizes the 'Boke of Philip Sparrow' as
'an exquisite and original poem.' It evinces Skelton's
powers as a humorist; the genial pleasantry of praying for
the bird's soul, and summoning all manner of birds to the
funeral, had not been equalled in the range of middle-ages
poetry, and has perhaps not been surpassed in modern
times, even by Sterne's celebrated 'Ass,' and Southey's
'Maggot in a Kernel;' such delicate flowers of fancy only
belong to the most fruitful and genial minds; a special
development is required for this humour, which can be

produced by those men alone who have gone through the whole range of ideas, have beheld human nature under all its aspects. As, according to the ancient tradition, stags become youthful by feeding on serpents, such minds are led into humour by their habits of moral scepticism; which by acting and reacting on more delicate feelings, give rise to a gentle satire, which will not be found in the early stages of literature, which differs from the Fox Satires by its tenderness and from the early fables by a less glaring simplicity. Gresset and La Fontaine (2) have given examples of this spirit, which also appears in several passages of Shakespeare.

'Speke Parrot,' is another poem in which the hero is a bird, but it is a satirical rather than humorous work, as the parrot vehemently declaims against the clergy. In the 'Bowge of Courte,' and the 'Garland of Laurell,' Skelton displays his talent for serious poetry. The former is an allegorical poem, which he wrote after the example of the ancient poets.

[Quotes 'Bouge of Court', lines 8-14.]

His minor poems include a fierce invective against the 'Scottes,' an ode 'On Time,' and some hymns to the Persons of the Trinity. He also wrote several plays, of which the 'Magnificence' alone survives; it is certainly superior to the masques and mysteries of the time, and has been con- sidered as entitling Skelton to rank among the fathers of the English drama.

Skelton had some literary quarrels in his day. He was no doubt the assailant in some of those squabbles, for according to Churchyard, he was inclined to talk as he wrote (Dyce); and Fuller observes that he had too much wit, and that his satirical spirit unfortunately lighted on 'three *noli me tangere's*, viz., the rod of a school- master, the cowls of friars, and the cap of a cardinal. The first gave him a lash, the second deprived him of his livelihood, the third almost outed him of his life.' Henry no doubt encouraged Skelton to attack Garnesche, the poems against whom purport to have been written 'by the kynges most noble commaundement.' Garnesche had been the first assailant, as appears from the opening lines of the first poem against Garnesche:-

Sithe ye have me chalyngyd, Master Gar-
    nesche,
Rudely revilyng me in the kynges noble
    hall.   [lines 1-2]

This Garnesche was a knight, gentleman usher to the king;
he attended the Princess Mary to France in 1514, and performed a feat of gallantry when she was wrecked at Boulogne: 'Her shippe with greate difficultie was brought to
Bulleyn, and with great jeopardy at the entryng of the
haven, for the master ran the shippe hard on shore, but
the botes were redy and reseyved this noble lady, and at
the landyng Sir Christopher Garnysche stode in the water,
and toke her in his armes, and so caryed her to land.' In
these days vessels who go ashore near Boulogne go to pieces
pieces immediately, and no lifeboats are ready.

Other adversaries of Skelton's were Gagwynne or Gaguin,
the French ambassador, who was a good historian for the
age; William Lily, the grammarian, who charged Skelton
with having no knowledge and being no poet; Dunbar, the
great Scotch satirist, wrote a 'flyting' against Skelton,
to which the Laureate replied; but these compositions seem
to have been prompted by rude and boisterous bantering
rather than personal hatred. The most celebrated of Skelton's literary quarrels was that between the Laureate and
Barclay. This writer, whose most widely known work is a
translation of Sebastian Brandt's 'Ship of Fools,'
attacked the dirge of 'Philip Sparrow;' but Skelton
retorted in no harsher terms than the following allusion -

[Quotes 'Garland of Laurel', lines 1257-60.]

Barclay also left a poem 'Contra Skeltonum,' which has
perished. In his fourth Eclogue, however, may be read
some of the most scurrilous invectives which envy could
devise. He classed Skelton among a 'shamfull rabble' of
'rascolde poets.'

In subsequent ages, Skelton has been depreciated by
Meres, Puttenham, Warton, and Hallam; on the other hand,
he has been praised by Disraeli, Coleridge, Southey.
Every one knows Pope's line, about heads of houses quoting
Skelton; from which it would seem that Skelton was as popu-
popular in the eighteenth century as Pope is in our age.

In the 'Garland of Laurell' Skelton gives a complete
list of his writings. He wrote that poem in praise of
himself, with the egotism of old age. He was at that time
sojourning at Sherifhotten Castle, Yorkshire, then in
possession of the Duke of Norfolk, the father-in-law of
Lady Surrey, mother of the great poet, and patroness of
the Laureate. It seems that some ladies had agreed to
crown the old poet with a garland of laurel; and it is
pleasant to think that he was honoured and befriended in
his old age. Skelton seems to have resided for some years
at Diss, as some short poems indicate, which he wrote at

the expense of his parishioners. According to Fuller he
was suspended from his ecclesiastical office through the
influence of the monks, who were bent on retaliating for
his attacks. 'Such foul Lubbers,' says Fuller, 'fell
heavy on all which found fault with them.' The sly Laureate had run away with a lady, and married her secretly.
His diocesan, Nix, Bishop of Norwich, a cruel and licen-
tious man, prompted by the friars, availed himself of this
adventure to suspend Skelton; in those days the marriage of
a priest was considered a far greater crime than his
having a concubine. The poet next succumbed in his
unequal struggle with Wolsey, who had not forgotten the
'Why come ye not to court?' This Cardinal sent officers
to capture Skelton, who, however, fled to the cloisters
of Westminster, where he took sanctuary. There he was
protected, and kindly treated by his old friend Abbot
Islip; and the old Laureate thus spent the remaining
years of his life in repose, amusing himself now and then
with writing verses to the memory of Henry VII., his
Queen, and other royal personages buried at Westminster.
He died June 21, 1529, and was buried in the chancel of
St. Margaret's.

   His memory shared the fate which always befalls great
writers whose satirical character has made a strong
impression on their time. A great number of apocryphal
pranks and comic writings were ascribed to him, as afterwards to Rabelais. Anthony Wood charges him with having
in his living and throughout the diocese, been 'esteemed
more fit for the stage than for the pew or pulpit.' The
'Merie Tales of Skelton' are a series of buffoonic stories composed after his death, relating singular antics
as having been performed by him; thus he is described as
coming to an inn, calling for drink, not being attended
to, crying 'Fire!' in order to arouse the people, and
pointing to his throat when asked by a terrified crowd
where the conflagration was. Such are the traits which
delighted the readers of the time, who sought for
'pleasaunt recreacion of minde' without caring much about
the truth. Far other, however, is the man as he appears
in his writings. He indeed appears, especially to our
age, to have indulged in vulgarity and coarseness. The
fastidious Elizabethan critics censured him for those
faults; but they wrote when Italian polish had already
profoundly leavened the English taste; Wyatt's satire had
been diluted by a refined sentimentalism, and Surrey had
imitated Petrarch. Skelton had not travelled, like the
son of his patroness; he had not seen a Geraldine at
Florence, or become imbued with the Italian spirit. He
was the product of an earlier and coarser age, and must not

be charged with the blemishes of his time. He performed
the necessary work of his age - a work which Surrey,
Wyatt would have had to perform had they lived under the
same circumstances and had the same ability. Satire was
sufficiently coarse as late as the eighteenth century; in
this age there is no satire at all; and to charge Skelton
with the faults of his age and vocation is to charge the
ichthyosaurus with uncouthness. His instrument, the language, was very imperfect; his attempts to improve it, and
his consciousness of its roughness, were weighty evidences
of his literary penetration. His embarrassed phraseology
is the result of his desperate endeavour to enrich the
literary dialect by graftings from the vernacular tongue.
    In writing he had two purposes to accomplish - to write
as 'ornately' as possible, but especially to make his
language popular, in order that his satire might be widely
relished. Wyatt and Surrey, on the contrary, were mere
court poets, comparative purists whose only care was to
prune their language of 'ragged' words and imitate the
flow of Italian verse. Had Skelton been less copious and
popular he would have been more polished; but what he
would have gained in elegance, he would have lost in
power, candour, and variety of expression. Even his predecessors, such as Chaucer, and many of his contemporaries, Roy, Lindsay, Barclay, are not so tattered and
rugged, merely because they did not make that effort to
popularity of language, which Skelton did. He probably,
like Sir Thomas More, studied the vernacular speech in
streets and markets. It was he who gave the modern impulse to the fixation of the language, by exhibiting its
vernacular power in its fullest aspect. and demonstrating
the extreme ruggedness of that speech; he showed from what
the language was to be purified before it could become a
perfect vehicle of literary expression. In his writings
are seen shoals of vernacular words such as fysgygge,
flirt; blother, to gabble, tunning, brewing, &c. His
writings are like Roger Bacon's optic tube, in which
future events were discerned; in Skelton's verse is fore-
shown the excellence which a succeeding generation attained.
But as for himself, he was not bent on writing agreeable
sentimental verses inspired from Petrarch. He had studied
Juvenal much more than Petrarch, and was bent on imitating
the satirist and not the sonnet-poet. His mission was to
express the rough, unsettled, and transitionary side of
the age. The language presents both power and beatuy;
Skelton expressed its power, and left the beauty to be
evinced by his younger successors; but in casting his
speech in the popular mould he was as great and useful a
neologist as those who assumed the Italian manner. His

works are like the great geological strata, which are the
pillars of the earthly crust - the deposits where uncouth
and gigantic creations, ichthyosauri, plesiosauri, ptero-
dactyls, are found; these layers must not be expected to
yield brilliant peals and precious stones, but the sau-
rians are, to philosophic eyes, more valuable than many
diamonds, because they bear witness to great evolutions in
the history of the globe. Far above them are the alluvial
fields that produce fruits and flowers, but each series of
layers has its own importance, is a thought of God, intimately linked to the great whole. It is thus in literature, where every phase must be understood and nothing
depreciated. Skelton was the ablest representative of the
reforming and satirical spirit of his age; More, the only
Englishman of his time who could have vied with the Laureate in learning and wisdom, adheres to a conservative
and mystical spirit. Both those great men lived at court;
both were humorists; but More was an ascetic and mystic;
Skelton a cynic. That good-nature, which is often com-
patible with the most apparently severe cynicism, made him,
however, always ready to regret the violence which his
fervid temperament imprinted to his attacks; impulsive,
but not virulent, his anger stings but does not fester in
the wound; his pugnacity, as evinced in the quarrel with
the Scotch poet, is often the effect of strength and buoy-
ant spirits rather than deliberate hostility. He had no
pride or undue vanity, but the amiable and harmless egotism of an aged literary man surrounded by a friendly
coterie. That garland of laurel, which ladies wove for
him in his time, has now been somewhat withered and forgotten in the rush of ages; Abbot Islip, Wolsey, Nix, the
Benedictine friars, the old Laureate, have passed away;
but Skelton's phantom can still be evoked from his writings, while his body is undergoing its changes under St.
Margaret's Church; around which gin shops disperse their
'tunning,' and the tide of human nature flows continually.

Notes

1 These lines were appended to the 1624 edition of
   'Elynor Rumming'; they are reprinted in Dyce, II,
   p. 155.
2 Jean-Baptiste-Louis Gresset (1709-77), French satiric
   poet and dramatist, and Jean de la Fontaine (1621-95),
   author of 'The Fables'.

46. JAMES RUSSELL LOWELL ON SKELTON AND 'PHILIP SPARROW'

1875, 1889

(a) From an article entitled Spenser in the 'North
American Review', CXX (1875), pp. 334-94; this extract is
from p. 340.
   Lowell (1819-91) was a distinguished American poet and
critic.

One genuine English poet illustrated the early years of
the sixteenth century, - John Skelton. He had vivacity,
fancy, humor, and originality. Gleams of the truest
poetical sensibility alternate in him with an almost
brutal coarseness. He was truly Rabelaisian before
Rabelais. But there is a freedom and hilarity in much of
his writing that gives it a singular attraction. A breath
of cheerfulness runs along the slender stream of his
verse, under which it seems to ripple and crinkle, catch-
ing and casting back the sunshine like a stream blown on
by clear western winds.
   But Skelton was an exceptional blossom of autumn. A
long and dreary winter follows.

(b) From Lowell's Address to the Modern Language Association of America in 1889, as printed in 'Publications of
the Modern Language Association of America', V (1890),
pp. 5-22; this extract is from p. 15.

Shall I make the ignominious confession that I relish
SKELTON'S 'Philip Sparowe', pet of SKELTON'S Maystres
Jane, or parts of it, inferior though it be in form,
almost as much as that more fortunate pet of Lesbia?
There is a wonderful joy in it to chase away what SKELTON
calls odious Enui, though it may not thrill our intellectual sensibility like its Latin prototype.

47. JOHN CHURTON COLLINS ON SKELTON

1880

From 'The English Poets', edited by Thomas H. Ward (1880),
I, pp. 184-5.
The scholar and critic John Churton Collins (1848-1908)
contributed these introductory notes to a selection of
Skelton's works.

Skelton's claims to notice lie not so much in the intrinsic excellence of his work as in the complete originality
of his style, in the variety of his powers, in the peculiar character of his satire, and in the ductility of his
expression when ductility of expression was unique. His
writings, which are somewhat voluminous, may be divided
into two great classes - those which are written in his
own peculiar measure, and which are all more or less of
the same character, and those which are written in other
measures and in a different tone. To this latter class
belong his serious poems, and his serious poems are now
deservedly forgotten. Two of them, however, 'The Bowge
of Court', a sort of allegorical satire on the court of
Henry VIII, and the morality of 'Magnificence', which
gives him a creditable place among the fathers of our
drama, contain some vigorous and picturesque passages
which have not been thrown away on his successors. As a
lyrical poet Skelton also deserves mention. His ballads
are easy and natural, and though pitched as a rule in the
lowest key, evince touches of real poetical feeling. When
in the other poems his capricious muse breaks out into
lyrical singing, as she sometimes does, the note is clear,
the music wild and airy. 'The Garlande of Laurell' for
example contains amid all its absurdities some really exquisite fragments. But it is as the author of 'The Boke
of Colin Cloute', 'Why come ye nat to Court', 'Ware the
Hawke', 'The Boke of Philipp Sparowe', and 'The Tunnyng
of Elinore Rummyng', that Skelton is chiefly interesting.
These poems are all written in that headlong voluble
breathless doggrel which, rattling and clashing on through
quick-recurring rhymes, through centos of French and
Latin, and through every extravagant caprice of expression, has taken from the name of its author the title of
Skeltonical verse. The three first poems are satires.
'Colin Clout' is a general attack on the ignorance and

sensuality of the clergy. The second is a fierce invective against Cardinal Wolsey, and the third is directed
against a brother clergyman who was, it appears, in the
habit of flying his hawks in Skelton's church. These
three poems are all in the same strain, as in the same
measure - grotesque, rough, intemperate, but though gib-
bering and scurrilous, often caustic and pithy, and sometimes rising to a moral earnestness which contrasts
strangely with their uncouth and ludicrous apparel.

[Quotes 'Colin Clout', lines 53-8.]

And the attentive student of Skelton will soon discover
this. Indeed he reminds us more of Rabelais than any
author in our language. In 'The Boke of Philipp Sparowe'
he pours out a long lament for the death of a favourite
sparrow which belonged to a fair lay nun. The poem was
probably suggested by Catullus' Dirge on a similar occasion. In Skelton, however, the whole tone is burlesque
and extravagant, though the poem is now and then relieved
by pretty fancies and by graceful touches of a sort of
humorous pathos. In 'The Tunnyng of Elinore Rummynge' his
powers of pure description and his skill in the lower
walks of comedy are seen in their highest perfection. In
this sordid and disgusting delineation of humble life he
may fairly challenge the supremacy of Swift and Hogarth.
But Skelton is, with all his faults, one of the most versatile and one of the most essentially original of all our
poets. He touches Swift on one side, and he touches
Sackville on the other.

48. RICHARD HUGHES ON SKELTON

1924

The Introduction to Hughes's edition of 'Poems by John
Skelton' (London, 1924), pp. ix-xv. One footnote has been
deleted.
    Hughes (1900-76) achieved his greatest recognition as
the author of such novels as 'A High Wind in Jamaica' and
'Fox in the Attic'.

It happens from time to time that some poet almost forgotten suddenly comes into his own. There is nothing strange and freakish about this: and it does not really give us license to crow over our fathers. The colour of the reading mind changes from one generation to another, as it changes from man to man: in becoming able to appreciate something our fathers found incomprehensible, or unpleasant, we generally lose our appreciation of something they found estimable. The ground shifts under us.

Certain poets have to wait a long time for the advent of a sympathetic generation: Skelton has had to wait four hundred years. Yet, you might say, in his own day his reputation was international: Oxford, Cambridge, and Louvain crowned him with laurel: he was tutor to Henry VIII and *Orator Regius*: Erasmus, Caxton, and other smaller fry praised him whole heartedly: and he was a sufficiently popular figure for a whole cycle of myth to have accumulated about his personality. But the learned admired him for his learning, and the people admired him as one of the most amusing and boisterous writers of any century: Skelton, knowing himself to be not only a scholar and a jocular but a poet, looked to Posterity for nice appreciation. The quality of poetry in Skelton was one of which it was impossibility absolute, in the rudimentary state of criticism and aesthetic theory, for the age of Henry VIII to have any inkling. (That they called him a poet, being deceived into a true verdict by irrelevancies, is nothing.) And so he placed his faith in Posterity: and Posterity has played the jade with him: never quite giving him his *congé*, she has kept him dangling after her through century after century - has been to him a sort of everlasting Fannie Brawne.

The reason for this neglect is simple and superficial. In the first place, he wrote at a time when the pronunciation of English was on the eve of a drastic change, and the dropping of the final *e* in so many words soon rendered his rhythms unintelligible. In the second, he came close before one of the greatest revolutions that ever transformed the surface of literature - the Elizabethan Era. Precurring signs of that revolution were already in the air: and he set his face against them. It is easy for us now, prejudiced by a knowledge of what was to come, to blame him: it is easy to explain after the race why such and such a horse won. But it would have been impossible to guess, at that time, from the stilted Italianate compositions of the opposite camp that the unaccountable Spirit of the Lord would choose such dry bones for its dwelling. Judged by themselves, they were worthless, and Skelton was right in condemning them. But he backed a

loser: and has paid for his misfortune with four centuries
of neglect and incomprehension.

For four centuries he has lain in his grave, food for
the grammarians.

Largely, they are to blame. If the critic is a man who
has failed at one of the arts, the scholar is generally a
man who has failed at criticism. He looks for no aesthetic worth in his subject-matter: for his purposes it is
irrelevant, hardly even an encumbrance.* If he made this
position clear, one would not blame him, one would not ask
blood from a stone. But he does not; he pretends to
criticism for form's sake: he accepts ready-made the
judgment of the general, damning with one hand what he
edits with the other: he takes his judgment from the
general, while the general imagine that they are taking
their judgment from him. They respect him: he has read
all these unheard-of people, he knows: if there was any
good in them, he would announce it. But he does not
announce it, because he could not see it, even if it were
shown him. God help any poet who hopes to be rescued
from oblivion by the scholars! His only hope is to be set
some day before a sympathetic generation in some form un-
encumbered by excess of learning, that his readers may
discover him for themselves. Even then, not till the very
servant-girls devour him by candle-light will it occur to
his editors that the subject of their life's work had any
intrinsic value of its own.

Their treatment of Skelton has been particularly
scurvy. Only one, the Rev. Alexander Dyce, has taken him
at all seriously. Such editions as appeared before the
time of Dyce were almost unintelligible conglomerations
of naïvely-accepted miscopyings. Dyce undertook the great
and necessary work of putting the text into an intelligible form: and gave half his life to it. Dyce's edition
is a fine piece of scholarship, and the standard text on
which all future work must be based. But it is doubtful
whether even Dyce realised the full aesthetic value of
Skelton's poetry. As for the others, they deserve all
opprobrium. The writers of literary histories have been
content to repeat with parrot-like persistence, one after
the other, that Skelton was a witty but coarse satirist,
having occasionally a certain rude charm, but in the main
bungling, disgusting, prolix, and tedious: and they have

_____

* One gentleman, to whom the Editor was told to apply for
information, answered that his interest in Skelton lay in
the possibility of reconstructing the Church of Diss from
the description of it in 'Ware the Hauke'. That was at
any rate frank: the literary historians are not. See the
'D.N.B.', etc.

relegated him to that most damning of insignificancies, the part of an 'influence.' They have been content to leave Dyce's edition, published eighty years ago, not only unrevised, but out of print and now practically unobtainable. But, truly, Skelton is a poor satirist compared with his powers as a poet: his influence is negligible when compared with the value of his original work: and simply regarded as a rhythmical technician he is one of the most accomplished the language has ever known. There is more variety of rhythm in Skelton than in almost any other writer.

Take, for example, the first piece published in this book, 'Speke, Parot'.* They regard it as an unintelligible piece of political satire, interesting only for its references to Wolsey and the Introduction of Greek! Those last three stanzas, which set the pointer to the parable, which tell us that

> Parot is my owne dere harte...   [line 213]

- they are entirely overlooked. Yet no one who bears those those three stanzas in mind can misread the rest, can fail to see the beauty of the whole conception. Shakespeare did not misread it: as his 'Phoenix and Turtle' bears witness.

So much for the core of the poem. But alas!

> Crescent in immensum me vivo Psittacus iste: [line 513]

> [That Parrot will grow to a boundless extent while I
>   am alive]

Skelton, finding the Parot so convenient a mouthpiece for his views on things in general, has later hidden the sensitive mystery of his poem under a great deal of additional matter that is simply concerned with mundane affairs. (For it is generally admitted that the poem, as

* The sole reference to this poem in the 'Dictonary of National Biography' is to say that it is 'written in Chaucer's well-known stanza': which is not only inadequate, but also untrue. The rhyme-scheme is certainly that of Rhyme-royal: but the metre had never been used before; and so far as I am aware, has only once been used since - in 'Rocky Acres', by Robert Graves. I know of no other poem with more originality, more beauty, more subtle variety of rhythm than this same 'Speke, Parot'.

But if I were to continue quoting the stupidities uttered about Skelton in high places, there would never be an end.

it has reached us, is a hodge-podge composed at many different dates.) Admittedly it is a difficult poem: but the
extraordinary sense of rhythm, the extraordinary intellectual grasp that not only makes every word significant but
every juxtaposition of words, every possible turn and
shade of meaning, render it one of those few poems that
can be read with increasing admiration, increasing compre-
hension and delight year after year. The more one reads
it, the more one learns of its meaning, the more certain
one is of never getting to the bottom of it. It is a
living thing, its roots branching innumerably: comprehen-
sion of it is interminable. And, as all fine poetry must,
it baffles eulogy.

  Far simpler, far more easily popular, is the 'Boke of
Phyllyp Sparowe'. Here is no high lyrical mystery; only,
in the words of Coleridge, 'A beautiful and romantic poem':
very simple and pathetic. Jane Scroupe, a school-girl of
Carowe, mourns for her dead pet. It is remarkable that at
a time when Elizabethan drama was still below the horizon
Skelton should have so *characterised* the poem, have
brought Jane so vividly into our minds, not by description
but by the very words she speaks. In two things the mediaeval poets excelled, even the dullest of them - in the
description of birds and young girls: Skelton, if in the
senses he is the first of the Georgians, in another is the
last of the mediaevals: he has brought these two things to
a climax in 'Phyllyp Sparowe'

[Quotes lines 115-26.]

  It is a pretty thing.

  Next, one is faced with

  The topsy-turvy tunnyng
  Of Mistress Elynour Rummyng.

  The weak stomach will be turned by it: but those with a
gizzard for strong meat will find it a remarkable piece.
I do not speak of it as a precursor of the 'realistic'
school of poetry: it is more valuable than that. It is
the processional manipulation of vivid impressions, the
orchestration, the *mental* rhythm which strikes me. So far
from calling it a realistic poem, I would call it one of
the few really abstract poems in the language. Its aesthetic effect is that of a *good* cubist picture (or any
picture dependent on form for its value).

  It would be foolish to take each of his poems in turn:
but one word should be said for the 'Garlande of Laurell'.

'This,' say the historians, 'is the longest poem ever
written by a poet in his own honour.' They accuse the
author of pomposity and vanity in consequence. I only ask
you to read it: I do not think he makes any claims in it
which are not justified: after all, he *is* the finest poet
in England (Scotland is *hors concours*) between Chaucer and
the Elizabethans, and he cannot be blamed for knowing it.
If he errs, it is in attaching too much reverence to Gower
and Lydgate, not to himself. Anyhow, the whole is very
pleasant reading: and some of the incidental lyrics are
wholly delightful.

What wonderful plays, one thinks after reading 'Phyllyp
Sparowe', he might have written: what easy characterisa-
tion! That he did write plays is known: and one, 'Magnyfycence', has survived. The others, like a great many
of his poems, have unhappily vanished. The nineteenth
century dubbed it 'the dullest play in any language.'
From the point of view of the nineteenth century the
judgment was admissible, seeing the ideal of drama it
serves was not then invented: but not from the point of
view of the twentieth. It is an abstract play, a sort of
morality - still, even at the date I write, a little
ahead of the times: but I believe that if the language
were modernised and the whole produced with skilful
expressionistic lighting it could not fail to create a
sensation. Not in England, perhaps, for another twenty
years or so: but I confidently recommend it to the notice
of Berlin and Prague - and perhaps New York....

49. EDMUND BLUNDEN ON SKELTON'S 400th ANNIVERSARY

1929

From the 'Times Literary Supplement', 20 June, 1929,
pp. 481-2; an unsigned review to mark the 400th anniversary of Skelton's death.
    Blunden (1896-1974) was an English poet and man of
letters.

Charles Lamb's thesis on the sociable nature of antiquity
rises in the memory on the four-hundredth anniversary of
the death of 'Master Skelton, Poet Laureate,' a being so

little destroyed in his individuality by the passage of
this long period as to commend exactly the sweet reason-
ableness of the words, 'Surely the sun rose as brightly
then as now, and man got him to his work in the morning.'
Scarcely less than Chaucer, Skelton habitually sets forth
like a cheerful sunrise and a jolly workman; there is sunshine and there is action in his ancient and modern verse.
Speaking across so wide a range of time, society, science
and creed, the tutor of Henry VIII and the too candid
friend of Wolsey has power to bring us to our windows with
all the freshness of a known and sudden voice. What has
age to do with Skelton?

[Quotes 'Garland of Laurel', lines 1004-22.]

Nothing could be more instantaneous, though in our date
we have not quite the same inbred notion of the nobility
of falcons.
    This song of Skelton's, springing out from the fif-
teenth century into the twentieth, will not be refused as
a realisation of poetical ubiquity, nor do I quote an
unfamiliar poem. But we must proceed to the admission
that, in spite of his carolling intimacy, Skelton suffers
considerably from the malady of being registered among
the 'old authors.' Between posterity and antiquity there
is always a distorting mist. There are faults on both
sides. In the instance of Skelton, the faults of posterity have been more than usually stubborn and unkind.
The character of the man, which must always imply for the
majority the worth of the poet, has been scribbled upon
with an indolent vaingloriousness. Had he been living in
the eighteenth century, he would have been estimated in
the same vein of cordiality as were Arbuthnot and Gay.
In the nineteenth there would have been little to with-
hold from him a name of breezy honesty and eccentric
virtue, akin to that of Edward FitzGerald. In the twentieth, one may picture him in the sphere of Mr. Chester-
ton, or Mr. Shaw. But being demonstrably an 'old author'
he fell under the careless lash of Pope (himself not the
most infallibly offenceless of wits), and was put in his
place:

    Chaucer's worst ribaldry is learned by rote,
    And beastly Skelton heads of houses quote.

Fifty years later came Thomas Warton, from whom a critical
and personal good-fellowship might have been anticipated
towards a predecessor whom he was professing to have read;
but what had Warton to say? 'It is vain to apologise for

the coarseness, obscenity, and scurrility of Skelton,
by saying that his poetry is tinctured with the manners
of his age. Skelton would have been a writer without
decorum at any period.' Epithets like these of Pope and
Warton, fostered by negligent reading, have overgrown the
simple honour of Skelton the original. While most of us
shrink from active elucidation of the works, we apprehend
that they are not as ingenuous as they might be. Our
minds have been obscurely assured that Skelton was guilty
of producing 'The Tunning of Elinor Rumming.'
      And indeed it is one of his considerable works. Even
Dyce, who stood up so valiantly in defence of Skelton,
glances at its darker reputation with uncertainty: 'If few
compositions of the kind have more coarseness or extravagance, there are few which have greater animation or a
richer humour.' Strong and bitter are its ingredients.
It is rhyming Rowlandson. But I mistake greatly if it is
not as a whole a sharp medicine, and no concoction for the
perverted taste of the insolent. Elinor Rumming is a
witch, her alehouse a den, and the poor slatterns who are
fascinated into it are as the victims of Circe. It is not
Skelton's fault that his startling talent for sketching
human peculiarity makes the poem incidentally a mirror of
low life, nor that his genial preferences come in to vary
his pitiless facsimiles with milder humour. His object
was to show what intemperance can do with the female sex;
to present the contrast between his merry Margarets and
his Margery Milkducks; even (for he was the parson as well
as the laureate) to show some of his congregation, in a
more penetrative form than sermons, the ruinous costliness
of the tavern:

[Quotes 'Elynor Rumming', lines 600-6.]

Let us accord to Skelton the credit given in ordinary to
an author, and consult his own Latin postscript to 'The
Tunning of Elinor Rumming' for his stated intention in the
satire. 'The poet,' he declares, 'invites all women, who
are either too fond of the bottle, or are notorious for
their sluttishness, or their disgraceful indecencies, or
their gossip and clack, to pay attention to this little
book.'
      Skelton was capable of furious and relentless
onslaughts on those who challenged him. Once roused, he
became a human battery of hoarse and hasty invective,
hurling out expressions of contempt by the dozen, serious
and comic mixed, against 'false stinking serpents,'
'Moorish manticors,' 'mockish marmosets.' In that there
is nothing vicious. Rude railing has been practised by

later poets, even Byron and Swinburne, and they are
appreciated. In brief, I may express the conviction that
'beastly Skelton' never mounted the pulpit at Diss, never
set Latin exercises to a Royal pupil; though, at the same
time, we may be grateful for one or two of the nonsensical
remarks made against our poet on the assumption of his
beastliness. So the dear authoress of the 'Lives of the
Queens of England' gathered her forces for a crushing comment: 'It is affirmed that Skelton had been tutor to Henry
VII. in some department of his education. How probable it
is that the corruption imparted by this ribald and ill-
living wretch laid the foundation for his Royal pupil's
grossest crimes!' The final reply to Pope and Warton and
Agnes Strickland, and our own inherited legend, is the
collected poetry of Skelton, whether we consider what has
chiefly produced the misunderstanding - his satire against
drunken women - or his fine, wise and humane allegory
'Magnificence,' or those songs of April and innocence
which seem so like this year's, or that deep-toned direct
utterance of the Crucifixion:

[Quotes 'Wofully Araid', lines 1-6.]

Thus far of the false barrier between us and the manly
truth of Skelton; I come now to the other conditions which
have troubled the understanding between this poet and ourselves. Pope, with another purpose, indicates them:

Authors, like coins, grow dear as they grow old;
It is the rust we value, not the gold. (1)

Yet, though the passion for the antique may preserve some
precious relics of old glory, its process is often only a
disguised limitation. Posterity, which is a very busy
and breathless monster, naturally stands aloof from matter
which it fears to be nearly unintelligible. The scholar
is left to work out the assumed abracadabra of discarded
speech, orthography, interest and allusion. At first
sight, most of the pages of Dyce's Skelton appear too
cryptic to come within the scope of our common reading and
our leisure for it; and Dyce himself only ventured to
offer his two volumes to 'a very limited class of readers.'
Two poets of the younger school, Mr. Robert Graves and Mr.
Richard Hughes, have particularly endeavoured to clear the
air and show Skelton as a living and communicative poet;
for my part I may observe that a great deal of his writings is as natural in style and as clear in significance
as could be wished. The medieval spelling which indeed
veils the outlines or varnishes the hues of his poetry

can with a little labour be made no veil at all; one may
think Skelton into modern English, for long passages
together, with no more strain than that of transliterating
'braynsycke frantycke folys' into 'brainsick frantic
fools.' In my present quotations I have done as much,
taking what perhaps the canon of scholarship may censure
generally as permissible here at least, because the effect
of Skelton's presence is felt on ripened acquaintance
without much accidental interruption: obsolete formalities
do not belong to him; he lives in an essential approach-
ableness. One must see him, if at all, as a friend of
poetry and humanity and not as a perplexing fragment in a
curiosity shop.

  Among the British poets Skelton is remarkable for his
metrical, as for his emotional, independence; his restless
and whimsical nature expresses itself in a volleying
succession of rapid rhythms, made more brilliant by the
fund of alliteration, assonance and unexpected rhyme which
he flings forth. But in his appearance of abandon there
is an art concealed. His free verse is not what Warton
superficially calls it, 'this anomalous and motley mode
of versification.' It is founded on a decisive feeling
for accent, and those 'strong and fastened' syllables
which will carry a play of less obvious ones through a
long composition. It is the literary employment of the
popular song-metre, which requires always a colloquial
indifference, though that is controlled by mood and intention. Swinging, dancing, dodging; laughing, clowning measures are instinctive with Skelton. Thus he seems to
carry on a perpetual campaign against the philosophical
and cloistered iambic, which has obtained so overwhelming
a position in the verse-history of our poets. He cannot
or he will not tread in its ordered placidity. He may
sometimes attempt it, but is soon springing round its
track with incorrigible variations. The secret of this
is perhaps discoverable in his own words:

[Quotes from 'A Replycacion ...', lines 365-78.]

The classic observation of Dr. Harvey as he laid down his
Virgil may more readily be applied to Skelton; he has a
demon, and only a few other writers (such as the poet of
'Hudibras,' or of 'Don Juan') give the same impression of
audacity and urgency. The vigour of syncopation did not
begin with our day; Skelton takes the lead:

[Quotes 'Magnificence', lines 1039-54.]

Under such a merry-andrew fusillade, to be sure, the poet

is not the only one to grow dizzy; and the defect of Skelton is his superfluity of noise and phrase. But while we
admit the monotony into which his voluble ecstasies lead
us, we must allow that his spirit and his metre do yield
graver and sweeter melodies. After the fun of the Skel-
tonian fair comes another voice, and none has exceeded its
mild purity:

[Quotes 'Garland of Laurel', lines 985-92.]

Or the laconic lines will assume a dignity in which the
impossible seems about to happen, and Skelton for a
moment, turned Solomon, dreams of the sublime:

[Quotes 'Upon a Deedmans Hed', lines 7-11.]

For the young poet, wondering at the mystery of words
and attempting the instrument of English verse, in such a
season of discovery as that which sent Keats delighted
through Chapman's Homer, the works of Skelton might be no
unlucky recommendation. A mind naturally safe from excess
of imitative enthusiasm could only win resource and com-
prehension from the diction and music of Skelton's poetical festivity. In the singular poem called the 'Garland
of Laurel,' where occur the faultless lyrics in praise of
Margaret Hussey and Isabel Pennell and other ladies, the
technique of the poet is perhaps most versatile and impressive. The 'Garland of Laurel,' again, is acceptable
to the general friend of Skelton because it displays him
with harmless vanity - indeed, with that pride which
belongs to health and hopefulness - warming both hands
before the fire of his poetic life, and sketching his own
various bibliography with affection. Paler light invests
our later considerations of poetry as a profession. We
have grown timid as writers and as readers. Both as
writer and as reader of his own verse, John Skelton was
radiant with contentment. He blessed his stars that he
was a poet, and that he was a good one.
  Of one of his major performances, and some of his shorter yet not less notable achievements, I have already
taken notice. In commemorating Skelton four hundred years
after his death, it is just to review his principal poems,
so far as they are known to us; and actually, in spite of
his volubility, the total extent of his surviving verse
need not deter anyone from knowing him better. His
closing years were themselves a proof of the influence of
his poetry; they were passed in sanctuary at Westminster,
away from the indignation of Wolsey, who had 'read the
book with interest.' Skelton opened fire on this

prodigious grandee in his 'Colin Clout,' which begins with
a pleasing pretence of the futility of proceeding, since

> The devil, they say, is dead,
> The devil is dead.   [lines 36-7]

Yet, Skelton proceeds, the devil is not dead. He is in the
the Church. Then follows a great catalogue of his mis-
doings, each one stated in short, sharp definition. The
sensual profits which he is making are reckoned; the
luxuries of his new mansions are imagined with lively
irony. These denunciations are at length concentrated
unmistakably,

> For one man to rule a king!   [line 991]

Throughout the whole work Skelton combines solidity of
sense, earnestness of heart and courage of opinion; moreover, the turns of the satire are dramatically forcible,
and the argument is maintained as though by a bioscope of
actual incidents and persons: 'look on this picture - and
on this!'
    In 'Speak, Parrot' the invective against Wolsey is
fearlessly increased; although, had we nothing more of the
poem than the delicate, gay and ingenious overture, we
might be content. Here is the parrot once and for all
among the birds of the British poets, sparkling with
rogue vitality

[Quotes lines 17-23.]

But Skelton's main object is not to vie in verse with
Edward Lear's paintings of parrots. 'Ware the cat,
Parrot, ware the false cat!' Wonderfully does the poet
manipulate his invention. The parrot is put forward with
his little wanton eye - but there are certain things he is
pre-eminently able to detect. He also earns several presents of dates by describing those things with masterly
anger. They are the characteristics of one who

> carryeth a king in his sleeve, if all the world fail;
>   [line 423]

whose

> Wolves' head, wan, blue as lead, gapeth over the crown.
>   [line 428]

'Why Come Ye Not to Court?' is the further exposure of

Wolsey. The tone is curt and final. These, says Skelton,
are the facts; and what will England do to counter them?

[Quotes lines 289-96.]

There could hardly be a more dangerous and momentous calm-
ness than that which Skelton affects by way of a change in
his appeal to the people - the 'simple Hodge' manner:

[Quotes lines 398-406.]

It was no idle fancy in 'Colin Clout' that the author, as
he wandered through the streets, had the knack of hearing
what people said. Skelton is rich in the tune and term of
shop door, ale bench, market-place; quaintly learned and
of a wide-roaming fancy, he brings his subject home with
the sudden directness of language immediately conceived
in necessities. If in this part of his poetic method he
draws upon the harsher weapons of the vulgar tongue, I
hold that his natural brightness of character remains un-
sullied; his 'anger has a privilege'; and so, in his last
condemnation of Wolsey, the occasional brutality is to be
regarded as marking his complete belief in the mission of
his satire. The marvel is that he escaped; had he been
what he has been counted, a mere buffoon, there would have
been no marvel; but Skelton wrote with an inspired per-
secution, comparable with the voice that cried in the
wilderness.
    Two admirable productions of Skelton's on the large
plan remain for my annotation. 'Philip Sparrow,' which
Coleridge (who never confused ancient date with vanished
value) found 'exquisite and original,' is his prettiest
work. It combines a dirge for a pet bird with a song in
honour of the bird's owner; and, although Catullus had
shown what beautiful caprice could be expressed on such an
occasion, it might not have been thought that a new poet
would so enrich and illumine and berhyme the matter as
Skelton does. Orthodoxy might demur at his parody of the
service book, which nevertheless demanded genius, of
humour as of metre:

    De pro fun dis cla ma vi
    When I saw my sparrow die.   [lines 145-6]

All that is noticed of the sparrow is touched with a
choice Lilliputian lightness, and with a mythological play
that here and there adventures into the higher air of
romance. The funeral congregation of birds, too, though
doubtless of an heraldic rather than ornithological

circumstance, is a profusion of 'sounds and sweet airs.'
And at last when the poet turns from the lament for Philip,
while the sun with sympathetic leave-taking sinks west-
ward, then he surprises us after his many inventions by
discovering a strong and happy impulse, culminating in the
song to her who

> Flourisheth new and new
> In beauty and virtue:
> Hac claritate gemina
> O gloriosa femina.   [lines 896-99]

Gems and blossoms, which he chooses in order to express
this lady's grace, might be the images of his own style in
a singing so matins-like.

The interlude 'Magnificence' is Skelton's most serious
imaginative design. In this play the characters are
abstractions, as Felicity, Liberty, Measure, Counterfeit
Countenance, Crafty Conveyance; but there is no thin
abstract monotony in their dialogues or speeches. The
campaign of integrity and decency against licence and
sharp practice is fought out with freedom of incident and
keenness of stroke; excellent fooling makes the didactic
and moralising passages more agreeable. The pleasure of
Skelton's shrewdness, and of his mastery of aphorism, pro-
verb and the wit of the crowd, is deepened by his apparently invincible skill in rhyme, with which he points and
quickens the dialogues as though our ordinary talk ran
that way:

[Quotes lines 1152-7.]

Such byplay contributes to the ultimate sobering of magnificence with 'sad circumspection,' and the whole may
make us grieve that the interlude ascribed to Skelton by
Warton, on a Necromancer, has either disappeared, or as
some sceptical observers of Warton declare (as though
avenging Skelton for the view of him in the 'History of
English Poetry') never existed.

Skelton at all events existed. No necromancy placed
him there between Chaucer and Marlowe, an erratic luminary darting his fireworks, in defiance of all other
poetic rays and splendours, as the whim struck,

> From Ocean the great sea
> Unto the Isles of Orcady,
> From Tilbury ferry
> To the plain of Salisbury.   ['Philip Sparrow',
>   lines 318-21]

He has been regarded as a decidedly unheavenly body.
Among folks of this world, however, I take him to have
been a genuine worthy and entirely a man to have on one's
side - an anticipation, in some measure, both of the temper and the talents of Swift. There was in him, however,
a greener leaf than that great nature could put forth.
When these and other attempts at an estimate of Skelton
have been made, one thing remains certain: it is long
enough since the item, 'of Mr. Skelton for viii. tapers
o1. 2s. 8d.' was entered in the churchwarden's accounts
of St. Margaret's Westminster, but still we find a pathos
in the substitution of those dim lights at last for the
sunlight so heartily enjoyed and glorified by the
laurelled Skelton.

Note

1 Pope, 'Imitations of Horace', Epistle II, i, 35-6.

50. HUMBERT WOLFE ON SKELTON'S INNOVATION

1929

From 'Notes on English Verse Satire' (London, 1929),
pp. 42-8. Wolfe (1885-1940) was a poet and essayist.

Time, on the whole, is a trusty critic. Not frequently,
nor for long periods, will he slight a great talent. On
the rare occasions that he does full atonement is made, as
with Herrick, whose star burns ever brighter after a dusky
first ascension. Of diamonds he is as expert a cutter as
those of Holland, though he may sometimes permit a semi-
precious stone to be mislaid among featureless pebbles.
But John Skelton is one of Time's errors, and he must be
sternly impeached for this lack. In a book claiming some
authority, 'The English Poets', edited by Thomas Ward,
Mr. Churton Collins writes thus of Skelton: 'Skelton's
claims to notice lie not so much in the intrinsic excellence of his work as in the complete originality of his
style, in the variety of his powers, in the peculiar
character of his satire, and in the ductility of his

expression when ductility of expression was unique.' He
continues with amiable condescension, 'These poems [the
Satires] are all written in that headlong voluble breathless doggerel ... often caustic and pithy, and sometimes
rising to a moral earnestness which contrasts strangely
with their uncouth and ludicrous apparel.' But lest we
should concede too much to the rogue, Mr. Collins notably
concludes in respect of 'Elinore Rummynge' that 'In this
sordid and disgusting delineation of humble life he may
fairly challenge the supremacy of Swift and Hogarth.'
[See No. 47.] In his mild and obscure way Mr. Collins
seeks to do for Skelton what Morley with greater publicity
did for Swinburne. (1) But the task of Collins was
easier, because his was the less heroic task of flogging a
dead lion.

It is not difficult to understand why Victorian shabby
gentility waved a black-gloved hand severely at this
shameless friend of naked truth. The period which sub-
stituted 'too much of nothing' for the Greek 'nothing too
much' could not but have sought to damn him with faint
praise. But why did the Elizabethans ignore him, why had
he no place in the Augustan age, and why is he still known
only to the learned and the curious?

Something must, as with Dunbar, be due to the mere difficulty of his language, though it is nearer to us than
that of the Scots poet. But more to the inopportunity of
his birth. The dates of his birth and death are conjec-
turally placed at the middle of the fifteenth and at the
end of the third decade of the sixteenth century. He was
born, therefore, in the queasy time of the Yorkists, was
in the twenties when Richard fell at Bosworth, and lived
to see the eighth Henry, and what is even more to the
point, bitterly to attack the great Cardinal Wolsey.
These were times too unsettled for the poet. Civil War
and Reformation are not nurses of the Arts. It was his
misfortune to be one of the strong that had lived before
Agamemnon. The Elizabethans, beginning with Marlowe,
seemed to step ready-armed from the head of the virgin
Queen. They were too dazzled with the light of their own
splendour to look back to the preceding dark. Their eyes
were on Italy and on Spain. They might (as Shakespeare
often did) hear echoes of country chanties. But for the
rest Italy and the Renaissance served their need.

Skelton suffered too because he was as English as
Hogarth, and as great a master of his craft. Mr. Collins
makes the comparison almost by way of cursing. But any
writer (or painter) who can sustain that comparison is
blessed indeed. Skelton, when all were for foreign
examples, was unshakably English. That would not commend

him. But more than that he was a sturdy innovator in
verse forms. What Mr. Collins calls headlong doggerel is
on the contrary a quite startling mastery of prosody.
Not only had nobody before Skelton used the form he so
brilliantly applied in such poems as those against Garnesche, but no one has been able completely to master it
since. Doggerel? What is the test of a verse-form? That
it should fit the matter and express the mind of the
maker, and that it should both move and sing. Did ever
any verse more completely fulfil these criteria than such
as this in the lament on Philip Sparowe?

[Quotes lines 127-37.]

Every trick, not excluding that of enjambement, is there.
This is not writing about the sparrow. It is the sparrow
in a verse that jerks it as neat as his two strutting
feet. Nor does it fit only the rapid narrative. It can
be slow in denunciation, as:

> That vengeaunce I ask and crye
> By way of exclamacyon
> On all the hole nacyon
> Of cattes wild and tame!
> God send them sorrow and shame!   [lines 273-7]

And it can even rise to a certain mock-heroic tragedy
with:

> Farewell, Phillyp, adeu!
> Our Lorde thy soule reskew!
> Farewell, without restore!
> Farewell for evermore!   [lines 331-4]

Doggerel! I wish that we had more English poets capable
of writing it.
     As an innovator he was, however, doubly unfortunate.
All such are opposed in their beginnings, but it happens
often that they become the dogma of the succeeding age.
Skelton suffered from the strange accident that he was
immediately succeeded by innovators as violent as himself, and of greater genius. It seemed, indeed, as
though Fate itself had decided that to be three times
Laureate was not merely an end but a termination in
itself.
     Professor Collins, in the passage dismissing 'the in-
trinsic excellence' of Skelton's work, calls attention
among instances of its lack of intrinsic excellence to
'the peculiar character of his satire.' The adjective is

not ill-chosen. Like the rest of his work Skelton's
satire is 'peculiar' in the sense that he was the first
Englishman to write so. Chaucer, his master in the form
of such a poem as 'The Bowge of Court', could and indeed
did teach him nothing in the form of 'Colin Cloute'.
While Dunbar - the best of his predecessors - hit the mark
with a cross-bow, Skelton was rattling away with a machine-
gun. His is the very ecstasy of vituperation, but with a
mock breathlessness for ever regaining its second wind.
If ever a man hated heartily and honestly, if ever a man
had the gift to brand that clearly and ringingly, that man
was Skelton. Hear him 'Against the Scottes'

[Quotes lines 99-102.]

Or in the tremendous denunciation of 'Colin Cloute', that
hits all the harder for the scornful laughter implicit in
its very form

[Quotes lines 595-7, 644-53, 666-72.]

And still another and harsher mood let Parotte 's'en va
complayndre':

[Quotes 'Speak Parrot', lines 470-6.]

   This is unhappily not the place to deal with Skelton's
qualities as a lyric poet. Professor Collins is good
enough to observe that he 'deserves mention' in this
regard. He does. Here it is sufficient to let his
satires mention themselves - in no uncertain tone.
   At the end of one of the most barren periods in all
English verse Skelton is the sown at the edge of the
desert. Unhappily time has permitted the sand-storms
behind to overwhelm him. In front in brilliant contrast
stretch the green uplands of Elizabeth. That is his great
misfortune, but ours is greater still if we permit it to
continue. We cannot claim that he influenced the course
of literature after this time. His immediate successors -
Wyatt and Surrey - wrote as though Skelton had never
existed. Nor is there a trace in Hall and Marston - the
Elizabethan satirists - of his influence. He remains
unique. There are worse fates.

Note

1 John Morley, the Victorian critic, who launched a
   savage and influential attack on Swinburne's 'Poems and
   Ballads' in the 'Saturday Review' (1866).

51. ROBERT GRAVES ON HENDERSON'S EDITION OF SKELTON

1931

Originally published as An Incomplete Complete Skelton in
'Adelphi', III (1931-2), pp. 146-58. This article is a
review of Philip Henderson's 1931 edition of Skelton.
    Graves (1896-) is former Oxford Professor of Poetry and
a distinguished poet, scholar and critic.

Mr. Philip Henderson, in the introduction to his edition
to 'The Complete Poems of John Skelton,' tells that it is
only in the last ten years that Skelton has begun to be
rediscovered popularly as a poet. The first and the most
enthusiastic modern rediscoverer was, let me say at once,
myself; and if I had not done so much to create a demand
for a Complete Skelton this book would not be here for me
to review. So I have no hesitation in complaining on
Skelton's behalf and on my own that Mr. Henderson has
bungled his job. I only wish he had bungled it much
worse: I have read several reviews of the book and none
of the reviewers seem to have realised what is being put
over on them. They are just blankly grateful that at last
they have a Complete Skelton to fill that blank on their
shelves. And so the book will sell and nobody will think
of asking for a better one. Except myself.
    But first about Skelton. He was born about 1460 and
died in 1529. Henry VII made him tutor to Henry, Duke of
York, afterwards Henry VIII, for whom he wrote a handbook
of princely behaviour called 'Speculum Principis,' and
who appears to have had great personal fondness for him,
making him his Poet Laureate when he succeeded to the
throne. Skelton was a famous scholar and a friend of
Erasmus. But without pedantry. He was opposed to the
Greek cult in the universities because it was too academic:

[Quotes 'Speak Parrot', lines 150-2.]

He was Laureate of Oxford, Cambridge and Louvain, an
aggressive enemy of Church abuses, rector of Diss in
Norfolk, and the only man in England who had the courage
to stand up against Cardinal Wolsey when he was at the
height of his power and tell him what he really thought of
him. For instance, that he was a cur, a butcher's dog,

that he hated religion, that he suffered from the pox,
that the Pope had given him a special indulgence for
lechery on account of his natural incontinence, that he
knew no Latin, that his pride was immense and insane, that
one day he would lose the King's favour and come to complete ruin, and that he was an obscene Polyphemus.
Against Wolsey he wrote popular verse-satires which had
a wide circulation among the common people. They were not
intended as serious poetry but were put in easy rhyme for
the convenience of ballad circulation. Though 'Colin
Clout' and 'Why Come Ye Not to Court?' have a strong historical appeal which tempts professors of literature to
misrepresent them as Skelton's most important work, and
though Skelton took a lot of trouble with them –

   To makë such trifles it asketh some cunning –

it is not on their account that Skelton has been rediscovered. They are still trifles. Wolsey was slow in
taking action against Skelton, whose position at Court was
extremely strong. He was the privileged buffoon, compan-
ion to Henry in his adventures among the common people and
playfellow of the young Court ladies. His open jealousy
of Wolsey's political influence with the King seems to
have been regarded at Court as a standing joke. Wolsey
would be thought a dull fellow if he did not laugh too,
especially when the joker was so obviously at his mercy –
a priest subject to his princely authority as Cardinal.
Finally Wolsey seems to have entered into the spirit of
the joke, which was not a joke really. No more of a joke
than that other part of Skelton's buffoonery, his glori-
ous self-admittance in 'The Garland of Laurel' to the
House of Fame. For Skelton knew perfectly well how good
a poet he was, and Wolsey knew perfectly well what real
dislike Skelton had for him. Wolsey sent him to prison.
Skelton refused to take this as a joke and complained
loudly to his friends, who brought the news to Wolsey.
The story is that Wolsey then sent for him and abused
him at length. Skelton, kneeling with mock humility,
asked for a boon. Wolsey refused it. Some court offi-
cials, aware of the joke that wasn't really, tried to
ease things by persuading Wolsey to grant the boon. 'It
may be a merry conceit that he would show to your Grace.'
It was. 'I pray Your Grace to let me lie down and wallow,
for I can kneel no longer.'
   Skelton had a 'musket' to whom he was devoted (secretly
his wife) and by whom he had several children. He did not
believe in the celibacy of the clergy and used his buffoon's reputation as a way of keeping her with him. He

obeyed the Bishop's order to send her out of his door but
took her back through the window. He brought his child
into church and told the congregation that they had no
good cause to complain about him, as they had done. It
was a very nice-looking child, he said, not a monstrous
birth, with a calf's or a pig's head, or with wings like
a bird. They were unreasonable. 'And if you cannot be
contented that I have her (his wife) still, some of you
shall wear horns.'

Skelton went too far with his satires, and his privileged position counted for nothing when the King was so
dependent on Wolsey for raising money and arranging his
divorce. He was finally compelled to take sanctuary at
Westminster, where he lived six years until his death,
being buried obscurely in a neighbouring church. Wolsey's
fall came soon after.

Skelton's poems. About a third of his works survive.
The titles of those that have been lost raise regrets.
'The Ballad of the Mustard Tart.' 'A Devout Prayer to
Moses' Horns.' 'John Jew.' 'The Grunting of the Swine.'
'The Pageants of Joyous Garde.' 'Minerva and the Olive
Tree.' 'Apollo Whirléd Up His Chair.' But there is still
that surviving third, and the range of poetry in them is
very wide. There is the 'Tunning of Elinor Rumming,'
written at Henry's request about an ale-wife at an inn
near Leatherhead. It is very pleasantly piggish and has
given Skelton a bad name. The ale was so good - not only
malt went into it but other accidental farmyard ingredients which gave it body - that all the women for miles
around came to the Tunning (brewing) to get drunk on it.
They paid Elinor in kind:

[Quotes 'Elynor Rumming', lines 244-8, 303-8.]

and soon lost all modesty.

Then there is 'Philip Sparrow,' a long nonsense
elegy for little Jane Scrope's bird which was killed by
a cat in the Black Nuns' convent at Carow where Jane was
at school.

[In this fore-runner of 'Who Killed Cock Robin?' occur,
by the way, some seventy first-mentions in English of
different bird-species.]

[Quotes lines 386-402.]

Then there are Skelton's popular songs. 'Lullay,
lullay, like a child,' 'Mannerly Margery Milk and Ale,'
and 'Rutterkin, Hoyda.' And his satire on the Scots.
And 'Magnificence,' a lively play in the morality style

but with no religious characters in it. Among Skelton's
other distinctions is that he was the originator of the
English secular drama. Then his 'Prayer to the Father of
Heaven':

[Quotes lines 1-8.]

And his poem 'Woefully Array'd' about the Crucifixion,
beginning:

[Quotes lines 1-6.]

And the early 'Elegy for the Death of King Edward IV.'
And the macaronic 'Trentale on the Death of Old John
Clarke sometimes called The Holy Patriarch of Diss,' which
ends:

> *Sepultus est* among the weeds,
> God forgive him his misdeeds!
> With hey, ho, rumbelbow,
> *Rumpopulorum*
> *Per omnia saecula saeculorum.*   ['A Devoute Trentale',
>   lines 18-19, 61-3]

And then 'Speak Parrot' in which, as if to resolve
these apparent contradictions, the Philip Sparrow sentiment and the Father of Heaven sentiment and the Colin
Clout sentiment and all the other sentiments fuse in a
great parrot-confusion of serious gibberish. The joke
once more that is not really a joke; and Skelton's most
peculiar poem. Why has Skelton been forgotten so long?
It has not been merely because of his reputation for
beastliness - Urquhart's translation of Rabelais has
always been deservedly popular among the educated classes.
It is that he has always been too difficult, not only in
his language, so full of obsolete words, but in his
metres, which became unintelligible as soon as the iambic
metre and syllable-counting overcame the native English
style of writing, musically, in stresses.
    In the late eighteenth century Chaucer was rediscovered
in spite of his obsolete vocabulary; but then Chaucer
wrote iambics. The early nineteenth century was so pre-
occupied with the Elizabethans that it could afford to go
no further back than Wyatt and Surrey in the direct line
of English Poetry, except to Chaucer as to an unaccountable Melchizedek. Skelton was over the boundary-line in
the pre-sonnet, that is to say, in the pre-poetry epoch.
From 'Beowulf' to Skelton was the province of the antiquary, not of the reader of poetry.

But the antiquarians had consciences, and the Reverend
Alexander Dyce spent twenty years or so on an antiquarian
edition of Skelton's complete works. That was in 1843, and
and he did his job extraordinarily well. But there has
not been a re-issue of the book. A Dyce's Skelton, if you
are lucky enough to get one, will cost you at least five
pounds. Since 1843 there has been a great extension of
the boundaries of English poetry. Henrysoun and Gavin
Douglas have been rediscovered and Child's 'British
Ballads' and Chambers and Sidgwick's 'Early English
Lyrics' have appeared. And even 'Beowulf' has been recognised as a real poem. And in the later traditional line,
too, certain misfit poets who did not seem to belong because they wrote too personally have been given garlands
of laurel and published popularly in decent collected editions. Blake and Donne, for example. Skelton was misfit
as well as pre-sonnet, so his rediscovery has been the
longest delayed.

Dyce was a very capable antiquarian. He routed out all
the manuscripts and all the black-letter books he could
hear about and reprinted the texts in their original
spelling, letter by letter. And so anyone who has money
and buys a Dyce and is prepared to recognise any poetry
that there may be there waiting for him will find it very
hard to keep the poetry sense of what he is reading when
he has to deal with words like 'puplysshyd' (published),
'ffylty' (filthy), 'preuye' (privy), and 'Diologgis of
Ymagynacioun' (Dialogues of Imagination). He will almost
certainly give it up.

I read the Parrot's: 'With my beke I kan pyke my
lyttel praty to' several times before I recognised that
he meant that he could peck his little pretty toe.

In 1915 someone gave me a Skelton and I made the discovery
and wrote about it. Ever since I have been asking for a
Complete Skelton, an improvement on Dyce's book, with his
notes re-edited in the light of recent antiquarian research, and newly discovered poems added, and the spelling
modernised enough to make it at least as readable as the
Globe edition of Chaucer. A publisher wanted me to do the
job myself, but I refused because I had not the time or
the research equipment to do it worthily. The only Skelton I have edited since is a sixpenny book of extracts for
the 'Augustan' Series, and that was merely more ground-
bait for an improved Dyce.

In 1924 Richard Hughes, to whom I had introduced Skelton when he was still a schoolboy, undertook, without
mentioning his intention to me, to prepare an edition.
He had never done the necessary research work, but he

borrowed a copy of Dyce from an Oxford Library and sat
down in a remote cottage in North Wales to do the sort of
book that needed only an intelligent copyist. Among the
curious omissions of Mr. Hughes's edition are 'Lullay,
lullay, like a child,' and the 'Addition to Philip
Sparrow,' which is almost the best part of the poem....

Mr. Philip Henderson is a young poet, as Mr. Richard
Hughes was in 1923; but Mr. Hughes had at least the
enthusiasm of a young poet. Mr. Henderson, without any
of the equipment of a scholar, has made a tedious bluff
of being one - writing as if with a scholar's moderation.
He has put a little more work into the job than Mr.
Hughes. He has visited the British Museum and consulted
the recent authorities and put in two short new pieces
which he found in Brie's 'Skelton-Studien.' But he has
not apparently been to the trouble of studying the original manuscripts and printed texts, even in this country -
taking Dyce's word for variant readings; still less has he
found an American correspondent to help him with readings
from the many important black-letter Skelton texts in the
United States. Worse than not being a scholar, or getting
the co-operation of scholars, he has not even shown a
common-sense consistency in presenting his modernisations
of Dyce. And he has proved himself to be without any true
ear for Skelton's rhythms. He has had the effrontery to
write of Skelton (who was, to say only that, one of the
most skilful metrists in English) that 'Skelton's line
should not be read as iambics even when they approximate
to such smoothness, which is not often, for by attempting
to read them in that way we shall turn what, in its own
time, *was fairly regular and artistic verse* into wretched
halting stuff.' He has been explaining about the final e
which in Skelton's time was being less frequently sounded
than in the time of Chaucer. He admits that he often
cannot be sure in Skelton's lines whether the Elizabethan
printers of Skelton (whose manuscripts have mostly been
lost) have not omitted terminal e's from their editions
which Skelton intended to be sounded. So he is content,
he says, to mark only those which are necessary for scansion. Fairly artistic scansion only. The fact is, that
scansion is not as easy with Skelton as with Chaucer, for
readers without ears. Chaucer's syllable-counted iambics
allow no mistake.

Whan that Aprillë with her shourës sootë can only be
read one way. With Skelton, readers without ears can
make mistakes. He wrote by stress.

Let me explain what I mean, by analogy. Nursery
rhymes are written by stress. Take the rhyme:

Misty moisty was the morn,
    Chilly was the weather:
There I saw an old man
    Dressed all in leather ...

Suppose that, being mediaeval in composition, this rhyme
had survived only as an Elizabethan broadside, reading
there:

Myste moiste was the morn,
    Chylle was the weather ...

It would then be *possible* to modernise it, disregarding
the final *e* as:

Mist-moist was the morn,
    Chill was the weather;

but obviously *wrong* to do so, because of the general needs
of the rhythm. Or take the last line of 'Humpty-Dumpty,'
to which common nursery usage rightly gives an extra bar
(so as to mark the catastrophe with a long-drawn out sad-
ness), by putting the stress on *Couldn't* instead of on
put. If this were modernised into 'Couldn't put Humpt-
Dumpt together again' that also would be obviously wrong.
Mr. Philip Henderson has made far too many misty-moisties
into mist-moists and Humpty-Dumpties into Humpt-Dumpts.
To take the first four lines in his book, the opening
stanza of the 'Elegy on the Death of King Edward IV.'
He prints:

Miseremini me, ye that be my friends!
    This world hath conforméd me down to fall.
How may I endure, when that everything ends?
    What creature is born to be eternall?   [lines 1-4]

There is a misprint in the first line, *me* for *mei*.
'Down to fall' is sheerest Humpt-dumpt. There must be a
sounded *e* at the end of 'down.' Edward did not fall like
a sack of coals; it is a tragic not a comic piece. The
original reading of 'friends' is 'frendis,' and the word
should be kept two-syllabled, and so should 'endis.'
'Creature' was in Skelton's time pronounced 'Crëature' and
'eternall' was pronounced 'aeternall' with an accent on
all three syllables. Mr. Henderson elsewhere makes
'creature' three-syllabled by dotting the *e*, so that it is
clear that he reads it here as only two. And he does not
give 'born' a final *e*. What is the result? Humpt-dumpt-
mist-moist, fairly artistic, wretched, halting stuff!

About that Latin misprint. Mr. Henderson seems to have
been dependent on an uncle for 'worrying out' the meaning
of the Latin parts of Skelton's poems; and to have only a
rudimentary knowledge of Latin himself. (Also of Greek
and Spanish, which he mistranslates.) But he might have
taken the trouble to copy the texts properly for the
benefit of others who are better educated. For instance,
Skelton's obscure Latin hexameter cypher in the satire
'Ware the Hawk' is made more obscure than ever by the
omission of four separate letters (including lines over
vowels which indicate terminal consonants) in the four
lines.

Modernisation should be consistent. Mr. Henderson has
no consistency. The word written 'toote' by Skelton,
meaning to peer, is sometimes made 'toot' and sometimes
'tote.' He sometimes spells the three-syllabled 'ladyes'
like that, and sometimes makes it two-syllabled, as
'ladies.' He modernises 'denty' as 'dainty,' except
in 'prickmedenty,; where he does not apparently recognise
it. Prick-me-dainty is a word used to describe one of
Elinor Rumming's customers who behaved coyly and affect-
edly, as if she were ashamed of finding herself in such
low company. There are women like her in the private-
bars of London public-houses every Saturday night. To
turn the coarse 'prick-me-dainty' into a refined 'per-
nicketty,' as Mr. Henderson does in a foot-note, is
doing the situation an injustice. In another footnote to
'Elinor Rumming' Mr. Henderson has invented a mediaeval·
verb, 'I tun, thou tunnest, he tuns,' meaning 'I fall,
thou fallest, he falls,' by a misreading of a simple
passage to which Dyce has, for once, given no note.
About the hens contributing their share to the brew:

> And dongĕ, when it comĕs,
> Into the ale tunnĕs.   ['Elynor Rumming', lines 193-4]

He has mistaken 'dongĕ' for a noun and 'ale; for a noun
on its own, and 'tunnes' for a verb. Whereas 'dongĕ' is
the verb, and 'ale-tunnĕs' are the ale tuns in which
Elinor was doing her tunning. Scholars are not supposed
to guess at words like that. On another occasion we find
him incorporating an explanatory note in the text:-

> Also a Devout Prayer to Moses' Hornĕs
> Metrified merrily, meddelĕd with scornĕs   ['Garland of
>   Laurel', lines 1381-2]

Mr. Henderson has explained 'meddelĕd' to himself as
'minglĕd' and then accidentally put 'mingled' up into the

line. This is wrong from every point of view. It spoils
the rhythm by removing a syllable, it spoils the succession of short *me*'s, and Skelton did not write it. These
instances could be multiplied. He has not, I think, left
out any of Skelton's verses, except those which preface
his 'Book of Three Fools' - he should have put those in,
of course. But he has left out Skelton's Latin marginal
notes to 'Speak Parrot,' 'A Replication' and the 'Garland
of Laurel,' and that is bad. To go on saying the same
thing, I am afraid that these omissions and the many in-
accuracies mentioned above and all the other faults will
not be noticed, or considered important enough, if
noticed, to justify the competitive publication of the
really Complete Skelton that has been so long wanted.
Mr. Henderson has probably delayed that for another ten
years or more.

But that pretending mature sobriety, for which, on the
jacket of this book Arnold Bennett praised his 'First
Poems,' and which is really so disgraceful in a young
poet! It even allows him to write here:

Although no one would pretend that Skelton was a
great poet, one hesitates to apply to him the epithet
'minor.' One feels all the while that he worked at
a disadvantage -

What is wrong with Mr. Henderson? What difficult emotion is he suppressing? One feels that one hesitates to
guess, but that it is probably so. One suspects, in fact,
that *Mr. Henderson is a Proud Scot*. Especially when he
writes:

Skelton's savage exultance over the Scottish defeat
at Flodden is sufficient to show that for all his culture, he still had a good deal of the unredeemed bar-
barian in him.

Skelton disliked the Proud Scots very heartily and
pleasantly. He would have disliked Mr. Henderson particularly, as being also one of those:

Stoicall studiantes and friscaioly younkerkyns much
better bayned than brained, surmised unsurely in their
perihermenial principles to prate and preach proudly
and lewdly and loudly to lie.

Yes, that is almost certainly right about the Scottish-
ness. The unusual and nervous display of foot-notes to
Skelton's 'Against the Scots' cannot be a coincidence.

I will take a risk on it. So:

> Walk, Scot,
> Walk, sot,
> Rail not so far!   ['...Dundas ... Caudas contra
>   Angligenas', lines 61-3]

Not that Mr. Henderson rails. With a scholar's moderation
he merely scoffs.

52. W.H. AUDEN ON SKELTON 'THE ENTERTAINER'

1935

John Skelton by Wystan Hugh Auden, included in 'The Great
Tudors', edited by K. Garvin (London, 1935), pp. 55-67.
This essay has not hitherto been reprinted: several
corrections subsequently made to the text by Auden are
included here for the first time.
   Auden (1907-73) was one of the foremost twentieth-
century poets as well as an important critic.

To write an essay on a poet who has no biography, no
message, philosophical or moral, who has neither created
characters, nor expressed critical ideas about the literary art, who was comparatively uninfluenced by his predecessors, and who exerted no influence upon his successors, is not easy. Skelton's work offers no convenient
critical pegs. Until Mr. Robert Graves drew attention to
his work some years ago, he was virtually unknown outside
University-honour students, and even now, though there
have been two editions, in the last ten years, those of
Mr. Hughes and Mr. Henderson, it is doubtful whether the
number of his readers has very substantially increased.
One has only to compare him with another modern discovery,
Hopkins, to realise that he has remained a stock literary
event rather than a vital influence.
   My own interest dates from the day I heard a friend at
Oxford, who had just bought the first Hughes edition,
make two quotations:

> Also the mad coot
> With bald face to toot ['Philip Sparrow', lines 410-11]

and

> Till Euphrates that flood driveth
> me into Ind,   ['Speak Parrot', line 4]

and though I should not claim my own case as typical, yet
I doubt if those to whom these lines make no appeal are
likely to admire Skelton.

Though little that is authentic is known of Skelton's
life, a fairly definite portrait emerges from his work: a
conservative cleric with a stray sense of humour, devoted
to the organisation to which he belonged and to the cultural tradition it represented, but critical of its
abuses, possibly a scholar, but certainly neither an aca-
demic-dried boy or a fastidious highbrow; no more unpreju-
diced or well-informed about affairs outside his own province than the average modern reader of the newspapers,
but shrewd enough within it, well read in the conventional
good authors of his time, but by temperament more
attracted to more popular and less respectable literature,
a countryman in sensibility, not particularly vain, but
liking to hold the floor, fond of feminine society, and
with a quick and hostile eye for *pompositas* in all its
forms.

Born in 1460, he probably took his degree at Cambridge
in 1484, and was awarded a laureate degree by Cambridge,
Oxford, and Louvain, which I suppose did not mean much
more then than winning an essay prize or the Newdigate
would to-day, became tutor to the future Henry VIII, was
sufficiently well known socially to be mentioned by
Erasmus and Caxton; took orders at the age of thirty-
eight, became Rector of Diss, his probable birthplace,
about 1500; began an open attack on Wolsey in 1519, and
died in sanctuary at Westminster in 1529. Thus he was
born just before Edward IV's accession, grew up during the
Wars of the Roses, and died in the year of Wolsey's fall
and the Reformation Parliament. In attempting to trace
the relations between a poet's work and the age in which
he lived, it is well to remember how arbitrary such deduc-
tions are. One is presented with a certain number of
facts like a heap of pebbles, and the number of possible
patterns which one can make from them are almost infinite.
To prove the validity of the pattern one chooses, it would
be necessary first to predict that if there were a poet in
such and such a period he would have such and such poetical qualities, and then for the works of that poet to be
discovered with just those qualities. The literary historian can do no more than suggest one out of many possible views.

Politically Skelton's period is one of important
change. The Plantagenet line had split into two hostile

branches, ending one in a lunatic and the other in a
criminal. The barons turned their weapons upon each other
and destroyed themselves; all the English Empire in France
except Calais was gone; the feudal kind of representative
government was discredited and the Church corrupt. The
wealth of the country was beginning to accumulate in the
hands of the trading classes, such as wool merchants, and
to be concentrated in the cities of the traders. Traders
want peace which gives them liberty to trade rather than
political liberty, secular authority rather than a religious authority which challenges their right to usury and
profit. They tend therefore to support an absolute mon-
archy, and unlike a feudal aristocracy with its international family loyalties, to be nationalist in sentiment.
Absolute monarchies adopt *real politik* and though Machia-
velli's 'Prince' was not published till 1513, his principles were already European practice.

Skelton's political views are those of the average man
of his time and class. A commoner, he had nothing to lose
by the destruction of the old nobility; like the majority
of his countrymen, he rejoices at royal weddings and
national victories, and weeps at royal funerals and
national defeats. With them also he criticises Henry
VII's avarice.

Immensas sibi divitias cumulasse quid horres?   ['Elegy
                                     on Henry VII', line 15]

[Why were you shocked that you had accumulated great
                                              riches?]

Like a good bourgeois he is horrified at the new fash-
ions and worldliness at Henry VIII's court, but cannot
attribute it to the monarch himself, only to his companions; and hates the arrogance and extravagance of Wolsey,
who by social origin was no better than himself.

In religious matters he is naturally more intelligent
and better informed. Though Wyclif died in 1384, his doctrines were not forgotten among the common people, and
though Skelton did not live to see the English Reformation, before he was fifty Luther had pinned his protest to
the church door at Wittenberg, and he lived through the
period of criticism in the Intelligentsia ('The Praise of
Folly' was written in 1503) which always precedes a mass
political movement.

The society of Colet, Grocyn, Linacre, and More was an
intellectual and international one, a society of scholars
who, like all scholars, overestimated their capacity to
control or direct events. Skelton's feelings towards them

were mixed. Too honest not to see and indeed in 'Colin Clout' unsparingly to attack the faults of the Church, he was like them and like the intelligent orthodox at any time, a reformer not a revolutionary, that is to say, he thought that the corruptions of the Church and its dogmatic system were in no way related; that you could by a 'change of heart' cure the one without impairing the other; while the revolutionary, on the other hand, attributes the corruption directly to the dogmas, for which he proposes to substitute another set which he imagines to be fool-proof and devil-proof. Towards the extremists he was frightened and hostile.

[Quotes 'Colin Clout', lines 542-3, 548-52.]

His difference from the early reformers was mainly temperamental. He was not in the least donnish and, moving perhaps in less rarefied circles, saw that the effect of their researches on the man in the street, like the effect on our own time, for example of Freud, was different from what they intended.

He has been unjustly accused of opposing the study of Greek; what he actually attacked was the effect produced by the impact of new ideas upon the average man, never in any age an edifying spectacle.

[Quotes 'Speak Parrot', lines 146-52.]

As a literary artist, it is difficult to escape the conclusion that Skelton is an oddity, like Blake, who cannot be really fitted into literary history as an inevitable product of the late fifteenth century. There is every reason for the existence of Hawes or even Barclay as the moribund end of the Chaucerian tradition; it is comparatively easy to understand Elizabethan poetry as a fusion of the Italian Renaissance and native folk elements; but the vigour and character of Skelton's work remains unpredictable.

One may point out that the Narrenschiff influenced the 'Bouge of Court,' that Skeltonics may be found in early literature like the Proverbs of Alfred,

> Ac if pu him lest welde
> > werende on worlde.
> Lude as stille
> > His owene wille, (1)

or that the style of his Latin verses occurs in Goliardic poetry or Abelard.

> *Est in Rama*
> *Vox audita*
> *Rachel fluentes*
> *Eiolantes*
> *Super natos*
> *Interfectos.*

But that a writer should be found at that particular date
who would not succumb to aureate diction, and without
being a folk writer, should make this kind of rhythm the
basis of work, would seem, if it had not occurred,
exceedingly improbable.

Excluding 'Magnificence,' Skelton's poetry falls
naturally into four divisions: the imitations of the
'aureate' poetry of Lydgate and similar fifteenth-century
verses, such as the elegy on the Duke of Northumberland
and the prayers to the Trinity; the lyrics; the poems in
rhyme royal such as the 'Bouge of Court' and 'Speke
Parrot'; and those like 'Elinor Rumming,' 'Philip
Sparrow,' and 'Colin Clout,' written in skeltonics.

Of the first class we may be thankful that it is so
small. The attempt to gain for English verse the sonority
of Latin by the use of a Latinised vocabulary was a failure in any hands except Milton's, and Skelton was no Milton. It was dull and smelt of the study, and Skelton
seems to have realised this, and in his typically ironical
way expressed his opinion.

[Quotes 'Philip Sparrow', lines 769-73, 800-7, 811-12.]

and in the 'Duke of Albany' he rags the aureate vocabulary by giving the long words a line a piece.

[Quotes lines 446-51.]

As a writer of lyrics, on the other hand, had he chosen
he could have ranked high enough. He can range from the
barrack room. ''Twas Xmas day in the workhouse' style of
thing, to conventional religious poetry like the poem
'Woefully arrayed' and the quite unfaked tenderness of the
poem to Mistress Isabel Pennell, and always with an un-
failing intuition of the right metrical form to employ in
each case. Here is an example of his middle manner.
Fancy's song about his hawk in 'Magnificence',

[Quotes lines 984-95, 1000-3.]

Skelton's use of Rhyme Royal is in some ways the best
proof of his originality, because though employing a form

used by all his predecessors and contemporaries and at a
time when originality of expression was not demanded by
the reading public, few stanzas of Skelton's could be
confused with those of anyone else.

The most noticeable difference, attained partly by a
greater number of patter or unaccented syllables (which
relate it more to a teutonic accentual or sprung rhythm
for verse) lies in the tempo of his poetry. Compare a
stanza of Skelton's with one of Chaucer's:

> Suddenly as he departed me fro
>   Came pressing in on in a wonder array
> Ere I was ware, behind me he said 'BO'
>   Then I, astoned of that sudden fray
> Start all at once, I liked nothing his play
>   For, if I had not quickly fled the touch
> He had plucked out the nobles of my pouch.   ['Bouge of
>   Court', lines 498-504]

> But a word, lordlings, herkeneth ere I go:
> It were full hard to finde now a dayes
> In all a town Griseldes three or two
> For, if that they were put to such assayes,
> The gold of hem hath no so bad aloyes
> With brass, that though the coyne be fair at ye,
> It would rather breste a-two than plye. (2)

In Chaucer there is a far greater number of iambic
feet, and the prevailing number of accents per line is
five; in the Skelton it is four.

Indeed, the tempo of Skelton's verse is consistently
quicker than that of any other English poet; only the
author of 'Hudibras,' and in recent times Vachel Lindsay,
come anywhere near him in this respect.

It seems to be a rough-and-ready generalisation that
the more poetry concerns itself with subjective states,
with the inner world of feeling, the slower it becomes,
or in other words, that the verse of extrovert poets like
Dryden is swift and that of introvert poets like Milton
is slow, and that in those masters like Shakespeare who
transcend these classifications, in the emotional crises
which precede and follow the tragic act, the pace of the
verse is retarded.

Thus the average pace of mediaeval verse compared with
that of later more self-conscious ages is greater, and no
poetry is more 'outer' than Skelton's.

His best poems, with the exception of 'Speke Parrot,'
are like triumphantly successful prize poems. The
themes - the death of a girl's sparrow, a pub, Wolsey,

have all the air of set subjects. They may be lucky
choices, but one feels that others would have done almost
equally well, not, as with Milton, that his themes were
the only ones to which his genius would respond at that
particular moment in his life; that, had they not occurred
to him, he would have written nothing. They never read as
personal experience, brooded upon, and transfigured.
        Considering his date, this is largely to the good.
Pre-Elizabethan verse, even Chaucer, when it deserts the
outer world, and attempts the subjective, except in very
simple emotional situations, as in the mystery plays,
tends to sentiment and prosy moralising. Skelton avoids
that, but at the same time his emotional range is limited.
The world of 'The soldier's pole is fallen' is not for him.

[Quotes 'Upon a Deedman's Heed', lines 5-8.]

is as near as he gets to the terrific. This is moralising,
but the metre saves it from sententiousness.
        The skeltonic is such a simple metre that it is surpris-
ing that fewer poets have used it. The natural unit of
speech rhythm seems to be one of four accents, dividing
into two half verses of two accents. If one tries to
write ordinary conversation in verse, it will fall more
naturally into this scheme than into any other. Most
dramatic blank verse, for example, has four accents rather
than five, and it is possible that our habit of prefacing
nouns and adjectives by quite pointless adjectives and
adverbs as in 'the *perfectly* priceless' is dictated by our
ear, by our need to group accents in pairs. Skelton is
said to have spoken as he wrote, and his skeltonics have
the natural ease of speech rhythm. It is the metre of
many nursery rhymes.

        Little Jack Horner
        Sat in a corner;

or extemporised verse like the *Clerihew*:

        Alfred de Musset
        Used to call his cat pusset;

and study of the Woolworth song books will show its
attraction to writers of jazz lyrics:

        For life's a farce
        Sitting on the grass.

No other English poet to my knowledge has this

extempore quality, is less 'would-be,' to use a happy
phrase of D. H. Lawrence.

It makes much of his work, of course, quite unmemorable
- it slips in at one ear and out at the other; but it is
never false, and the lucky shots seem unique, of a kind
which a more deliberate and self-conscious poet would
never have thought of, or considered worthy of his singing
robes:

> Your head would have ached
> To see her naked.   ['Elynor Rumming', lines 478-9]

Though much of Skelton's work consists of attacks on
people and things, he can scarcely be called a satirist.
Satire is an art which can only flourish within a highly
sophisticated culture. It aims at creating a new attitude
towards the persons or institutions satirised, or at least
at crystallising one previously vague and unconscious. It
presupposes a society whose prejudices and loyalties are
sufficiently diffuse to be destroyed by intellectual
assault, or sufficiently economically and politically
secure to laugh at its own follies, and to admit that there
is something to be said on both sides.

In less secure epochs, such as Skelton's, when friend
and foe are more clearly defined, the place of satire is
taken by abuse, as it always is taken in personal contact.
(If censorship prevents abuse, allegorical symbolism is
employed, e.g. 'Speke Parrot.') If two people are having
a quarrel, they do not stop to assess who is at fault or
to convince the other of his error: they express their
feelings of anger by calling each other names. Similarly,
among friends, when we express our opinion of an enemy by
saying 'so and so is a closet' we assume that the reasons
are known:

> The Midwife put her hand on his thick skull
> With the prophetic blessing, 'Be thou dull,'

is too much emotion recollected in tranquillity to be the
language of a quarrel. Abuse in general avoids intellectual tropes other than those of exaggeration which
intensify the expression of one's feelings such as,
'You're so narrow-minded your ears meet,' or the genea-
logical trees which bargees assign to one another.

Further, the effect on the victim is different. Abuse
is an attack on the victim's personal honour, satire on
his social self-esteem; it affects him not directly, but
through his friends.

Skelton's work is abuse or flyting, not satire, and he

is a master at it. Much flyting poetry, like Dunbar's and
Skelton's own poems against Garnesche, suffer from the
alliterative metre in which they were written, which makes
them too verbal; the effect is lost on later generations,
to whom the vocabulary is unfamiliar. The freedom and
simplicity of the skeltonic was an ideal medium.

[Quotes 'Dundas ... Caudas contra Angligenos', lines
50-63.]

   Later literary attempts at abuse, such as Browning's
lines on Fitzgerald or Belloc's on a don, are too self-
conscious and hearty. Blake is the only other poet known
to me who has been equally successful.

   You think Fuseli is not a great painter; I'm glad
   This is one of the best compliments he ever had. (3)

   With his capacity for abuse Skelton combines a capacity
for caricature. His age appears to have been one which
has a penchant for the exaggerated and macabre, and he is
no exception. His description of a character is as accurate in detail as one of Chaucer's, but as exaggerated as
one of Dickens's. Compared with Chaucer he is more violent and dramatic; a favourite device of his to inter-
polate the description with remarks by the character
itself.

[Quotes 'Bouge of Court', lines 344-50, 365-71.]

   This has much more in common with the Gothic gargoyle
than with the classicism of Chaucer; 'Elinor Rumming' is
one of the few poems comparable to Breughel or Rowlandson
in painting. The effect is like looking at the human skin
through a magnifying glass.

[Quotes lines 418-35.]

   All Skelton's work has this physical appeal. Other
poets, such as Spenser and Swinburne, have been no more
dependent upon ideas, but they have touched only one
sense, the auditory. The Catherine-wheel motion of Skelton's verse is exciting in itself, but his language is
never vaguely emotive. Indeed, it is deficient in over-
tones, but is always precise, both visually and tactually.
He uses place-names, not scientifically like Dante, or
musically like Milton, but as country proverbs use them,
with natural vividness:

> And Syllogisari was drowned at Sturbridge Fair. ['Speak
> Parrot', line 170]

Naturally enough the figures of classical mythology
which appear in all mediaeval work (just as the Sahara or
Ohio appears in modern popular verses) occur in Skelton
also, but he is never sorry to leave Lycaon or Etna for
the Tilbury Ferry and the Plains of Salisbury. The same
applies to the Latin quotations in 'Philip Sparrow'; not
only have they dramatic point, but being mainly quotations
from the Psalter, they make no demands upon the erudition
of his audience, any more than would 'Abide with me' upon
a modern reader.

Of Skelton's one excursion into dramatic form, 'Magnificence,' not much need be said. It is interesting,
because he is one of the few dramatists who have
attempted, and with success, to differentiate his characters by making them speak in different metres, thus
escaping the tendency of blank verse to make all the
characters speak like the author; which obliged the
Elizabethans to make their comic characters speak in
prose; for the future of poetic comedy it may prove important. Its fault, a fatal one in drama, is its prolix-
ity, but cut by at least two-thirds it might act very much
better than one imagines.

Skelton's reputation has suffered in the past from his
supposed indecency. This charge is no longer maintained,
but there are other misunderstandings of poetry which
still prevent appreciation of his work. On the one hand,
there are those who read poetry for its message, for great
thoughts which can be inscribed on Christmas calendars; on
the other, there are admirers of 'pure' poetry, which
generally means emotive poetry with a minimum of objective
reference. Skelton satisfies neither of these: he is too
carefree for the one, and too interested in the outer
world for the second.

If we accept, and I think we must, a distinction between the visionary and the entertainer, the first being
one who extends our knowledge of, insight into, and power
of control over human conduct and emotion, without whom
our understanding would be so much the poorer, Skelton is
definitely among the entertainers. He is not one of the
indispensables, but among entertainers - and how few are
the indispensables - he takes a high place. Nor is
entertainment an unworthy art: it demands a higher standard of technique and a greater lack of self-regard than
the average man is prepared to attempt. There have been,
and are, many writers of excellent sensibility whose work
is spoilt by a bogus vision which deprives it of the

entertainment value which it would otherwise have had; in
that kind of pride Skelton is entirely lacking.

Notes

1 'Proverbs of Alfred': cf. the edition of O. S. Arngart
   (1955), lines 233-6.
2 Chaucer, 'Clerk's Tale', lines 1163-9.
3 'Verses to Robert Hunt', in 'The Poems of William
   Blake', ed. W. H. Stevenson (1971), p. 594.

53. G. S. FRASER ON SKELTON

1936

Originally published as Skelton and the Dignity of Poetry
in 'Adelphi', XIII (1936-7), pp. 154-63.
    Fraser (1915-80) was a British poet and critic. This
essay was written while he was still an undergraduate.

The fifteenth century is the dullest period in the history
of English poetry. But anatomy is easy on the dead model,
and the period has a fascination for the critic. For him,
its interest is that it shows, with extraordinary clearness, the dangers of an unbroken tradition. After Chaucer
had died, Gower went on writing like Chaucer, and not so
well. After Gower had died, Lydgate and Hoccleve went on
writing like Chaucer and Gower, and not so well. They,
too, had died. And at the very end of the fifteenth century, poor Stephen Hawes went on writing like Chaucer and
Gower and Lydgate and Hoccleve - and not so well. Hawes
is the final dilution of the pure Chaucerian spring, the
last splash of soda in the stale nectar. Chaucer was to
be, after Hawes, a dead influence, until Spenser recreated
him, looking on him with an eye not dazed by custom. It
is easy to point out, by taking a random sample of his
verse, just how and why Stephen Hawes is not good. Consider the rhymes of this stanza.

    The boke of fame, which is sentencyous
    He drewe himself on his own invencyon:

And than the tragidyes so pitous,
Of the XIX ladyes was his translation;
And upon his ymaginacion
He made also the tales of Canterbury:
Some vertuous, and some glad and mery. (1)

It is a complicated stanza, and Hawes is writing a long
poem, 'The Pastime of Pleasure.' He makes the rhymes
ridiculously easy. There is a predominance especially of
rhymes on the weak and meaningless suffixes of words, an
unnatural predominance, since even in these days and even
with borrowed French words (naturalised, mostly, since
Chaucer's day) the beat of English words was on the root.
Hawes is always racking the natural accent of English.
It is too painful to keep up this distortion in reading,
and one tends to read Hawes with as little emphasis on the
beat as possible, a modulation more or less syllabic and
French, a dreary slurring, a drawl on the unimportant.
This fault also, of course, affects Hawes' vocabulary.
For the sake of rhyme he uses the trite adjective,

And than the tragidyes so pitous,   [line 1326]

the heavy abstraction,

Over the waves of grete encombraunce,   [line 1299]

the abstraction almost resoundingly hollow of meaning,

Remember thee of the trace and daunce
Of poetes old, with all the purveyance. [lines 1315-16]

With all the purveyance! With all, one supposes charitably, that the poets purveyed, but what an effect of hope-
less floundering. Typically, too, Hawes uses this damp,
trailing word 'purveyance' to close a couplet with, instead of the sharp, suitable word (which he has to hand),
'daunce.' For anyone who cares for the craft of poetry,
Stephen Hawes is a depressing study.
    Now Hawes, as I have said, was simply following a
tradition. It is easy, of course, to blame tradition.
One does not suppose that, with the best of advantages,
poor Hawes would have become a very exhilarating poet.
Yet it does seem that there comes a stage in every tradition when it is quite fully diluted. Every great and
original poet gets such a crowd of second-rate imitators
that other great and original poets, following him, react
against his influence, and go back to some other and older
tradition. They break, that is, with the immediate past

if it does influence good poets, often influences them
from a foreign source. The fifteenth century is anything
but the dullest period in the history of Scottish poetry.
It is probably the greatest period. Yet James I, Dunbar,
Henryson, 'good Gawaine Douglas, Bischop of Dunkell'
were, like Lydgate, like Hoccleve, like Hawes, Chaucer-
ians. The difference is that for [them] the Chaucerian
tradition was a foreign influence, a grafting, what the
second Samuel Butler calls a 'cross.' In England,
unfortunately, there was no tradition older than Chaucer
for a man like Hawes to fall back on. There was no alter-
native, foreign tradition, Chaucer was France and Italy
and England, an all-embracing orthodoxy. Skelton is the
one living poet of the fifteenth century in England. He
is living only because he managed without a tradition.
He is that very rare thing, an original artist.
    'Skeltonic' is a word still used for any jogging dog-
gerel metre. Skelton's metre is, in itself, an anomaly.
There are no rules for it except that it shall have go,
push, vigour. This metre is perfectly intelligible, however, if one considers it as a reaction against the deca-
dent Chaucerian tradition, against the verse of people
like Hawes. Skelton is determined, above all things, not
to be dreary. The tendency of Hawes' verse, we have seen,
is to rack the natural accent of English, to approximate
unhappily to syllabic modulation and French. Skelton
completely ignores syllables. His lines move wholly on
the beat. He emphasises this by his rhymes: unlike Hawes'
rhymes, they are usually rhymes on short, sharp, single-
syllabled words. The same rhyme is carried on, often,
for five or six lines. The effect is like tap-dancing
or rub-a-dub.

[Quotes 'Colin Clout', lines 16-26.]

There is no more music in that than in a percussion drum.
On the other hand, like the dancing of Fred Astaire, (2)
the repetition of one small trick, again and again, till
it surprises and interests us, the sudden finish,

    Or if he speak plain,   [line 26]

a transition, in the poem, from patter to anger, it is
undeniably an evidence of training and skill. This is
language in trim, Hawes' verse is language run to seed.
It is not, perhaps, wholly fantastic to see in Skelton's
doggerel line Hawes' sorry, slurring iambic pentameter
squeezed: all the superfluous epithets, cumbrous abstractions, 'aureate terms,' wrung out of the bag; a hard,

tough curd of language left.
    There is a current phrase, originally used about some
of Mr. Auden's productions - 'buffoon-poetry.' (There is
something exhilarating, said Baudelaire, about the company
of buffoons.) This phrase applies very well to Skelton.
It is not that he has not beauty. He has, quite frequently; the cock, for instance, in 'Philip Sparrow,' who
was never taught

> by Ptolemy,
> Prince of Astronomy,
> Nor by Haly;
> And yet he croweth daily
> And nightly the tides
> That no man abides,   [lines 503-8]

the other birds,

> The goose and the gander,
> The swan of Menander,   [lines 435, 434]

the phoenix,

> The bird of Araby
> That potentially
> May never die.   [lines 513-15]

these creatures, undeniably have a brittle and angular
beauty. The verse, too, is skilful. The passage about
the phoenix shows Skelton's use (very 'modern' and with
him sometimes highly successful) of repetition: the
'phoenix kind' -

[Quotes lines 540-9.]

It is the echo 'plain, plain' that gives a sort of sinister and resonant tone to this passage, the muttered
repetition of that one short line - 'Plain matter indeed'
[line 548] - casts a quiver of doubt *back* on the firm climax,

> Saving that old age
> Is turned into courage
> Of fresh youth again,   [lines 544-6]

and this doubt, again, seems half resolved by the new
firmness, the sharp, flat

> Whoso list to read.   [line 549]

This may seem fanciful. But if other people agree with me
that the lines do express this ambivalent mood, they will
agree with me that Skelton can use verse, when he cares,
with quite subtle skill. But both beauty and subtlety are
incidental, are perhaps even accidental in Skelton's poems.
They are by-products. Of what?

It is hard to put it precisely. Anyone reading Skelton
can see just what he was aiming at, but the proper word
for it, the exact, just phrase is, somehow, elusive. Fun,
satire, energy? Energy is perhaps nearest it. There is
fun, it is true; Skelton has an astonishing eye, an astonishing gusto. But the scenes he chooses are often not
intrinsically funny. It is rather that he deliberately
makes them funny, that he sustains the reader's amusement
with his own energy of vision. On a much greater scale,
of course, Rabelais does the same sort of thing. Think of
the famous twenty-seventh chapter of 'Gargantua,' Friar
John's defence of the Abbey. It is an orgy of blood and
slaughter, bowels, brains, bones flying everywhere. Why
do we laugh at it, on the deepest analysis of the matter,
but because Rabelais wants us to? It is his amusement
which makes the scene comic, we laugh for company. This
ability then, to make one laugh at anything is not so much
the character of a humorist as of an orator; it is a way
not of increasing perception, but of exerting power.

This quality of Skelton's is seen very well in his
poem, 'The Tunning of Eleanor Rumming.' This picture of
ale-house manners is as good, in its way, as Rowlandson.
Nobody has ever seen, not even in Rowlandson, quite such
lewd carbuncular bloatedness in life. Nevertheless, while
we look at these exquisite drawings, Rowlandson's people
convince us. They seem portraits of monsters, not caricatures of men. They exist in their medium. As a mere
artist, Skelton is much the inferior of Rowlandson, who
can build up a complete effect of brutal strength by individual touches as light and sensitive as possible. But
Skelton's figures are also portraits not caricatures.
Eleanor Rumming, regrettably, exists:

[Quotes line 17-21.]

one sees vividly. Every detail (and the details grow more
and more unsavoury) adds to her reality. Skelton, moreover, knows exactly how people eat and drink:

[Quotes lines 303-8.]

How shocking that last couplet, how memorable, how true!
Finally, from this remarkable poem, let me quote the

description of a cheese.

[Quotes lines 431-5.]

'It was tart and punyete,' [line 435]. Does that not strike you as an unusually felicitous phrase? It is obvious, of course, that 'punyete' means 'pungent.' The odd thing about Skelton, however, is that he is continually using phrases which strike one as felicitous if one could fathom what they meant. It is this (too absolute an up-to-dateness, probably, in idiom) which prevents him from being a really witty poet. For instance, I have quoted already,

> But drink, still drink,
> And let the cat wink.   [lines 305-6]

Why let the cat wink? The phrase, perhaps because of the sly, conniving cat in 'Alice in Wonderland,' we are apt at first to let pass without question. But what does it really mean - and how does it manage, still, to convey a sense of comic mischief? There are other more obvious instances of this sort of phrase.

> What hath lay men to do
> The gray goose to shoe?   ['Colin Clout', lines 197-8]

This mocks the language of churchmen, we know by the context. We feel it has energy, we are at a loss about what it refers to? Even more obviously in, say,

> For a simoniac
> Is but a hermoniac,   ['Colin Clout', lines 298-99]

while the energy is still communicable, has the meaning lapsed. (When, with the aid of the professors, we do _root_ out the meaning of 'hermoniac' - Armenian and hence, possibly, heretic; there is still some doubt where the wit lies. 'Simony is only a kind of heresy.' 'Burglars are only Bolsheviks,' might be equivalent for us. This, of course, cuts both ways, according to your feelings about Bolsheviks, and so may have Skelton's joke.) It is here that Skelton is inferior to Samuel Butler, of 'Hudibras,' who, with a regular metre, is very like Skelton in energy of humour. Skelton is too profuse or too particular, he cannot gather himself together for the general statement. Compare Butler's

> This we among ourselves may speak.
> But to the wicked or the weak
> We must be cautious to declare
> Perfection-truths, such as these are. (3)

with

> Their mules gold doth eat,
> Their neighbours die for meat,   ['Colin Clout',
>   lines 321-2]

the embryo of an epigram, lost in the rush of Skelton's
rhymes. Yet Skelton is in many ways a pleasanter poet
than Butler. 'Hudibras' is too full of plums to be very
digestible. Butler has a dry, dull attitude towards his
characters. They are lay figures to build jokes around.
He has no charm. Skelton has charm, and his attitude towards his characters, a sort of mock identification of
himself with them, is much more sympathetic than Butler's.
    Skelton is damned for many people as a poet because he
lacks dignity. Hawes has, I suppose, in his dreary way,
dignity. His incompetence is heavy, is tragic with the
weight of a century's deterioration. He is, after all,
the last man of the Middle Ages, the last Chaucerian
voice. There is nothing of this atmosphere in Skelton,
this atmosphere of the breaking of gray daylight into a
heavy dream. 'Buffoon-poetry' is typical, always, of a
man living between two sets of values, two ways of looking
at life. Skelton lacks both the melancholy of the Middle
Ages and the grandiose manner of the Renaissance. He is a
man, for once, just writing as he likes, and giving us
verse for talk. He uses both Mediaeval theme and Renaissance learning. The catalogue of birds or beasts or
flowers is a favourite item in Mediaeval poems of the type
of 'The Romaunt of the Rose.' But in the 'Kingis Quhair,'
for instance, the effect of such a catalogue is that of
being conducted, too slowly, past dark and threadbare
tapestries. In 'Philip Sparrow,' the catalogue of birds
shows knowledge and imagination. The interest, however,
is not that of Faustus, 'the lust of the eye.' It is
rather, again, the interest of patter. What, another bird
still! How long will he keep it up?
    Is poetry an essence or a medium? That is the question
by which Skelton must stand or fall. Is poetry something
which is achieved only occasionally, achieved with great
difficulty - a blaze, as Mr. Peter Quennell has figured
it, which will flare up only for a second, after one has
been rubbing for ages together the dry sticks of verse?
So many estimable people (and particularly Platonists)

think. Or is poetry just a medium like prose (prose for
statement and poetry for expression, prose for thought and
poetry for feeling?) a medium which it is difficult to become a master in? The alternatives are crudely stated,
and most people will dislike intensely the implication
that prose which is expressive and emotional is poetry;
though nobody, again, so far as I know, has denied the
possibility of writing a 'prose poem.' I agree, however,
that most expressive and emotional prose is not poetry.
Poetry implies intensity, consistency, concentration, and
most writers, to attain these qualities when they are
expressing their feelings, require the discipline of
verse. I incline, myself, to the theory that poetry is a
medium. Such a theory, at least, leaves little room for
charlatanerie in critics. We can all judge pretty well
whether a poem expresses a man's personality with honesty
and economy. We will quarrel till doomsday about what
(and where) is 'beauty.' If poetry is a medium, Skelton,
is seems to me, is a fair master in it.

Skelton, in our day, has enjoyed a certain popularity.
He has interested and influenced Mr. Robert Graves. Mr.
Auden has written (in a compilation vaguely called 'The
Great Tudors') an essay about him, with a brilliant
choice of quotations. Skelton seems, also, to have
influenced Mr. Auden in his poems, particularly in his
'buffoon-poetry.' Like Skelton, Mr. Auden always misses
wit; his idiom is private, precious, and he is thinking
of too small and intimate an audience. Like Skelton, he
has charm. I do not think he beats Skelton at his own
game. Here are two passages for comparison, both expressing an exasperation at listless people.

This is Auden's.   This is Skelton's,
    Fitters and moulders,   He is but a fool
    Wielders and welders   Let him go to school,
    Dyers and bakers,   On a three-legged stool
    And boiler-tube makers,   That he may down sit
    Poofs and ponces,   For he lacketh wit:
    All of them dunces,   And if that he hit
    Those over thirty   The nail on the head,
    Ugly and dirty,   It standeth in no stead,
    What are they doing   The devil, the say, is
    Except just stewing? (4)   dead,
                                    The devil is dead
                          ['Colin Clout', lines 28-37]

The poor, the unemployed have, of course, more immediate
interest than the thick-skins whom Skelton is mocking.

On the other hand, Skelton's strategy of identifying
himself with the enemy is much cleverer than Auden's plain
grumble. Merely as verse, however, Skelton's passage
seems to me to have much more drive than Auden's. The
trochaic movement and feminine rhymes of Auden's passage
rob it, obviously, of a good deal of energy. You get a
slightly plaintive, querulous note, a thing fatal to
satire. Auden is trying to be tough about these people,
but they are getting into his nerves. It is Skelton's
voice which is better than Auden's for 'buffoon-poetry,'
on the whole. Auden's voice has the *miaulement* which
lurks at the bottom of the lyric, and a hint of that is in
his satire, giving it - I admit, on a second reading - a
slightly fractious air. I suppose this fractious tone (I
have noticed it in people expensively brought up) is a
legacy of the English public school. Skelton was more
like George Robey, (5)

[Quotes 'Colin Clout', lines 944, 946-49, 951.]

Auden's 'schoolmaster writing "Resurgam" with his penis in
the sand' is aimed at a more special and less central
audience.
     What is the justification for 'buffoon-poetry'? The
example of Skelton suggests that it is justifiable to
write 'buffoon-poetry' when a tradition is exhausted and
when there is no other obvious tradition to turn to.
This, I believe, was Auden's case as well as Skelton's.
What is remarkable about Auden is that, not content with
'buffoon-poetry,' he has also created for himself a tradition. A person of desultory reading, turning over
Auden's pages, will recognise uses of Freud, case-books
of psychology, geology, folk-plays, spy stories, military
manuals, and what not. Skelton (who was admired by Erasmus and Pico della Mirandola) had the same sort of harum-
scarum erudition. He had not the *miaulement*, the lyric
cry. He had not the *paranoia* (to use Salvador Dali's
term) by which all this discrepant stuff could be used to
illustrate one heroic obsession. He achieves, in his few
lyrics, only (as here and there throughout his longer
poems) a brittle and angular beauty:

[Quotes 'Garland of Laurel', lines 1004-7.]

He created no tradition, therefore. He is quite unique
in his kind. The great stream of English literature would
have taken much the same course if he had never written.
But I have never held to the theory that a poet is only
justified, in the end, by the saturation of his tradition,

by the number and final deadness of his imitators.
Shakespeare stands without Shirley. Skelton will always
remain an example for poets caught up in the coils of a
tradition, a decent way of writing, which they feel to be
constricting their lives. It is better, always, to be a
buffoon than a bore.

Notes

1   Hawes, 'Pastime of Pleasure', lines 1324-30.
2   An American film star and dancer.
3   'Hudibras', First Part, Canto II, lines 1099-102.
4   From Auden's 'The Orators' (1932), Ode III.
5   An English comic actor.

54. E. M. FORSTER ON SKELTON

1950

From E. M. Forster's 'Two Cheers for Democracy', first
published in 1951. I have followed the text of the Abin-
ger Edition (London, 1972), pp. 133-49.
   Forster (1879-1970) was one of the most distinguished
novelists of the twentieth century. His novels include
'The Longest Journey' (1907), 'Howards End' (1920) and
'A Passage to India' (1924). In addition he wrote volumes
of biography and criticism. The lecture printed below was
first given at the Aldeburgh Festival in 1950.

John Skelton was an East Anglian; he was a poet, also a
clergyman, and he was extremely strange. Partly strange
because the age in which he flourished - that of the early
Tudors - is remote from us, and difficult to interpret.
But he was also a strange creature personally, and whatever you think of him when we've finished - and you will
possibly think badly of him - you will agree that we have
been in contact with someone unusual.
   Let us begin with solidity - with the church where he
was rector. That still stands; that can be seen and
touched, though its incumbent left it over four hundred
years ago. He was rector of Diss, a market town which

lies just in Norfolk, just across the river Waveney, here
quite a small stream, and Diss church is somewhat of a
landmark, for it stands upon a hill. A winding High
Street leads up to it, and the High Street, once very
narrow, passed through an arch in its tower which still
remains.   The church is not grand, it is not a great
architectural triumph like Blythburgh or Framlingham.
But it is adequate, it is dignified and commodious, and
it successfully asserts its pre-eminence over its sur-
roundings. Here our poet-clergyman functioned for a time,
and, I may add, carried on.

Not much is known about him, though he was the leading
literary figure of his age. He was born about 1460,
probably in Norfolk, was educated at Cambridge, mastered
the voluble inelegant Latin of his day, entered the
Church, got in touch with the court of Henry VII, and
became tutor to the future Henry VIII. He was appointed
'Poet Laureat', and this was confirmed by the universities
of Cambridge, Oxford and Louvain.   In the early years of
Henry VIII he voiced official policy - for instance, in
his poems against the Scots after Flodden.   But,
unfortunately for himself, he attacked another and a
greater East Anglian, Cardinal Wolsey of Ipswich, and
after that his influence declined. He was appointed
rector of Diss in 1503, and held the post till his death
in 1529. But he only seems to have been in residence
during the earlier years. Life couldn't have been con-
genial for him there. He got across the Bishop of Norwich, perhaps about his marriage or semi-marriage, and he
evidently liked London and the court, being a busy con-
tentious fellow, and found plenty to occupy him there.
A few bills and documents, a few references in the works
of others, a little posthumous gossip, and his own poems,
are all that we have when we try to reconstruct him.
Beyond doubt he is an extraordinary character, but not
one which it is easy to focus. Let us turn to his poems.

I will begin with the East Anglian poems, and with
'Philip Sparrow'. This is an unusually charming piece of
work. It was written while Skelton was at Diss, and re-
volves round a young lady called Jane, who was at school
at a nunnery close to Norwich. Jane had a pet sparrow -
a bird which is far from fashionable today, but which
once possessed great social prestige. In ancient Rome,
Catullus sang of the sparrow of Lesbia, the dingy little
things were housed in gilt cages, and tempted with
delicious scraps all through the Middle Ages, and they
only went out when the canary came in. Jane had a
sparrow, round which all her maidenly soul was wrapped.
Tragedy followed. There was a cat in the nunnery, by

name Gib, who lay in wait for Philip Sparrow, pounced,
killed him and ate him. The poor girl was in tears, and
her tragedy was taken up and raised into poetry by her
sympathetic admirer, the rector of Diss.

He produced a lengthy poem - it seemed difficult at
that time to produce a poem that was not long. 'Philip
Sparrow' swings along easily enough, and can still be
read with pleasure by those who will overlook its volubility, its desultoriness and its joky Latin.

It begins, believe it or not, with a parody of the
Office for the Dead; Jane herself is supposed to be
speaking, and she slings her Latin about well if quaintly.
Soon tiring of the church service, she turns to English,
and to classical allusions.

[Quotes 'Philip Sparrow', lines 17-30, 36.]

Then - in a jumble of Christian and antique allusions,
most typical of that age - she thinks of Hell and Pluto
and Cerberus - whom she calls Cerebus - and Medusa and
the Furies, and alternately prays Jupiter and Jesus to
save her sparrow from the infernal powers:

[Quotes lines 115-17, 120-42.]

Jane proceeds to record his other merits, which include
picking fleas off her person - this was a sixteenth-
century girls' school, not a twentieth-, vermin were no
disgrace, not even a surprise, and Skelton always manages
to introduce the coarseness and discomfort of his age.
She turns upon the cat again, and hopes the greedy grypes
will tear out his tripes.

[Quotes lines 338-41.]

She goes back to the sparrow and to the church service,
and draws up an enormous catalogue of birds who shall
celebrate his obsequies -

[Quotes lines 428-31.]

- together with other songsters, unknown in these marshes
and even elsewhere. She now wants to write an epitaph,
but is held up by her diffidence and ignorance; she has
read so few books, though the list of those she has read
is formidable; moreover, she has little enthusiasm for the
English language -

[Quotes lines 774-83.]

Shall she try Latin? Yes, but she will hand over the job
to the Poet Laureate of Britain, Skelton, and, with this
neat compliment to himself, Skelton ends the first part of
'Philip Sparrow'.
    He occupies the second part with praising Jane:

[Quotes lines 1136-40.]

bypasses the sparrow, and enters upon a love poem:

[Quotes lines 1145-50.]

The rector is in fact losing his head over a schoolgirl,
and has to pull himself up. No impropriety is intended,
he assures us.

[Quotes lines 1133-5, 1251-9.]

Then he too slides into Latin and back into the Office of
the Dead: *Requiem aeternam dona eis Domine* [line 1238],
he chants.
    This poem of Philip Sparrow - the pleasantest Skelton
ever wrote - helps to emphasize the difference in taste and
and in style between the sixteenth century and our own.
His world is infinitely remote; not only is it coarse and
rough, but there is an uncertainty of touch about it which
we find hard to discount. Is he being humorous? Undoubtedly, but where are we supposed to laugh? Is he being
serious? If so, where and how much? We don't find the
same uncertainty when he read his predecessor Chaucer, or
his successor Shakespeare. We know where they stand,
even when we cannot reach them. Skelton belongs to an
age of break-up, which has just been displayed politically
in the Wars of the Roses. He belongs to a period when
England was trying to find herself - as indeed do we today, though we have to make a different sort of discovery
after a different type of war. He is very much the product of his times - a generalization that can be made of
all writers, but not always so aptly. The solidity of the
Middle Ages was giving way beneath his feet, and he did
not know that the Elizabethan age was coming - any more
than we know what is coming. We have not the least idea,
whatever the politicians prophesy. It is appropriate, at
this point, to quote the wisest and most impressive lines
he ever wrote - they are not well known, and probably they
are only a fragment. They have a weight and a thoughtful-
ness which are unusual in him.

> Though ye suppose all jeopardies are passed
>   And all is done that ye lookéd for before,
> Ware yet, I warn you, of Fortune's double cast,
>   For one false point she is wont to keep in store,
>   And under the skin oft festered is the sore;
> That when ye think all danger for to pass
> Ware of the lizard lieth lurking in the grass.
>   ['Dyuers Balettys and Dyties Solacious', lines 9-15]

It was a curious experience, with these ominous verses in
my mind, to go to Diss and to find, carved on the buttress
of the church, a lizard. The carving was there in Skelton's day; that he noticed it, that it entered into his
mind when he wrote, there is no reason to suppose. But
its appearance, combined with the long grass in the churchyard, helped me to connect the present with the past,
helped them to establish that common denominator without
which neither has any validity.

[Quotes ibid., lines 14-15.]

So true of the sixteenth century, so true of today! There
are two main answers to the eternal menace of the lizard.
One of them is caution, the other courage. Skelton was a
brave fellow - his opposition to Cardinal Wolsey proves
that - but I don't know which answer he recommends.
   But let us leave these serious considerations, and
enter Diss church itself, where we shall be met by a fantastic scene and by the oddest poem even Skelton ever
wrote: the poem of 'Ware the Hawk'. Like 'Philip Sparrow',
it is about a bird, but a bird of prey, and its owner is
not the charming Jane, but an ill-behaved curate, who took
his hawk into the church, locked all the doors, and pro-
ceeded to train it with the help of two live pigeons and
a cushion stuffed with feathers to imitate another pigeon.
The noise, the mess, the scandal, was terrific. In vain
did the rector thump on the door and command the curate
to open. The young man - one assumes he was young - took
no notice, but continued his unseemly antics. Diss church
is well suited to a sporting purpose, since its nave and
choir are unusually lofty, and the rood-loft was convenient for the birds to perch on between the statues of the
Virgin and St John. Up and down he rushed, uttering the
cries of his craft, and even clambering onto the communion
table. Feathers flew in all directions and the hawk was
sick. At last Skelton found 'a privy way' in, and managed
to stop him. But he remained impenitent, and threatened
that another day he would go fox-hunting there, and bring
in a whole pack of hounds.

Now is this an exaggeration, or a joke? And why did
Skelton delay making a poem out of it until many years
had passed? He does not - which is strange - even mention
the name of the curate.

[Quotes lines 38-42.]

That is moderately put. It was amiss. Winding himself up
into a rage, he then calls him a peckish parson and a
Domine Dawcock and a frantic falconer and a smeary smith,
and scans history in vain for so insolent a parallel; not
even the Emperor Julian the Apostate or the Nestorian
heretics flew hawks in a church. Nero himself would have
hesitated. And the poem ends in a jumble and a splutter,
heaps of silly Latin, a cryptogram and a curious impression of gaiety; a good time, one can't help feeling, has
been had by all.
   How, though, did Skelton get into the church and stop
the scandal? Perhaps through the tower. You remember
my mentioning that the tower of Diss church has a broad
passage-way running through it, once part of the High
Street. Today the passage only contains a notice saying
'No bicycles to be left here', together with a number of
bicycles. Formerly, there was a little door leading up
from it into the tower. That (conjectures an American
scholar) may have been Skelton's privy entrance. He may
have climbed up by it, climbed down the belfry into the
nave, and spoiled, at long last, the curate's sport.
   There is another poem which comes into this part of
Skelton's life. It is entitled 'Two Knaves Sometimes of
Diss', and attacks two of his parishioners who had dis-
pleased him and were now safely dead; John Clerk and Adam
Uddersall were their names. Clerk, according to the poet,
had raged 'like a camel' and now lies 'starke dead, Never
a tooth in his head, Adieu, Jayberd, adieu,' while as for
Uddersall, 'Belsabub his soule save, who lies here like a
knave.' The poem is not gentlemanly. Little that Skelton
wrote was. Not hit a man when he is down or dead?
That's just the moment to wait for. He can't hit back.
   The last East Anglian poem to be mentioned is a touching one: to his wife. As a priest, he was not and could
not be married, but he regarded his mistress as his legal
consort, and the poem deals with a moment when they were
parting and she was about to bear a child:

   'Petually
   Constrained am I
   With weeping eye
      To mourn and 'plain

That we so nigh
Of progeny
So suddenly
    Should part in twain.

When ye are gone
Comfort is none,
But all alone
    Endure must I
With grievely groan
Making my moan
As it were one
    That should needs die. (1)

There is a story about the birth of this child which was
written down after Skelton's death, in a collection called
'The Merry Tales of Skelton'. According to it, there were
complaints to the bishop from the parish, which Skelton
determined to quell. So he preached in Diss church on the
text *Vos estis*, you are, and suddenly called out, 'Wife!
Bring my Child.' Which the lady did. And he held the
naked baby out to the congregation saying: 'Is not this
child as fair as any of yours? It is not like a pig or a
calf, is it? What have you got to complain about to the
bishop? The fact is, as I said in my text, *Vos estis*, you
be, and have be and will and shall be knaves, to complayne
of me without reasonable cause.' Historians think that
this jest-book story enshrines a tradition. It certainly
fits in with what we know of the poet's fearless and abusive character.

Tenderness also entered into that character, though it
did not often show itself. Tenderness inspires that poem
I have quoted, and is to be found elsewhere in his gentle
references to women; for instance, in the charming 'Merry
Margaret', which often appears in anthologies.

[Quotes 'Garland of Laurel', lines 1004-10.]

And in the less known but still more charming poem 'To
Mistress Isabel Pennell' which I will quote in full. Isabel was a little girl of eight - even younger than Jane of
the sparrow. ('Reflaring', near the beginning of the
poem, is 'redolent'. 'Nept' means catmint.)

[Quotes 'Garland of Laurel', lines 973-1003.]

Women could touch his violent and rugged heart and make it
gentle and smooth for a little time. It is not the dying
tradition of chivalry, it is something personal.

But we must leave these personal and local matters, and turn to London and to the political satires. The main group is directed against Cardinal Wolsey. The allusions are often obscure, for, though Skelton sometimes attacks his great adversary openly, at other times he is covering his tracks, and at other times complimentary and even fulsome. The ups and downs of which have furnished many problems for scholars. Two points should be remembered. Firstly, Skelton is not a precursor of the Reformation; he has sometimes been claimed as one by Protestant historians. He attacked the abuses of his Church - as exemplified in Wolsey's luxury, immorality and business. He has nothing to say against its doctrines or organization and was active in the suppression of heresy. He was its loyal if scandalous son.

Secondly, Wolsey appears to have behaved well. When he triumphed, he exacted no vengeance. Perhaps he had too much to think about. The story that Skelton died in sanctuary in St Margaret's, Westminster, fleeing from the Cardinal's wrath, is not true. He did live for the last years of his life in London, but freely and comfortably; bills for his supper parties have been unearthed. And though he was buried in St Margaret's it was honourably, under an alabaster inscription. Bells were pealed, candles were burned. Here again we have the bills.

The chief anti-Wolsey poems are 'Speke Parrot', 'Colin Clout', 'Why come ye not to Court?' and the cumbrous Morality play 'Magnificence'.

Speke Parrot - yet another bird; had Skelton a bird complex? Ornithologists must decide - Speke Parrot is one of those convenient devices where Polly is made to say what Polly's master hesitates to say openly. Poor Polly! Still, master is fond of Polly, and introduces him prettily enough.

[Quotes 'Speak Parrot', lines 209-15.]

Skelton's genuine if intermittent charm continues into the next stanza.

[Quotes lines 216-22.]

The 'popinjay royal' - that is to say the bird of King Henry VIII, whose goodness and generosity Wolsey abuses. And parrot, given his beak, says many sharp things against the Cardinal, who 'carrieth a king in his sleeve' and plays the Pope's game rather than his liege's. Subtly and obscurely, with detailed attention to his comings and goings, the great man is attacked. It is a London poem, which could not have been written in a Norfolk rectory.

Much more violent is 'Why come ye not to Court?' where the son of the Ipswich butcher gets brutally put in his place.

[Quotes lines 398-406.]

And at Hampton Court Wolsey rules, with

[Quotes lines 488-91, 569-75.]

As for 'Colin Clout'. The title is the equivalent of Hodge or the Man in the Street, from whose point of view the poem is supposed to be written. It is a long rambling attack on bishops, friars, monks and the clergy generally, and Wolsey comes in for his share of criticism. I will quote from it not the abusive passages, of which you are getting plenty, but the dignified and devout passage with which it closes. Skelton was, after all, inside the church he criticized, and held its faith, and now and then he reminds us of this.

[Quotes lines 1250-67.]

It is a conventional ending, but a sincere one, and re-minds us that he had a serious side; his 'Prayer to the Father of Heaven' was sung in the church here, to the setting of Vaughan Williams. He can show genuine emotion at the moments, both about this world and the next. Here are two verses from 'The Manner of the World Nowadays', in in which he laments the decay of society.

[Quotes lines 169-76.]

'Magnificence', the last of the anti-Wolsey group, is a symbol for Henry VIII, who is seduced by wicked flatterers from his old counsellor (i.e. from Skelton himself). Largess, Counterfeit-Countenance, Crafty-Conveyance, Cloaked-Collusion and Courtly Abusion are some of the names, and all are aspects of Wolsey. At enormous length and with little dramatic skill they ensnare Magnificence and bring him low. By the time Stage 5, Scene 35 is reached he repents, and recalls his former adviser, and all is well.

Well, so much for the quarrel between Skelton and Wolsey - between the parson from Norfolk and the Cardinal from Suffolk, and Suffolk got the best of it. Skelton may have had right on his side and he had courage and sincerity, but there is no doubt that jealousy came in too.

At the beginning of Henry VIII's reign he was a very
important person. He had been the King's tutor, he went
on a semi-diplomatic mission, and as Poet Laureate he was
a mouthpiece for official lampoons. With the advent of
Wolsey, who tempted the king with pleasure, his importance
declined, and he did not live to see the days when Henry
preferred power to pleasure, and Wolsey fell.

The satires against the Scots, next to be mentioned,
belong to the more influential period of Skelton's life.
They centre round the Battle of Flodden (1513). King
Henry's brother-in-law, James IV of Scotland, had challenged him, had invaded England, and been killed at Flodden, with most of his nobility. Skelton celebrates the
English victory with caddish joy. In quoting a few lines,
I do not desire to ruffle any sensitive friends from over
the Border. I can anyhow assure them that our Poet Laureate appears to have got as good as he gave:

[Quotes 'Against the Scots', lines 91-4, 139-42.]

And still more abusively does he attack an enemy poet
called Dundas who wrote Latin verses against him.

[Quotes lines 1-10, 25-8, 54-5, 60-3.]

The accusation that Englishmen have tails is still sometimes made, and is no doubt as true as it ever was. I
have not been able to find out how Dundas made it, since
his poem has vanished. We can assume he was forcible.
Nor have I quoted Skelton in full, out of deference to
the twentieth century. He is said to have written it in
his Diss rectory. That is unlikely - not because of its
tone, but because it implies a close contact with affairs
which he could only have maintained at Court.

Our short Skeltonic scamper is nearing its end, but I
must refer to the 'Tunning of Elinor Rumming', one of the
most famous of Skelton's poems. Elinor Rumming kept a
pub - not in East Anglia, but down in Surrey, near
Leatherhead. The poem is about her and her clients, who
likewise belonged to the fair sex.

[Quotes lines 1-5, 7-11, 18-21.]

You catch the tone. You taste the quality of the brew.
It is strong and rumbustious and not too clean. Skelton
is going to enjoy himself thoroughly. Under the guise
of a satirist and a corrector of morals, he is out for a
booze. Now the ladies come tumbling in:

[Quotes lines 117-30.]

They get drunk, they tumble down in inelegant attitudes,
they trip over the doorstep, they fight. Margery Milk-
duck, halting Joan, Maud Ruggy, drunken Alice, Bely and
Sybil, in they come. Many of them are penniless and are
obliged to pay in kind, and they bring with them gifts
often as unsavoury as the drink they hope to swallow - a
rancid side of bacon for example - and they pawn anything
they can lay their hands on, from their husbands' clothes
to the baby's cradle, from a frying-pan to a side-saddle.
Elinor accepts all. It is a most lively and all-embracing
poem, which gets wilder and lewder as it proceeds. Then
Skelton pulls himself up in characteristic fashion.

[Quotes lines 618-21.]

And remembering that he is a clergyman and a Poet Laureate
he appends some Latin verses saying that he has denounced
drunken, dirty and loquacious women, and trusts they will
take his warning to heart. I wonder. To my mind he has
been thoroughly happy, as he was in the church at Diss
when the naughty curate hawked. I often suspect satirists
of happiness - and I oftener suspect them of envy. Satire
is not a straight trade. Skelton's satires on Wolsey are
of the envious type. In 'Elinor Rumming' and 'Ware the
Hawk' I detect a coarse merry character enjoying itself
under the guise of censoriousness

[Quotes 'Philip Sparrow', lines 1201-03.]

   One question that may have occurred to you is this:
was Skelton typical of the educated parish priest of his
age? My own impression is that he was, and that the men
of Henry VIII's reign, parsons and others, were much more
unlike ourselves than we suppose, or, if you prefer it,
much odder. We cannot unlock their hearts. In the reign
of his daughter Elizabeth a key begins to be forged.
Shakespeare puts it into our hands, and we recover, on a
deeper level, the intimacy promised by Chaucer. Skelton
belongs to an age of transition: the silly Wars of the
Roses were behind him; he appears even to regret them, and
he could not see the profounder struggles ahead. This
made him 'difficult', though he did not seem so to himself. His coarseness and irreverence will pain some
people and must puzzle everyone. It may help us if we
remember that religion is older than decorum.
   Of his poetry I have given some typical samples, and
you will agree that he is entertaining and not quite like

anyone else, that he has a feeling for rhythm, and a
copious vocabulary. Sometimes - but not often - he is
tender and charming, occasionally he is devout and very
occasionally he is wise. On the whole he's a comic - a
proper comic, with a love for improper fun, and a talent
for abuse. He says of himself, in one of his Latin verses,
that he sings the material of laughter in a harsh voice,
and the description is apt; the harshness is often more
obvious than the laughter, and leaves us with a buzzing
in the ears rather than with a smile on the face. Such a
a row! Such a lot of complaints! He has indeed our
national fondness for grumbling - the Government, the
country, agriculture, the world, the beer, they are none
of them what they ought to be or have been. And, although
we must not affix our dry little political labels to the
fluidity of the past (there is nothing to tie them on to),
it is nevertheless safe to say that temperamentally the
rector of Diss was a conservative.

On what note shall we leave him? A musical note com-
mends itself. Let me quote three stanzas from a satire
called 'Against a Comely Coistroun' - that is to say,
against a good-looking kitchen-boy. The boy has been con-
jectured to be Lambert Simnel, the pretender to the
crown of England. He was silly as well as seditious, and
he fancied himself as a musician and 'curiously chanted
and currishly countered and madly in his musicks mock-
ishly made against the Nine Muses of politic poems and
poets matriculate' - the matriculate being Skelton, the
Poet Laureate. Listen how he gets basted for his incompetence; you may not follow all the words, but you can
hear the blows fall, and that's what matters

[Quotes lines 22-42.]

Kitchen-boy Simnel, (2) if it be he, was evidently no
more a performer than he was a prince. Yet I would have
liked to have him here now, red, angry, good-looking,
and making a hideous noise, and to have heard Skelton
cursing him as he screeched. The pair of them might have
revived for us that past which is always too dim, always
too muffled, always too refined. With their raucous
cries in your ears, with the cries of the falconer in
Diss church, with the squawking of Speke Parrot, and the
belchings of Elinor Rumming, I leave you.

Notes

1 Not in fact by Skelton, but included in Henderson's

1931 edition of his works, p. 19.
2 Lambert Simnel, a pretender to the throne of Henry VII,
   was permitted to survive as Henry's kitchen boy.

55. C. S. LEWIS ON SKELTON, 'THE REALLY GIFTED AMATEUR'

1954

From C. S. Lewis, 'English Literature in the Sixteenth
Century Excluding Drama' (Oxford, 1954), pp. 133-43.
    Lewis (1898-1963) was a distinguished novelist, theo-
logical writer and literary critic. The following
extract is from his volume contributed to the Oxford
History of English Literature. Occasional footnotes have
been deleted.

But when all's said John Skelton (1464?-1529) is the only
poet of that age who is still read for pleasure. Skelton
was a translator, a laureate of more than one university,
tutor to Henry VIII, the satirist and later the client of
Wolsey, and a jest-book hero in Elizabethan tradition.
Pope's epithet of 'beastly' is warranted by nothing that
ought either to attract or repel an adult; Skelton is
neither more nor less coarse than dozens of our older
comic writers. His humanism is a little more important
than his supposed beastliness, but it did not amount to
much. It led him to translate 'Tully's Familiars' and
(from Poggio's Latin version) Diodorus Siculus, at some
date before 1490. These translations, which still remain
in manuscript, are said to abound in neologisms, often
successful, and it is plain from such scraps of Skelton's
prose as are accessible in print that he was a lover of
ink-horn terms. But his humanism extended only to Latin
and he was one of those who opposed the study of Greek
at the university and called themselves 'Trojans'. One
of his objections to Greek learning is of great historical interest. He complains that those who learn Greek
cannot use it in conversation, cannot say in Greek

How hosteler fetche my hors a botell of hay.
                                    ('Speeke Parot', 152.)

This shows that the very conception of a *dead* language, so familiar to us, was to Skelton a ridiculous novelty. The process of classicization which was finally to kill Latin seemed to him merely the improvement of a living tongue.

If the list of his own works which Skelton gives in the 'Garland of Laurel' is accurate he must have been one of our most prolific authors, and his lost books must have outweighed in volume those which have survived; indeed his 'Of Man's Life the Peregrination', if it was really a version and a complete version of Deguileville's 'Pèlerinage', would have done so by itself. But it is hard to believe that so busy and erratic a genius ever completed such a task. In what follows I must naturally base my judgement on the extant works; but it should be remembered that we know Skelton only in part and the part we do know is by no means homogeneous. We cannot be sure that the recovery of the lost works might not seriously modify our idea of him.

In his earliest surviving pieces Skelton appears as a typical poet of the late Middle Ages: a poet no better than Barclay and, in my judgement, inferior to Hawes. His elegies on Edward IV (1483) and on the Earl of Northumberland (1489) reveal nothing of his later quality. We may probably assign to the same period (and certainly relegate to the same oblivion) three heavily aureate poems addressed to the Persons of the Trinity, a poem on Time, and an amatory 'Go Piteous Heart'. The only effect of all these is to set us thinking how much better they did such things in Scotland.

With the 'Bouge of Court' (probably written in 1498 or 1499) we reach work which is of real value, but we do not reach the fully 'Skeltonic' Skelton. The 'Bouge' is just as characteristic of the late Middle Ages as the previous poems; the difference is that it is good. There is no· novelty, though there is great merit, in its satiric and realistic use of the dream allegory. The form had been used satirically by Jean de Meung and Chaucer and had always admitted realistic detail; in the 'Flower and the Leaf' and the 'Assembly of Ladies' it had offered almost nothing else. The merit of Skelton lies not in innovation but in using well an established tradition for a purpose to which it is excellently suited. The subject is a perennial one - the bewilderment, and finally the terror, of a man at his first introduction to what theologians call 'the World' and others 'the racket' or 'real life'. Things overheard, things misunderstood, a general and steadily growing sense of being out of one's depth, fill the poem with a Kafka-like uneasiness. As was natural in Tudor times the particular 'world' or 'racket' described in the court; but almost any man in any profession can recognize most of the encounters - the direct, unprovoked snub from Danger ('She asked me if ever I drank of sauces cup' [line 73]), the effusive welcome of Favell, the confidential warnings of Suspect. the apparently light-hearted good fellowship of Harvy Hafter (but the very sight of him sets your purse shivering), and the downright bullying of Disdain. It ends in nightmare with the hero leaping over the ship's side: his name, which is *Drede*, gives the keynote to the whole dream. The metre is chaotic, but the poem almost succeeds in spite of it.

So far, if my chronology is correct, we have seen Skelton working along the lines marked out for him by his immediate predecessors. He was to do so again in the Flyting 'Against Garnesche' (1513-14), in 'The Garland of Laurel' (1523), and in the huge morality play of 'Magnificence' (1515-16) which I surrender to the historians of drama. But in the next group of poems which we must consider we are confronted with a different and almost wholly unexpected Skelton. The pieces in this group cannot be accurately dated. 'Philip Sparrow' was certainly written before 1509. 'Ware the Hawk' was obviously written while Skelton was resident at Diss, and therefore probably between 1502 and 1511. The 'Epitaphe' (on 'two knaves sometime of Diss') cannot be earlier than 1506 when the will of one of the 'knaves' was proved. The 'Ballad of the Scottish King' and its revised version 'Against the Scots' must have been composed in the year of Flodden (1513). The 'Tunning' I cannot date, for the fact that the real Alianora Romyng was in trouble for excessive prices and small measures in 1525 does not much help us.

The most obvious characteristic of all the poems in this group is the so-called Skeltonic metre; 'so-called', for by some standards it is hardly a metre at all. The number of beats in the line varies from two ('Tell you I chill' ['Elynor Rummyng', line 1]) to five ('To anger the Scots and Irish keterings with all ['Against the Scots', line 83]) with a preference for three. The rhyme is hardly ever crossed and any given rhyme may be repeated as long as the resources of the language hold out. In other words there is neither metre nor rhyme scheme in the strict sense; the only constant characteristic is the fact of rhyming. Scholars have shown much learning in their attempts to find a source for this extraordinary kind of composition. Short lines with irregular rhyme have been found in medieval Latin verse, but they do not show the Skeltonic irregularity of rhythm. More recently attention has been drawn to the rhyming passages in later medieval Latin prose; and in an earlier

chapter we have noticed something faintly like Skeltonics
in such Scotch poems as 'Cowkelbie Sow' and 'Lord Fergus'
Gaist'. This is not the only affinity between Skelton and
his Scotch contemporaries; his 'Lullay, Lullay' (not to be
confused with the noble carol) and his 'Jolly Rutterkin'
may be regarded as poor relations of the comic lyric about
low life which we find in the Scotch anthologies. Skelton
himself would rise from the grave to bespatter us with new
Skeltonics if we suggested that he had learned his art
from a Scotchman: but these affinities may suggest (they
certainly do not prove) some common tradition whose documents are now lost but from which the lower types of early
sixteenth-century poetry, both Scotch and English, have
descended. But whatever view is finally taken it remains
true that there is nothing really very like Skeltonics
before Skelton, and that his practice alone gives them any
importance. Hints and vague anticipations there may have
been, but I suspect that he was the real inventor.
  The problem about the source of Skeltonics sinks into
insignificance beside the critical problem. A form whose
only constant attribute is rhyme ought to be intolerable:
it is indeed the form used by every clown scribbling on
the wall in an inn yard. How then does Skelton please?
It is, no doubt, true to say that he sometimes does not.
Where the poem is bad on other grounds the Skeltonics make
it worse. In the 'Ballad of the Scottish King' the rodo-
montade of the non-combatant, the government scribbler's
cheap valiancy, is beneath contempt, and qualifies the
poet for the epithet 'beastly' far more than 'Elinor
Rumming'; and in the revised version the sinister hint
that those who disliked the 'Ballad' must be no true
friends of the king adds the last touch of degradation.
Here the looseness of the form does not help matters: it
aggravates the vulgarity. This can be seen by turning to
the similar poem on 'The Doughty Duke of Albany' (1523)
where the 'Envoy', by dint of its strict trimeter quat-
rains, is much more tolerable than the main body of the
poem. Where thought grovels, form must be severe: satire
that is merely abusive is most tolerable in stopped cou-
lets. But, of course, there would be no problem if all
Skelton's Skeltonic poems had been on this level. The
real question is about 'Elinor Rumming' and 'Philip Sparrow'. I am not at all sure that we can find the answer,
but we may at least eliminate one false trail. They certainly do not please by the poet's 'facility in rhyme'
considered as virtuosity. On Skelton's terms any man can
rhyme as long as he pleases.
  In modern language the kind to which 'Philip Sparrow'
belongs may roughly be called the mock-heroic, though the

term must here be stretched to cover the mock-religious as
well. Requiem is sung for the pet bird. At the appropriate place in the poem, as in 'Lycidas', the mourner remem-
bers that 'her sorrow is not dead' and asks

> But where unto shuld I
> Lenger morne or crye?   [lines 594-5]

Solemn execration is pronounced on Gib our cat (mountain
of mantichores are to eat his brain) and on the whole
nation of cats. She calls on the great moralists of antiquity to teach her how to moderate her passion. Thus,
superficially, the humour is of the same kind as in 'The
Rape of the Lock': much ado about nothing. But Pope's
intention was ostensibly corrective; if Skelton had any
such intention it got lost early in the process of composition. It may indeed be thought that something of the
same kind happened to Pope, that he loved, if not Belinda,
yet her toilet, and the tea-cups, and the 'shining altars
of Japan', and would have been very little pleased with
any 'reform of manners' which interfered with them. But
if such love for the thing he mocks was one element in
Pope's attitude, it is the whole of Skelton's. 'Philip
Sparrow' is our first great poem of childhood. The lady
who is lamenting her bird may not really have been a child
- Skelton's roguish reference to the beauties hidden beneath her kirtle (itself a medieval commonplace) may seem
to suggest the reverse. But it is as a child she is
imagined in the poem - a little girl to whom the bird's
death is a tragedy and who, though well read in romances,
finds Lydgate beyond her and has 'little skill in Ovid or
Virgil'. We seem to hear her small reed-like voice
throughout, and to move in a demure, dainty, luxurious,
in-door world. Skelton is not (as Blake might have done)
suggesting that such 'sorrows small' may be real tragedies
from within; nor is he, in any hostile sense, ridiculing
them. He is at once tender and mocking - like an affec-
tionate bachelor uncle or even a grandfather. Of course,
he is not consistently dramatic and by no means confines
himself to things that the supposed speaker could really
have said: a good deal of his own learning is allowed to
creep in. The mood of the poem is too light to require
strict consistency. It is indeed the lightest - the most
like a bubble - of all the poems I know. It would break
at a touch: but hold your breath, watch it, and it is
almost perfect. The Skeltonics are essential to its perfection. Their prattling and hopping and their inconsequence, so birdlike and so childlike, are the best possible embodiment of the theme. We should not, I think,

refuse to call this poem great; perfection in light poetry, perfect smallness, is among the rarest of literary achievements.

In the 'Tunning of Elinor Rumming' the metre has a more obvious and, I think, less fruitful appropriateness to the subject. Skelton here lets himself loose on the humours of an inn presided over by a dirty old ale wife. Her customers are all women, confirmed drinkers, who mostly pay for their beer in kind - one brings a rabbit, another her shoes, another her husband's hood, one her wedding ring. We have noisome details about Elinor's methods of brewing, and there are foul words, foul breath, and foul sights in plenty. The merit of the thing lies in its speed: guests are arriving hotfoot, ordering, quarrelling, succumbing to the liquor, every moment. We get a vivid impression of riotous bustle, chatter, and crazy disorder. All is ugly, but all is alive. The poem has thus a good deal in common with 'Peblis to the Play' or 'Christis Kirk on the Green': what it lacks is their melody and gaiety. The poet, and we, may laugh, but we hardly enter into the enjoyment of his 'sort of foul drabs'. It is here that the metre most fully justifies Mr. Graves's description of Skelton as 'helter-skelter John'. The shapeless volley of rhymes does really suggest the helter-skelter arrival of all these thirsty old trots. But there is much less invention in it than in 'Philip Sparrow'. The technique is much more crudely related to the matter; disorder in life rendered by disorder in art. This is in poetry what 'programme music' is in music; the thing is legitimate, it works, but we cannot forget that the art has much better cards in its hand.

If I see these two poems at all correctly, we may now hazard a guess at the answer to our critical problem. The Skeltonic, which defies all the rules of art, pleases (on a certain class of subjects) because - and when - this helter-skelter artlessness symbolizes something in the theme. Childishness, dipsomania, and a bird are the themes on which we have found it successful. When it attempts to treat something fully human and adult - as in the Flodden poem - it fails; as it does also, to my mind, in 'The Duke of Albany' (1523) and the unpleasant 'Replicacioun' (1528). The other poems in which Skelton has used it most successfully are 'Colin Clout' and 'Why Come Ye Not to Court?' (1522).

All right minded readers start these two lampoons with a prejudice in favour of the poet: however he writes, the man who defies all but omnipotent government cannot be contemptible. But these poems have a real, and very curious, merit. I would describe it as anonymity. The

technique, to be sure, is highly personal; but the effect
produced is that of listening to the voice of the people
itself. A vast muttering and growling of rumours fills
our ears; 'Lay men say' ... 'Men say' ... 'the temporality
say' ... 'I tell you as men say' ... 'they crye and they
yelle' ... 'I here the people talke' ... 'What newes?
What newes?' ... 'What here ye of Lancashire?' ... 'What
here ye of the Lord Dacres?' ... 'is Maister Meautis dede?'
Thus to hand over responsibility to a vague *on dit* is no
doubt a common trick of satirists: but thus repeated, thus
with cumulative effect accompanying Skelton's almost end-
less denunciations, it acquires a strange and disquieting
potency. It may be the truth that Wolsey needed to care
for Skelton no more than Bishop Blougram for Gigadibs, and
that the forgiveness for which the poet paid heavily in
flattery was the forgiveness of tranquil contempt. But
our imaginative experience in reading the poems ignores
this possibility. In them Skelton has ceased to be a man
and become a mob: we hear thousands of him murmuring and
finally thundering at the gates of Hampton Court. And
here once again the Skeltonics help him. Their shapeless
garrulity, their lack of steady progression are (for this
purpose) no defect. But he is very near the borders of
art. He is saved by the skin of his teeth. No one wishes
the poems longer, and a few more in the same vein would be
intolerable.

But Skelton's abusive vein was not confined to Skeltonics. In the astonishing 'Speke Parot' (1521) he had
returned to rhyme royal. This poem exists in two widely
divergent texts; in the Harleian MS. it is mainly an
attack on Wolsey, in the early print, mainly an attack on
Greek studies; both are put into the mouth of the Parrot
and both are almost wholly unintelligible. The obscurity
is doubtless denser now than it was in 1521, but it was
there from the beginning and is certainly intentional.
Modern scholars have laboured with great diligence, and
not without success, to dissipate it, but a critical
judgement on the poem cannot be made with any confidence;
not that we have no literary experiences while we read,
but that we have no assurance whether they are at all like
those the poet intended to give us. The very first lines
have for me their own whimsical charm:

[Quotes lines 3-6.]

His curiously carven cage, his mirror for him to 'toot
in', the maidens strewing the cage with fresh flowers and
saying 'Speak parrot', the utter inconsequence (as it
seems to us) of the statement 'In Poperynge grew paires

when Parot was an egge' [line 72] - all this delights us
scarcely less than the voyage of the Owl and the Pussycat
or the Hunting of the Snark. The same crazy sort of
pleasure can be derived from lines like

> For Ierichoe and Ierseye shall mete together as sone
> As he to exployte the man out of the mone [lines 307-8]

or

> To brynge all the sea to a chirrystone pytte.[line 331]

This raises in some minds the question whether we are
reading the first of the nonsense poets, or whether Skelton is anticipating the moderns and deliberately launching
poetry on 'the stream of consciousness'. I believe not.
I fear the poem was not meant to be nonsense: it is nonsense to us because it is a cryptogram of which we have
lost the key. Our pleasure in it may be almost wholly
foreign to Skelton's purpose and to his actual achievement in 1521; almost, not quite, because unless his mind
had been stocked with curious images, even the disorder
into which they necessarily fall for us who know too
little of the real links between them, would not affect
us as it does. His modern admirers are thus really in
touch with a certain level of Skelton's mind, but probably
not of his art, when they enjoy 'Speke Parot'.
   In the 'Garland of Laurel' (1523) Skelton returns, as
far as the main body of the poem is concerned, to the
broad highway of medieval poetry. The occasion of the
poem was a desire to compliment the Countess of Surrey
and certain other ladies: its form, stanzaic allegory:
its characters, Skelton as dreamer, Pallas, Fame, Gower,
Chaucer, and Lydgate. The catalogue of 'laureate' poets
is enlivened by a refrain about Bacchus which has a
hearty ring, but the only other good passage (that where
Daphne, though already tree, quivers at Apollo's touch)
is from Ovid. All that is of value in this production is
contained in the seven lyric addresses to ladies which are
inserted at the end. Only one of these ('Gertrude
Statham') is exactly Skeltonic, though 'Margaret Hussey'
comes near to being so. 'Jane Blennerhasset' and 'Isabel
Pennell' have the short, irregular lines, but there is in
both a real rhyme-scheme. 'Margett Wentworth', 'Margaret
Tylney', and 'Isabel Knight' are in stanzas. Some of
these are very good indeed: what astonishes one is the
simplicity of the resources from which the effect has been
produced. In 'Margery Wentworth', which is twenty lines
long, the same four lines are thrice repeated. Of the

eight lines which remain to be filled up by a fresh
effort of imagination, one is wasted (and in so tiny a
poem) on rubble like 'Plainly I cannot glose'. Yet the
thing succeeds - apparently by talking about flowers and
sounding kind. 'Isabel Pennell' captures us at once by
the opening lines, which sound as if the 'baby' (whether
she really was an infant matters nothing) had been shown
to him that moment for the first time and the song had
burst out *ex tempore*. After that, the flowers, the April
showers, the bird, and 'star of the morrow gray' (only
slightly improved by the fact that *morrow* is now an
archaism) do the rest. 'Margaret Hussey' lives only by
the opening quatrain: just as that very different lyric
'Mannerly Margery Milk and Ale' (which Cornish set) lives
almost entirely on the line which makes its title.

The tenderness, though not the playfulness, of these
little pieces is found also in 'Now sing we', and also,
with much more elaborate art, in the fine devotional
lyric 'Woefully Arrayed'. If this is by Skelton it is the
only piece in which he does not appear to be artless.

It may naturally be asked whether this artlessness in
Skelton is real or apparent: and, if apparent, whether it
is not the highest art. I myself think that it is real.
The result is good only when he is either playful or
violently abusive, when the shaping power which we ordin-
arily demand of a poet is either admittedly on holiday or
may be supposed to be suspended by rage. In either of
these two veins, but especially in the playful, his lack
of all real control and development is suitable to the
work in hand. In 'Philip Sparrow' or 'Margery Wentworth'
he 'prattles out of fashion' but that is just what is
required. We are disarmed; we feel that to criticize
such poetry is like trying to make a child discontented
with a toy which Skelton has given it. That is one of
the paradoxes of Skelton: in speaking of his own work he
is arrogant (though perhaps even then with a twinkle in
his eye), but the work itself, at its best, dances round
or through our critical defences by its extreme unpretentiousness - an unpretentiousness quite without parallel in
our literature. But I think there is more nature than art
in this happy result. Skelton does not know the peculiar
powers and limitations of his own manner, and does not
reserve it, as an artist would have done, for treating
immature or disorganized states of consciousness. When
he happens to apply it to such states, we may get delightful poetry: when to others, verbiage. There is no building in his work, no planning, no reason why any piece
should stop just where it does (sometimes his repeated
envoys make us wonder if it is going to stop at all), and

no kind of assurance that any of his poems is exactly the poem he intended to write. Hence his intimacy. He is always in undress. Hence his charm, the charm of the really gifted amateur (a very different person from the hard working inferior artist). I am not unaware that some modern poets would put Skelton higher than this. But I think that when they do so they are being poets, not critics. The things that Mr. Graves gets out of Skelton's work are much better than anything that Skelton put in. That is what we should expect: achievement has a finality about it, where the unfinished work of a rich, fanciful mind, full of possibilities just because it is unfinished, may be the strongest stimulant to the reader when that reader is a true poet. Mr. Graves, Mr. Auden, and others receive from Skelton principally what they give and in their life, if not alone, yet eminently, does Skelton live. Yet no student of the early sixteenth century comes away from Skelton uncheered. He has no real predecessors and no important disciples; he stands out of the streamy historical process, an unmistakable individual, a man we have met.

Bibliography

The following works contain useful sections dealing with criticism of Skelton.

BISCHOFFSBERGER, E., 'Einfluss John Skeltons auf die englische Literatur' (1914).
CARPENTER, N.C., 'John Skelton' (1967).
DYCE, A., ed., 'The Poetical Works of John Skelton' (1843, repr. 1965).
NELSON, W., 'John Skelton, Laureate' (1939).
POLLET, M., 'John Skelton, Poet of Tudor England' (1971).

Index

This index is divided into three sections. I. General Index listing only literary figures (including critics) and works. II. Comparisons of Skelton with other figures. III. References to Specific Works of Skelton.

I. GENERAL INDEX

219